Leases for Lives

Many historians of insurance have commented on the disconnect between the rise of English life insurance companies in the early eighteenth century and the mathematics behind the sound pricing of life insurance products that was developed at about the same time. Insurance and annuity promoters typically ignored this mathematical work. Bellhouse explores this issue and shows that the early mathematical work was not motivated by insurance but instead by the fair valuation of life contingent contracts related to property.

Even the work of the mathematician James Dodson in the creation of the Equitable Life Assurance Society, offering sound, actuarially based premiums, did not change the industry in any significant way. The tipping point was a crisis in 1770 in which the philosopher and mathematician Richard Price, as well as other mathematicians, showed that a dozen or more recently formed annuity societies could not meet their financial obligations and were inviable.

David R. Bellhouse holds degrees in Actuarial Science and in Statistics. He has worked for over 40 years at the University of Western Ontario, where he is now Professor Emeritus. He has published extensively in the history of probability, statistics, and actuarial science. He has recently published a major biography of Abraham De Moivre. Bellhouse is a fellow of the American Statistical Association and has served as President of the Statistical Society of Canada. He is a recipient of Western's Gold Medal for Excellence in Teaching and was recently given the University of Manitoba Faculty of Science Honoured Alumni Award.

Leases for Lives

Life Contingent Contracts and the Emergence of Actuarial Science in Eighteenth-Century England

David R. Bellhouse
University of Western Ontario

CAMBRIDGE
UNIVERSITY PRESS

CAMBRIDGE
UNIVERSITY PRESS

University Printing House, Cambridge CB2 8BS, United Kingdom

One Liberty Plaza, 20th Floor, New York, NY 10006, USA

477 Williamstown Road, Port Melbourne, VIC 3207, Australia

4843/24, 2nd Floor, Ansari Road, Daryaganj, Delhi – 110002, India

79 Anson Road, #06-04/06, Singapore 079906

Cambridge University Press is part of the University of Cambridge.

It furthers the University's mission by disseminating knowledge in the pursuit of education, learning, and research at the highest international levels of excellence.

www.cambridge.org
Information on this title: www.cambridge.org/9781107111769
DOI: 10.1017/9781316282229

First published 2017

Printed in the United Kingdom by Clays, St Ives plc

A catalogue record for this publication is available from the British Library.

ISBN 978-1-107-11176-9 Hardback

To Louise

Contents

Preface

I studied actuarial science as an undergraduate and then gave it up to pursue statistics as a field of study. Throughout my entire career I maintained an interest in history to the point that eventually my research moved away from technical work in statistics to the history of statistics. I seem to have come full circle by researching and then writing a book on the history of actuarial science.

In one sense this book is a natural outgrowth of an article I wrote with my friend and colleague, Christian Genest, on the life of Abraham De Moivre, the eighteenth-century Huguenot mathematician working in London, England. De Moivre is best known for his work in probability theory, but is also seen as one of the fathers of actuarial science. After much more research I was able to write a full-length biography of De Moivre. In that book there is a chapter on De Moivre's actuarial work, beginning in 1725 with his book on life annuities. When I was researching that chapter, what intrigued me was that I found a number of manuscripts showing English mathematicians around the 1740s answering questions on life contingent contracts involving life annuities but related to property. These questions had nothing to do with the insurance and annuity industry. That was puzzling to me. At about the same time I was reading histories of insurance and found, to my surprise, another puzzle. Although the insurance industry started in England in the late seventeenth century, mathematicians were not involved in the industry until the 1750s or 1760s and then only peripherally. It was not until much later in the eighteenth century that mathematics became more engaged in the insurance and annuity industry. Apparently, mathematicians like De Moivre were neither needed not wanted by the industry. The manuscripts that I initially found marked the beginning of a long paper chase that has resulted in what I hope are solutions to these puzzles.

What I have shown is that mathematical work in actuarial science was initially motivated by problems in the valuation of life contingent contracts related to property: leases for lives, reversions on estates, and marriage settlements. There was one enterprising mathematician, James Dodson, who tried in the 1750s to translate his skills in these areas to the establishment of a life insurance company. He died before the company was finally founded in 1762. The company he worked to establish, the Society for Equitable Assurances, may have remained the outlier among life insurance companies had it not been for mathematicians in the 1770s pointing to the very shaky foundations of several organizations offering life annuities. Because of the work of these mathematicians, especially Richard Price, almost all of these organizations ceased operating and those remaining reformed the products they offered. This was the turning point in the mathematicians' involvement in the life insurance and annuity industries. Throughout this entire period mathematicians continued to work as consultants on life contingent contracts related to property.

Acknowledgments

Writing this book would not have been possible without the help of several librarians and archivists. For many of them I do not have names. These include staff members at Cambridge University Library, St. John's College Library Cambridge, Columbia University Library, London Metropolitan Archives, Exeter Cathedral Archives, and Canterbury Cathedral Archives. They were all very helpful when I visited them. Among these people one stands out. This is David Raymont, the librarian at the Institute and Faculty of Actuaries in London, England. We met on several occasions and corresponded many times. He was most helpful every time I visited him. My most memorable visit was when Mr. Raymont brought me a manuscript as I was working away at a table in the library and said something like, "You might be interested in this one. We recently purchased it." It turned out to be a previously unknown letter of Richard Price that illustrates Price's work as a consultant on the valuation of a marriage settlement. I never would have found that manuscript on my own.

Another librarian I would like to thank is my sister-in-law, Carol Budnick. At one point I was considering giving up working on the book. I did not know if the effort I was expending would actually result in a published book. A grant application that I had made to fund research for the book had been turned down twice. Carol encouraged me to make a proposal to a publisher. As a result of her encouragement, I contacted Diana Gillooly at Cambridge University Press. My proposal was accepted and Diana has been very encouraging and helpful in getting this book to press. I was also able to find some creative ways to fund the research I needed to finish the book.

I am grateful to Columbia University Library for providing me with the photographs from the Thomas Simpson correspondence that they hold. The photographs appear in Figures 6.1 and 6.7. The reproductions of newspaper advertisements in Figure 6.2 appear with permission of the British Library. I am also grateful to the London Metropolitan Archives for photographing an entry in the London Assurance

Corporation's policy books that appears in Figure 10.3. The photograph appears with permission of Royal & Sun Alliance Insurance plc.

For many years Stephen Stigler has encouraged me in my historical pursuits. In fact, without his initial encouragement I might never have taken the journey that has resulted in this book. With respect to the current work, I want to thank him for alerting me to the possible origins of Richard Price's interest in life annuities through John Eames.

Once I finished the manuscript I asked a few people to look at it. Harry Panjer, an actuary, and Roger Emerson, a historian of Britain in the eighteenth century, were both supportive of the finished product. Two anonymous readers for Cambridge University Press made several suggestions that have improved the manuscript.

Most importantly, I want to thank Christian Genest, my friend and statistical colleague, as well as my coauthor on three historical papers. At the point where I was no longer seeing words on the page after reading the manuscript many times, Christian went over what I had written very carefully and made several excellent editorial suggestions, which I hope I have followed closely.

1 Introduction

When I was a student taking courses in the mathematics of life insurance, or actuarial science, the textbook that we used, entitled *Life Contingencies*, made a brief historical reference to the origins of some mathematical models describing human mortality.[1] It was mentioned that Abraham De Moivre (1667–1754) proposed a model in 1724 in which the number of people living at any age decreased in a linear fashion until by age 86 no one was left alive. He used this model to simplify the calculation of the values of life annuities. Later I learned that 1725 was the correct date. When we were taught about the centrality of life tables to insurance calculations we learned in passing that the astronomer Edmond Halley (1656–1742) had constructed the first life table. My awareness of the connection between insurance and these two people was strengthened when I read some histories of statistics. One modern historian of statistics describes De Moivre's 1725 book on life annuities as "the first textbook on life insurance mathematics."[2] Delving into this a little further, I found that professional actuaries writing in the nineteenth century described all the mathematical progress that had been made in the techniques that they used to value life insurance contracts, including the work of Halley and De Moivre.[3] These early histories look like attempts to give legitimacy to the newly formed actuarial profession, as well as providing advertisements for the sound scientific basis on which the insurance industry was assumed to rest in the latter half of the nineteenth century.

It was a revelation to me to find that historians of science and social historians did not share this viewpoint. Through careful research these historians have shown a disconnection between mathematicians and the insurance industry as it developed in the eighteenth century. One of these historians, Lorraine Daston, has described the situation succinctly:[4]

Despite the efforts of mathematicians to apply probability theory and mortality statistics to problems in insurance and annuities in the late seventeenth and early eighteenth centuries, the influence of this mathematical literature on the voluminous trade in annuities and insurance was negligible until the end of the eighteenth century.

Another historian, Eve Rosenhaft, has described it as a puzzle:[5]

> The historical literature on the development of life insurance has paid close attention to the relationship between risk-taking and risk avoidance in the transition to economic and social modernity. A central puzzle in the history of life insurance is this: the market in life insurance emerged in England early in the eighteenth century, *before* the calculus was developed that would make it possible to apply known mortality rates to the calculation of premiums and benefits. After mid-century, a second wave of foundings of life insurance and pension funds coincided with the existence of more or less reliable systems of calculation, but their founders ignored them, often defying good advice. So what ought to have been systems for the 'taming of chance' in everyday life resisted the influence of the scientific discourses – statistics and probability – that would have made them effective.

This certainly is a puzzle. If the mathematicians who applied probability theory to the valuation of standard life contingent contracts in today's life insurance industry were not actually involved in the insurance industry, what were they doing?

The historical evidence, on which historians such as Daston and Rosenhaft have relied, as well as the actuaries writing their own history, is for the most part the corpus of books that mathematicians in the eighteenth century wrote about the subject, mainly on life annuities. Were these book writers writing merely for one another? Or, were they writing in the hope that the insurance and annuity industry would take note of them? Any hopes about these budding industries were dashed as those in the industry apparently made little use of their work, as Daston and Rosenhaft have demonstrated.

This all became even more of a puzzle when I discovered that there was a perceived demand for these books as seen from the point of view of their printers or publishers. John Nourse was the publisher for two of the many writers on life annuities in the eighteenth century. In September 1741 Nourse paid Thomas Simpson, author of several mathematical books, 17 guineas for the copyright to his book *Doctrine of Annuities and Reversions*, published in 1742. Nourse also paid the mathematician and accountant James Dodson £25 and 4 shillings for the copyright to the third volume of his *Mathematical Repository*, which was devoted almost entirely to problems in life annuities.[6] Dodson was also to receive 25 free copies of the book. Nourse gave Dodson an advance of 10 guineas at least a year and a half prior to the *Mathematical Repository*'s appearing in print in 1755. The amounts Nourse paid for the copyrights seem to have been based on the number of printed sheets of paper that went into the book. As laid out in the contract, he paid Dodson £1, 11 shillings and 6 pence per sheet. For Simpson, we can compare the 17 guineas he received for his *Doctrine of Annuities and Reversions* to the 73 guineas he received in 1750 for *Doctrine and Application of Fluxions*. At 576 pages, the book on fluxions is 4½ times as long as the 128-page book on annuities, while the copyright paid is just under the multiple of 4½. To put the amounts Dodson and Simpson received into perspective, a clerk in the late 1720s, working in a customs house tallying the collection of duties on imports and exports, made £40 to £50 per annum.[7] Based on that comparison, the copyright money that Nourse paid is not an insignificant amount as it might seem today. Clearly, Nourse was taking a financial risk in the publication of these books and thought he would make a profit from them. There must have been some market for these books – someone was buying them for some reason, or at least Nourse thought so.

For those unfamiliar with predecimal British currency here is a short account of it. Up until "Decimal Day," on February 15, 1971, British currency was expressed in pounds, shillings, and pence with the symbols l or £, s, and d, respectively. There were 20 shillings to the pound and 12 pence to the shilling. There were several other denominations in the currency (farthings and florins, for example), but the only other denomination that is relevant to annuities was the guinea, which was 21 shillings. In 1741 Nourse paid Simpson 17 guineas, or £17 17s. Dodson's contract with Nourse for the *Mathematical Repository* was £1 11s 6d per sheet. Typically when carrying out annuity valuations mathematicians decimalized their calculations. Sometimes they left their final result in decimal form and sometimes they converted the decimal value back to pounds, shillings, and pence.

A short solution to the enigma of the lack of interest shown by the insurance industry and yet considerable interest from book publishers is that mathematicians were doing something other than trying to set fair values to annuity and insurance contracts for the insurance and annuity industry. In fact, the mathematical activity up to about 1760 is the opposite side of the coin of the Daston–Rosenhaft insight. The mathematicians showed very little interest in the insurance and annuity industry. A hint at a little more detail of what they were doing is given in a 1752 paper in the *Philosophical Transactions* by the author of the 1755 *Mathematical Repository*, James Dodson.[8] Making no mention whatsoever of the insurance industry or government life annuity schemes, Dodson described the ubiquitous nature of life annuities in British society at the time. Many of the sorts of situations that he describes involving life annuities are treated in a general way by the mathematical writers on life annuities in the eighteenth century. These situations are related to something that was central to the British economy of the eighteenth century – property. Many of the patrons of these mathematicians had interests in property.

Since the Norman Conquest of 1066 all land in England technically has been owned by the Crown but held by individuals through freeholds or leaseholds.[9] Someone who holds a freehold (also called an estate in fee simple) has complete use of the estate and the rights to dispose of it. The freeholder holds the land in perpetuity. By the eighteenth century a variety of types of leaseholds had evolved out of the feudal system.[10] As there are today, there were leases for a fixed period of time, or in the jargon of the eighteenth century, these were estates held for a term of years absolute. The normal term was 21 years, but it could be as long as 99 years or perhaps more. Unlike what exists today, there were many leases that were life-contingent, typically running for the lifetimes of the persons named in the lease. There were copyhold estates that evolved from the manorial system, as well as other forms of life leaseholds. Leases for fixed terms were typical in the east of England and leases that were life-contingent were typical in the west of England.[11] Lands held by dioceses of the Church of England and by colleges at Oxford and Cambridge, as well as some endowed charities, were let to others as life leaseholds.

Income from estates held for a term of years absolute is a form of fixed-term annuity or what is often called an annuity certain. Income from a freehold is a perpetuity. The value of the estate would involve, in part, finding the present value of an annuity certain. In terms of valuation, a long-term lease was treated as equivalent to a freehold. The present value of rents from a 99-year lease is nearly numerically equivalent to the present value of a perpetuity.

The common copyhold or life leasehold was let for the duration of the life of the last survivor of up to three persons named on the lease. For a lease on three lives, those named might be the farmer working the land, his wife, and his oldest son. If one of the persons named on the lease died – the term used in the eighteenth century is that one of the lives dropped – then that person could be replaced by another on payment of a sum of money to the landlord, commonly called a fine. This leasing arrangement provided a means by which land could remain within a family for many years. It was also a form of life annuity for the lessor, but based on the lives of his tenants, not on his own life. Copyhold leases usually involved a large fine payable to enter the lease and similarly large fines on renewal, with a nominal annual rent.

During the eighteenth century there was a move among estate holders to convert their life leases to leases for a fixed period of time. Conversion allowed the landlord more flexibility in trying to maximize his rents and more flexibility with the development of the land. Life leases on church lands remained in place until well into the nineteenth century. The risks associated with this kind of life annuity are mainly tied up in the ability of the lessee to pay the rent. On non-payment of rent, the tenant could be evicted and the land rented to someone else to continue the annuity for the lessor. The land is always there, unlike a monetary fund set up by those operating a life annuity company that is not backed by land.

Other kinds of arrangement with respect to land might have life-contingent provisions. For a gentleman who holds a life tenancy on lands which he sublets to others for his source of income there might be dower rights attached. Should this tenant for life predecease his wife, she would have the right to half the estate during her lifetime. A similar situation could apply to a landowner. In this case it comes in the form of a marriage settlement which conveys a portion of the land to the widow for her use on the landowner's demise. On her death, the land would revert to the heirs of the estate. Income from dower rights or a marriage settlement is a form of life annuity for the widow.

If the mathematicians did not devise methods for the valuation of life contingent contracts until the 1690s or later, how were they valued before then? There was a long-established tradition for the valuation of leases for lives, coming out of a statute of Henry VIII related to leases which lumped together leases of 21 years and leases for three lives.[12] The tradition was to equate the length of a life, which is uncertain, to a fixed period of time, specifically 21 years to the last survivor among three lives, or 7 years to one life. Consequently, any valuation method that can be applied to fixed-term leases can also be applied to the valuation of leases for lives. Should a life drop in a lease for three lives, the fine to renew the lease was based on tacking an extra 7 years on to the end of the lease. When Halley carried out the proper valuation of life annuities in 1693, using the life table he constructed, the values turned out to be quite different from what had been established by custom. Custom was hard to break. Many were content with the "old ways." Despite advances made by mathematicians in the valuation of life annuities by the 1750s, in his 1752 paper Dodson hinted at a continuing tension between calculation and custom. There needed to be compelling reasons to discard the "old ways" and to adopt the new technology.

Closely linked to the valuation of life annuities, as well as life insurance, is the life table. Construction of a life table requires proper data, and these data were not always available during the eighteenth century.[13] And when the data were available there was the question of their soundness, reliability, and applicability. Near the end of the century, Jeremy Bentham summed up the problem succinctly and put forward the idea in some notes on annuities that it should be the government that should take responsibility for the collection of such data.[14]

> Mathematicians though themselves unerring may lead men into error, and will do so whenever the stock of data they have to work upon is imperfect or erroneous: but to furnish them with proper data, and proper data is not their own province but is a government concern.

The move to central registration of births and deaths and to a regular census to determine population size did not occur until the middle of the nineteenth century.[15] By the beginning of the nineteenth century insurance companies dealt with this problem by constructing life tables based on their own mortality experiences or on a mortality study carried out in a locality where sufficient information was thought to have been collected. Throughout the eighteenth century, mathematicians working as consultants for life-contingent contracts relied on published tables that were possibly "imperfect or erroneous," in the words of Bentham.

Once the life-insurance blinkers are removed when examining mathematicians and their work in life annuities during the seventeenth and eighteenth centuries, a whole new world of activity opens up. I have found several manuscripts and printed sources that support mathematical activity in life-contingent contracts related to property throughout the entire eighteenth century. It has been a fruitful paper chase. The result of this chase has provided new insights beyond the mathematics in standard works on life annuities such as De Moivre's *Annuities upon Lives* and Simpson's *Doctrine of Annuities and Reversions*. Throughout the book I will try to put this new world of mathematical activity, including the eventual adoption of it by the insurance and annuity industries, into its historical context.

One of the stumbling blocks in the valuation of life-contingent contracts is that it requires an enormous amount of calculation without the aid of a computer or even a mechanical calculator. This inspired mathematical ways to get around the burden of calculation, as well as the construction of tables to ease the burden. Since I have a computer at my disposal, I was inspired to look more closely at many of these calculations. When I let the numbers speak I got further insights into what these mathematicians were doing, the type of problems they solved, and the issues they faced.

To understand the mathematical work on life-contingent contracts, it is necessary to start at the beginning – the valuation of annuities as they relate to land in the seventeenth century.

2 Mathematics and Property in the Seventeenth Century

The mathematical valuation of leases is part of a process of what might be called the mathematization of land. The foundations for the subject were laid with the rise of the profession of estate or land surveyor during the sixteenth century. This profession, new to the sixteenth century, is intricately tied to the changing relationship between the landlord and the tenant, as the old feudal model broke down and gradually evolved into something different.[1] The traditional model of landlord–tenant relations was one in which the manor was a community held together by personal ties and religious beliefs supporting the social order, all of which involved obligations to the lord of the manor, who had obligations higher in the hierarchy. With the pressures of increasing population, inflation, and a developing private property market caused by Henry VIII's dissolution of the monasteries in the 1530s, there was a move during the sixteenth century to a more economics-based relationship between landlord and tenant. The surveyor figured into this change by providing the landlord with an accurate description of his holdings, the need for which was recognized in the first manual for land surveying, written by John Fitzherbert in 1523.[2] He says in his prologue:

> Howe & by what maner, do all these great estates and noblemen and women lyve and maynteyne their honour and degre. and in myne opinyon, their honour and degre is upholden and maynteyned by reason of their rentes, issues, revenewes, and profytes that come of their maners, lordshippes, landes & tenementes to them belonging. Than it is necessarye to be knowen howe all their maners, lordshippes, landes & tenements shulde be extended, surveyed, butted, bounded, and valued in every parte: that the said estates shulde nat be disceyved, defrauded, nor disheryted of the possessyons, rentes, customes, and servyces, the whiche they have to them reserved for mayntenaunce of their estates and degrees.

Simply put, the landowner should know what he owns in order to maintain his status, financially and socially, through a proper accounting and valuation of all sources of his income. This kind of argument is repeated in later surveying books. The accuracy of land surveys increased over the century as education improved and interest in geometry grew. The surveyor not only constituted a part of the changing relationship between landlord and tenant, but at the same time was one of the agents of change.

The regular rent paid on a lease is a form of annuity, payable to the landholder. The present value of the annuity represents part of the current value of the land for the landholder. If Fitzherbert's advice is to be taken, then it should be important for the landholder to have knowledge of the value of his leases.

Annuities, as well as interest on loans, have a long history, often unrelated to land, dating back to antiquity.[3] Given this history, it is necessary to discover the how and why of interest and annuity valuations in early modern Britain, and then how and when they relate to the value of leases. This can be pieced together through an examination of books on annuities as well as an examination of commercial arithmetic books, especially the corpus of examples that are used to illustrate the calculations underlying the valuations. Not all the examples in commercial arithmetic books involve merchants and merchandise, as may be expected when looking back from the present; some examples deal with land, leases, and lordships. The first published book treating annuity valuations comprehensively is not a commercial arithmetic book, but rather a book devoted solely to the evaluation of annuities. It is Richard Witt's 1613 *Arithmeticall Questions, Touching the Buying or Exchange of Annuities*.[4]

Some general observations on book publication in the sixteenth and seventeenth centuries and their relation to Witt's book are in order before delving into the book's contents. The relationship between author and publisher was a little different from how it is today. Unless the author was wealthy, so that he could cover the cost of printing himself, any monetary risk in publication was borne by the printer or the bookseller. These two roles were not necessarily separate and distinct. A bookseller could hire a printer to produce a book. A printer with a manuscript in hand ready for press might seek out a bookseller. There were also printers who were booksellers and booksellers who had printing presses. Successful booksellers and printers had to be on top of what the reading public wanted in order to judge the potential demand for printing a manuscript that came their way. For the author, there was very little money to be made from the publication of his book. The printer or bookseller owned the original manuscript once it was in his hands. The printer or publisher might pay the author only a few pounds and/or give him some copies of his own book, as John Nourse did later in the eighteenth century for James Dodson, as described in Chapter 1.

Authors often sought patrons, who were recognized in dedicatory letters at the front of the book. There were many reasons for recognizing this patronage: past financial support, monetary aid in getting the current book published, hope of a future patronage appointment, and political support, in the case of a book that could be subject to severe criticism.[5]

Arithmeticall Questions was printed by Humphrey Lownes for the bookseller Richard Redmer. Lownes was a well-established printer and prominent in the Company of Stationers, the London printers' guild. On the other hand, Redmer had finished his apprenticeship only within the 3 or 4 years just before the publication of the book and so was a relatively new independent tradesman. Mathematical work was not part of his normal stock in trade; he "dealt in plays and miscellaneous literature."[6] Redmer owned the copyright on the book; it was he who registered the book with the Company of Stationers on January 22, 1613.[7] Witt dedicated his book to John Herdson, citing his support for Witt's mathematical endeavors in the past and his general love of the science of arithmetic. This is probably the John Herdson who held a substantial amount of land in Folkestone, Kent. The son of a London alderman, Herdson died unmarried in 1622, leaving his estate to his nephew Basil Dixwell, who was later made a baronet.[8] Witt was also closely involved in the publication process for *Arithmeticall Questions*, since he handled the galley proofs and corrections himself. His reasons for writing the book might be summed up in a quotation from his preface:

> Experience itselfe shewes, that men cannot hold any trading with one another, without great use of Numbers: whereupon it followes, that the losses are not few, which men incurre by ignorance of the Arte of Numbers.

Consequently, a reasonable scenario might be that Witt wrote his book so that his readers would not make bad financial decisions when dealing with interest and annuities. He brought his manuscript to Redmer who, as a relatively new bookseller, was willing to take a chance on the publication although it was the first of its kind to be printed. Redmer then took the manuscript to a prominent printer, perhaps to have a high-quality publication.

The basic concept on which the whole of *Arithmeticall Questions* is based is that, under compound interest (interest is earned on the accrued interest as well as the capital) at an annual rate of interest i, an amount of money currently of value 1 is worth $1 + i$ the following year and $(1 + i)^n$ at the end of n years. One often wants the present value rather than the accumulated value. Using the basic concept, a value $\frac{1}{(1+i)^n}$ will accumulate to 1 after n years so that $\frac{1}{(1+i)^n}$ is called the present

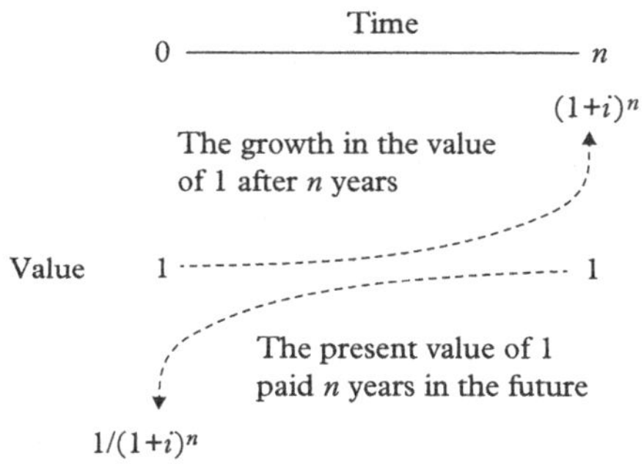

Figure 2.1. The growth in the value of money according to compound interest

value of 1 due to be paid in n years. This is illustrated in Figure 2.1. Upon this foundation, the entire elementary theory of interest and annuities is laid.

Consider, for example, annuities. The basic concepts can be used to find the present values of £1 paid at the end of every year for n years. The standard actuarial notation, or shorthand, for this value is $a_{\overline{n}\rceil}$. It is the sum of the present values of each of the n payments. I have provided a technical appendix (Appendix 1) showing how $a_{\overline{n}\rceil}$ is determined, as well as several other actuarial functions that will appear later in the book.

Scenarios can become more complicated and yet the same basic concept is applied to deal with each of them. For example, a yearly payment of £1 is to run for a certain number of years. What should the yearly payment change to if the annuity runs for fewer years while at the same time the present value of the annuity remains the unchanged? Or suppose the number of payments remains the same. What should the yearly payment change to if a lump sum is paid at the beginning followed by smaller annual payments later? Finally, what is the present value of an annuity whose first payment is deferred for a certain number of years and then runs for another period of time? In the seventeenth century this type of annuity was called a reversion. To put the value of the reversion into the shorthand notation, suppose the first payment is deferred for m years. Payments begin at the end of the next year and continue for $n - m$ years, so that the last payment occurs at the end of year n. The value of this reversion is $a_{\overline{n}\rceil} - a_{\overline{m}\rceil}$, the present value of n annual payments less the present value of the first m payments. What Witt called a reversion is closely related to the renewal of a lease for lives.

An act of Henry VIII allowed certain leases on land either for 21 years or for three lives.[9] It came to be interpreted that, in terms of valuation, a lease for three lives is the same as a lease for a fixed term of 21 years. If the rental value of the land is £1 per year, then the present value of the lease for 21 years or for three lives is $a_{\overline{21}|}$. The set of people first agreeing to enter into the lease for three lives would pay the full value of the lease or an entry fine of $a_{\overline{21}|}$. Should one of the people die, or "a life drop," using the terminology of the seventeenth and eighteenth centuries, then the life could be replaced and the lease renewed, based once again on three lives. With a single life equivalent to 7 years (3 lives ≡ 21 years) the lease without renewal would be seen as a lease with 14 years remaining. The addition of the new life was considered the equivalent of adding another 7 years to the end of the lease, extending the lease from 14 to 21 years. Consequently, the cost to renew the lease, or the renewal fine, is the present value of the last seven payments of £1. The value of these payments is $a_{\overline{21}|} - a_{\overline{14}|}$, which is a special case of Witt's reversion. Under this system, landlords with extensive holdings leased on lives would have much of their annual income in renewal fines as lives dropped and were replaced on the leases. This was the custom that James Dodson found firmly in place in the 1750s and was trying to dislodge. At a 10% annual rate of interest, the legal rate in England from 1545 to 1625, the renewal fine $a_{\overline{21}|} - a_{\overline{14}|}$ would be about £1.28 (or £1 5s 8d) and the entry fine $a_{\overline{21}|}$ would be about £8.65 (or £8 13s). The customary renewal fine on leases for lives in the seventeenth century and even in some places into the early eighteenth century was one "year's purchase" (the rent for 1 year – in general "years' purchase" is the number of years of rental payments equivalent to the lump sum payment) for lands held by dioceses in the Church of England. At 11½% interest annually, the renewal fine $a_{\overline{21}|} - a_{\overline{14}|}$ is a little more than 2 pence (2d) greater than £1.

Throughout *Arithmeticall Questions*, Witt does not present any symbols as I have done, or any formulas. Rather, he illustrates all the rules and results numerically and then follows his rules with several examples. Initially he uses a 10% annual rate of interest, the statutory maximum rate of interest at the time. After a discussion of how to calculate $(1 + i)^n$ and related interest functions, Witt considers a number of numerical examples of many of the scenarios I have described. This part of the book appears to be more pedagogical than practical.

If Witt had ended his book at this point, it may have had little practical interest or impact. A person who had difficulty making lengthy arithmetical calculations might be at a loss to evaluate interest functions according to Witt's verbal directions. Even the person who was capable at arithmetic would find the calculations tedious and would perhaps make a numerical error. Only an astute arithmetician would find Witt's rules and solutions satisfactory. Calculation of $(1 + i)^n$ or $1/(1 + i)^n$ requires a lot of steps. What was needed were tables that could be applied to several situations with minimal additional calculation.

To illustrate the need for tables, consider a modern annuity based on the mortgage amortization tables that are still available in one form or another in bookstores today, or on the Internet. Table users do not need to know the theory behind the numbers. They need only simple directions for the use of the table and at most some very simple arithmetic to obtain a desired result.

In the second part of his book, Witt provides various forms of annuity tables in abundance. There are four tables at an annual rate of 10%:

1. the present value of an amount of £1 payable at the end of a given number of years;
2. the present value of an annuity of £1 payable at the end of each year for a given number of years;
3. the accumulated value of the annuity described in item 2 valued at the end of a given number of years; and
4. the annual payment made at the end of the year for a given number of years that a purchaser could obtain with a single payment of £1.

The tables are calculated for periods up to 30 years. Witt repeats these four tables for an annual interest rate of 6¼%. Each of these tables eases the arithmetical burden for someone making annuity valuations. For each of several other rates of interest (6%, 7%, 8%, and 9%) Witt provides only a table for what an amount of £1 would be worth at the end of each year up to 30 years. At 5% interest annually, he gives his table for up to 50 years.

There is a section in the book that contains a practical aspect of interest and annuities that only a few others have considered before or after him. Conforming to the statutory 10% rate of interest, suppose that payments are made quarterly rather than annually. One would think that the effective quarterly rate would be 2.5%. However, from the basic concept of compound interest an amount of 1 would accumulate to $1.1^{1/4}$, or 1.0241 approximately, after 3 months, so that the quarterly interest rate is about 2.41%.[10] The quarterly rate of 2.5% is equivalent to an annual rate of 10.38% approximately. Properly done, quarterly payments are arithmetically more difficult to handle when given the annual rate of interest. Witt provides two tables each for semi-annual and quarterly payments at an annual interest rate of 10%. The first table shows the value of an amount £1 determined at the end of each of

6 months or 3 months as appropriate. The second table is the accumulated value of £1 paid at each of the time periods.

Witt ends his book with a topic directly related to the purchase of land. He considers two typical cases: land could be bought at 20 years' purchase or at 16 years' purchase. Witt's use of the term "years' purchase" differs from normal usage in the eighteenth century; he equates the reciprocal of "years' purchase" to the annual interest rate to be used in his calculations. When land was bought at 16 years' purchase, for example, the yearly rent received was 1/16 of the purchase price or 6¼%, and the interest rate used in calculations was then 6¼%. The 16 years' purchase is the value of a perpetuity of £1 annually at 6¼% interest. If rent is paid semiannually or quarterly, then it is 1/32 or 1/64, respectively, of the purchase price. This is the reason for his earlier table calculations at 5% (20 years' purchase) and 6¼% (16 years' purchase). Witt also provides tables for 20 years' purchase with semiannual rents and for 16 years' purchase with semiannual or quarterly rents. In each case there is a table showing the value of a unit of rent determined at the end of the period, and another table with the accumulated value of all the rental amounts of £1 paid at each of the time periods.

Witt provides 123 worked numerical examples in his book. About one third are generic questions concerning interest and annuities, one third relate mainly to loans but also to other business transactions, and the final third deal with land (leases and rents). Here is one example dealing with a lease:[11]

> There is a Lease of 30. years yet to come, whereof the present yearly profit, al[l] out-rents paid, is 10 l. but after 21 yeares it will yeelde 28 l. yearely, all out-rents paid. This lease is offered in sale: the Question is, What may be given for it, reckoning 10. per Cent per Ann. Interest, and interest upon Interest?

What this example shows, in addition to the equivalence of leases and annuities, is the complexity of the landholding system. What appears to be happening here is that the lessee is renting from a landowner, perhaps an endowed charity, a parish church, a diocese, or a college at Oxbridge, and then subdividing the land to sublet to small tenant farmers. After paying rent to the landowner (the out-rent), the lessee can clear £10 per annum and later £28 per annum from rents received from his tenant farmers.

Shortly after its publication *Arithmeticall Questions* was joined by a number of imitators and competitors. Like Witt's, these publications usually mix problems about loans with problems about leases and land. Perhaps this was done to appeal to a wider readership. Going against the general flow, the first publication after Witt, entitled *A Chorologicall*

Discourse with subtitle *Certaine Briefe and Necessarie Tables for the Valuation of Leases, Annuities, and Purchases, either in Present or in Reversion*, deals only with land. Written by the surveyor and mathematics teacher, Thomas Clay, it came out in print perhaps as early as 1619, but definitely by 1622.[12] The 1622 edition contains four tables. Two are similar to Witt's tables: the present value of an annuity of £1 and the present value of a single payment of £1, both evaluated at the statutory maximum interest rate of 10% per annum for up to 40 years. Two tables are devoted to finding the present value of deferred annuities or reversions, one at a 10% rate of interest and the other in terms of years' purchase (12, 16, and 20). These tables could be used to calculate renewal fines either in leases for lives (or 21 years) or in other common fixed-term leases. In 1624, Clay put out a revised edition. Other tables were added: the accumulated value of a single payment of £1 and the accumulated value of an annuity of £1 per year. Each table is accompanied by at least one example of its usage. At the end of the new edition there are an additional six difficult questions that show the range of situations facing a landlord. Here is one of them:

> A Tenant taketh a Lease for 21 yeares, and payeth for it 30 l Fine, and 80 l per annum: at 8 yeares end being through many losses and hindrances grown behind hand, & rent-run for three yeares: he agreeth with his Land-lord, by exchanging his old lease, and taking another for the residue of his terme, worth onely 20 l per annum above the rent, to satisfie the old debt, and to give a Fine for the new Lease: the Question is, what money is due betweene them, and to whether partie.

The chorological discourse part of the book is a description of the roles and duties of various personnel involved with estate management such as surveyors, stewards and solicitors.

The printer for all three editions of *A Chorologicall Discourse* was George Eld. He was joined in the final edition by Miles Flesher, who eventually took over Eld's printing presses. Eld ran two printing presses and produced a large number of books.[13] Since it was Eld who registered the book with the Company of Stationers on November 26, 1618, and hence held the copyright,[14] he probably recognized the demand for this kind of book, first satisfied by Richard Witt. Thomas Clay had his own monetary reasons for writing, which become apparent from his dedicatory prefaces and other introductory material at the beginning of each of the three editions of the book. Initially, Clay appears to have been looking for any patron. He dedicated his book to "all the Right Honorable, Noble and Worshipfull Lords, Owners, Possessors, and Purchasers of Revenue." He appealed to their higher calling through their purse by harking back to his fellow surveyor Fitzherbert's description 100 years before of the importance of surveying. Honor and nobility, Clay said, are created by virtue and revenue. In order to sustain honor and nobility, revenue should be organized to the best advantage and the least cost. By the third edition in 1624, Clay had found a high-ranking patron, a member of the Privy Council, who would support some of the cost of publication – Edward Somerset, Earl of Worcester. This time he appealed to the justice of his method of valuing leases and other properties, a theme that was to return in later years.

Clearly Redmer and Eld, perhaps along with their authors Witt and Clay, had recognized the potential demand for a book dealing with the valuation of leases. The question is: Since the system of leasing was not new to the seventeenth century, why was there a demand for this kind of book and at this particular time? Surveyors had been valuing land for the previous 100 years and would continue to do so for hundreds of years to come. And the mathematics behind the valuation of annuities is much simpler than the mathematics of surveying, although the arithmetic involved can be quite tedious. I put forward the premise that the demand for books and tables on the valuation is connected to a variety of issues concerning land management.

The biggest nongeological seismic event concerning land in England and Wales was Henry VIII's dissolution of the monasteries between 1536 and 1539. As a prelude to the dissolution, Thomas Cromwell, Henry's secretary and chief minister, commissioned the Valor Ecclesiasticus in 1535. This was a survey of the property and income of the Church in England and Wales. Following this compilation of Church wealth, the smaller monasteries were closed in the years 1536–38. The remaining monasteries were closed between 1538 and 1540. The Crown took over these ecclesiastical lands; some remained part of Crown land and the remainder were sold to raise money for the Crown, which was spent on waging a war with France. During the reign of Elizabeth I, the administration of Crown land as a source of revenue for the monarch was not well handled. Peculation was common. Records were not well kept. And there was the issue of what are called "concealed lands." These were lands that were supposed to have gone to the Crown at the time of the dissolution of the monasteries, but for one reason or another had not attracted the Crown's attention at the time.

One immediate effect of the Valor Ecclesiasticus, soon followed by the closing of the smaller monasteries, is that beginning in 1535 many monasteries started looking for liquid capital. One way to obtain it was to offer security to the tenant through long-term leases, 40–100 years, at a cost that was a high entry fine. When the property was transferred

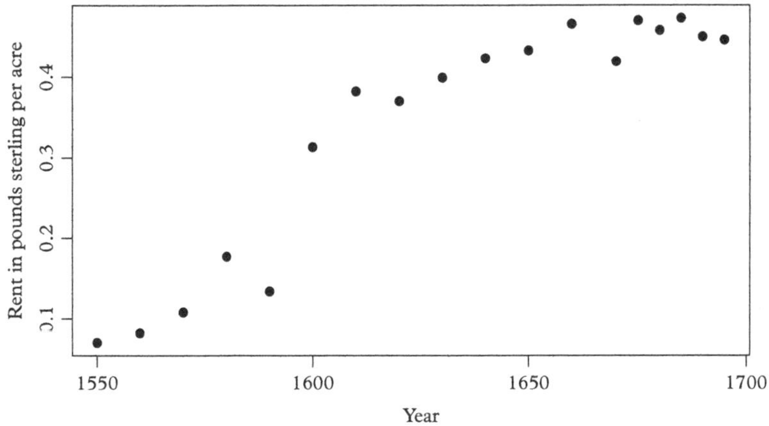

Figure 2.2. English land rental values, 1550–1700

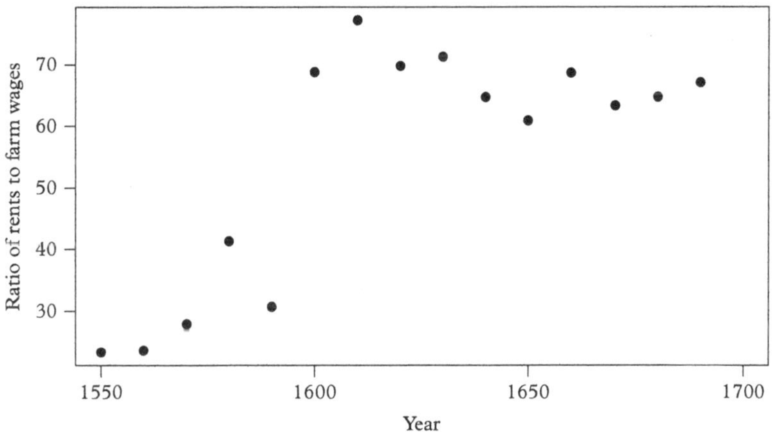

Figure 2.3. Rental values/farm wages, 1550–1700

to the Crown and from the Crown to a waiting purchaser, these long-term leases were usually confirmed. Some of these leases came due in the early seventeenth century and needed to be renegotiated at that time.[15]

One of the things that had changed in the land market during this 50–60-year period was that rent slowly increased during the latter half of the sixteenth century and then jumped significantly in the early seventeenth century. This is shown in Figure 2.2.[16] At the same time, farm wages did not keep pace. Figure 2.3 shows the ratio of the value of the rent to the value of wages during the same period.[17] Taking both of these graphs into account, it is evident that those whose incomes depended on rents were doing better economically than those who had to pay the rent. Landlords could only extract more rent from their tenants when the leases came due and the terms of the lease were renegotiated.

Reform of the Elizabethan approach to the administration of Crown lands began in 1598 after the death of Elizabeth's long-serving secretary of state, William Cecil, Lord Burghley. This accelerated during the reign of James I; as a result of his expenditures, James's appetite for ready money was voracious. There was a marked move, which involved increasing the use of land surveyors, to get an accurate assessment of the values of Crown estates with a view to improving revenue to the Crown from these estates.[18] The end result was a shift from long-established rents to rents and fines based on the value of the land. James was always in need of money, and his ministers looked for ways to provide it. Some of the Crown estates were sold as fee-farms, providing perpetuities to the Crown in rents much higher than what had been previously obtained. The relationship between the Crown as landlord and its tenants changed dramatically over the reign of James I.

Another factor in the changing face of land management was the move from the common field system of agriculture that was in place in more than half of England in 1500 to enclosed fields and the disappearance of common property rights.[19] In the common field system, there were subdivided fields with common property rights such as the right to graze animals on pasture land or on stubble after harvest. With enclosure came private property rights, in which all aspects of the farm operation were under the control of a single farmer. Enclosure could involve changes in field layouts and boundaries, and the amalgamation of farms.[20] What accompanied enclosure was the annulment of all leases associated with the common field system that it replaced. This could mean that some tenants no longer had land to farm and the tenants who remained paid a higher rent. As mentioned already, it has been estimated that slightly less than half of the land in England had been enclosed by 1500.[21] Enclosure during the sixteenth century was a slow process; only an additional 2% of the land was enclosed during this century. However, during the seventeenth century there was a big jump. A further 24% was enclosed in this century, which probably resulted, in part, in the upward pressure on rents seen in Figures 2.2 and 2.3. It may also have given impetus to landlords and prospective buyers of leases paying greater attention to the valuation of leases.

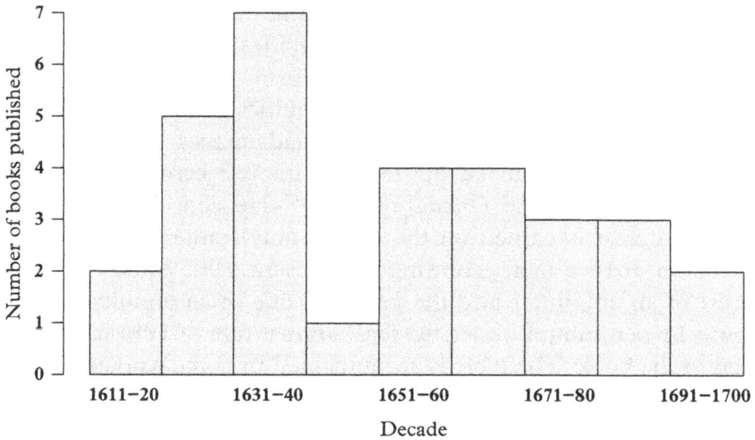

Figure 2.4. Number of books devoted mainly to lease and annuity valuations

Either Witt or his printer Redmer, or both, were correct in their assessment of the demand for the topic of lease valuations. After Witt's initial publication there was a steady stream of books about annuity and lease valuations. More than thirty books devoted mainly to these subjects, with accompanying tables, were published between 1620 and 1700. There was a flurry of activity in the 1620s and 1630s, followed by a publication every 3 or 4 years afterward, with the exception of the decade of the English Civil War. This is shown in Figure 2.4. The list of publications includes new editions of old ones. Witt, for example, died in 1624. His book *Arithmeticall Questions* was republished, or possibly pirated, in 1635. There was a new printer and it was distributed through a new bookseller. Another mathematical practitioner, Thomas Fisher, made some additions to the book, mainly by providing tables at the new statutory maximum annual rate of interest of 8%.

Material on interest and annuities also appears in commercial arithmetic books. These books had been available for many years prior to Witt's 1613 *Arithmeticall Questions*, but had quite a different flavor from Witt's book. First published in 1543, *The Ground of Artes Teachyng the Worke and Practise of Arithmetike* was a highly influential arithmetic book that went through at least 15 editions before 1600 and at least 50 editions by 1699.[22] This large number of editions speaks to the popularity of the book and the demand for access to the mathematical techniques contained in it. The author, Robert Record (ca 1512–58) was university educated and at the same time had extensive experience in the practice of mathematics, initially through work with the Bristol Mint.

There is no treatment of interest or annuities in the early editions of Record's book. It was John Mellis, a mathematics teacher living in Southwark, who introduced the topic of interest earned on money in the 1582 edition of the *Ground of Artes*.[23] He considers only simple interest (interest is earned on the capital only) rather than compound interest. In 1615 a table, showing the present value under compound interest of an amount 1 and the present value of an annuity paying an amount £1 per annum under the legal annual rate of 10% interest, was added to the book. The table is accompanied by some worked problems that use the table. For the 1623 edition, someone known as "R.C." computed four tables (present values and accumulated values of single payments and of annuities) that are in line with what Richard Witt had done.[24] A few examples are given to illustrate the use of each table; only one deals with land.

Several commercial arithmetic books include material on annuities after the venture into the field of the writers of Record's *Ground of Artes*. Typically, the topic appears at the end of these early books. There are often brief discussions of how the calculations are done and there are always brief tables of the values of single payments and annuities, both present and forborne values, at the appropriate annual rates of interest. Usually, no attempt is made to cover semiannual or quarterly payments and only a few examples deal with land.

One of the most influential commercial arithmetic books coming out of this tradition is Edmund Wingate's *Arithmetique Made Easie*. First published in 1630, it continued to be published until 1760. The printer for the first edition was Miles Flesher, who was one of the printers for the final edition of Thomas Clay's *Chorologicall Discourse*. Given the long run of the book, Flesher appears to have had a good eye for the market. Flesher's son printed the second edition. The first edition of *Arithmetique* falls into the mold for interest and annuities established by other commercial arithmetic writers by having an appendix dealing with the topic of interest and annuities.[25] Like Clay, Wingate had worked as a land surveyor.[26] For the second edition, Wingate handed off the book to the mathematician John Kersey. In the second edition, published in 1650, Kersey greatly enlarged the section on interest and annuities.[27] He describes in detail how interest and annuity calculations are carried out, including semiannual and quarterly payments, and provides several sets of tables at various annual rates of interest. Of all the numerical examples that Kersey provides, only the final three deal with leases.

One of these examples is reminiscent of one that Richard Witt had used earlier:[28]

> There is a Lease of certain Lands worth 32 l. per annum, more than the rent paid to the Lord for it, of which Land there is a Lease yet in being for seven years, and the Lessee is desirous to take a Lease in reversion for 21 years, to begin when his old Lease is expired. The question is, what summe of money is to be paid for this Lease in reversion, accompting compound interest at the rate of 6 per centum per annum?

Again, this is an example of the two-tiered system in land. A lord leases his land to a middle man for a certain rent. The middle man leases some of his land to a farmer. If the middle man wants some ready cash at the time when the farmer wants to renegotiate his lease and sells the reversion, the answer to the question is the sale price.

When the corpus of commercial arithmetic books is examined as a whole, there are distinct differences between them and the manuals used to evaluate leases and annuities. The two groups were aiming at different audiences. The tone throughout commercial arithmetic books is pedagogical; a student is taught how the calculations are done and how to use various mathematical tables, including those on interest and annuities. The emphasis is on mathematical or arithmetical training. Like modern mortgage amortization tables, the lease valuation manuals were meant to provide lessors and lessees with the easiest ways to determine entry or renewal fines.

Leases for lives received no mention in the annuity literature or the commercial arithmetic books until the 1650s. There was probably no need to mention these leases; everyone knew they were each equivalent to a 21-year lease. The first mention I can find is in Henry Phillippes's 1653 *The Purchasers Pattern Shewing the True Value of Any Purchase of Land or Houses, by Lease or Otherwise*. Phillippes writes:[29]

> There is another way of purchasing Land or Houses, by buying Lives therein, And this is the ordinary rule for it. One Life in any thing is accounted of equall worth to a Lease of seven years. Two Lives are worth as much as a Lease of 14 years. Three Lives are worth as much as a Lease of 21 years. And so still increasing by seven years for every Life.

Phillippes goes on to recognize the uncertainty of life and how this custom could result in inequality. He rationalizes the custom by commenting that after a person dies he need not care about the lease and that a younger person who might have a life expectancy of 20 or 30 more years would be taking on a good bet. Despite the rationalization he goes on to suggest an alternative that he thought would be more equitable: one life should be worth 12 years, two lives 23 years in total, three lives

33 years, and so on, decreasing the length of any additional life by 1 year. This suggestion does not seem to have caught on, and probably for good reason. Most of the yearly income for a landlord leasing land on lives would come from renewal fines. Renewal fines for leases with a yearly rent of £1 held by several Church of England dioceses (evaluated at 11½% annually) would fall from £1 to 12s 11d. Renewal fines evaluated at the legal rate of interest in 1653 (8% annually) would fall from £1 15s 6d to £1 9s 11d.

There was one other thing that Phillippes brought to the table. From the perspective of Fitzherbert, and Clay in his early publications, proper lease valuations were for the purpose of having the landlord know the value of his property in order to obtain the income necessary to maintain his honor and social status. Later writers on the subject say only that they were responding to the change in the statutory maximum rate of interest – a reduction to 8% per annum in 1625 and then to 6% in 1651. In his preface to the reader, Phillippes expands greatly on Clay's idea of justice in the valuation of leases. He begins with a theological discussion of justice that concludes with:[30]

> For Justice is a giving to every one his due: and that gives God his due, and his neighbour his due, doth all things which both the Law and Gospel require.

This theological opening is followed by a criticism of the usual image of the goddess of justice, veiled and holding a sword and scales, one in each hand. The veil can signify ignorance, not impartiality, Phillippes says, and ignorance may not lead to justice. His tables and calculations should dispel ignorance,

> so that all men may make their bargains without fear or danger, and receive just, true and mutuall profit and gain thereby.

The theme of just calculation runs through the evaluation of life-contingent products, related to both annuities and leases, throughout the eighteenth century.

The set of tables that became the standard by the end of the seventeenth century is called *Tables for Renewing & Purchasing of the Leases of Cathedral-Churches and Colleges, According to Several Rates of Interest*, first published in 1686. Although his name appears nowhere in the book, the author is George Mabbut, who was a steward for King's College, Cambridge.[31] The book was printed by John Hayes, printer to Cambridge University. Hayes was responsible for printing a second edition of *Tables for Renewing & Purchasing of the Leases* in 1700, well after Mabbut's death in 1689. Inside the front cover of the 1686 and 1700 editions, there is a "seal of approval" of the book by Isaac Newton.[32]

At least four more editions of the book appeared in the eighteenth century, some of them pirated. Because of Newton's note in the early editions, later editions of the book were often attributed to Newton.

Mabbut's tables cover a variety of practical situations at annual rates of interest of 5%, 6%, 8%, 10%, and 12% and for lease lengths of 10, 20, 21, and 40 years. Once again, the 21-year lease is the standard equivalent for a lease for three lives. Each table shows the fine for renewing the lease when the lessee is already a certain number of years into the lease. In a nutshell, Mabbut's tables contain values of $a_{\overline{n}|} - a_{\overline{m}|}$ for the various values of n (10, 20, 21, 40) and i (0.05, 0.06, 0.08, 0.10, and 0.12), where m takes on all integer values up to n. Like Phillippes, Mabbut did not think it equitable that a lease for three lives be treated as equivalent to a lease for 21 years. His proposal is similar to Phillippes's, differing only in the numbers: one life is equivalent to 10 years, two lives to 19 years, and three lives to 27 years. Mabbut provides tables to handle his proposal. Like Phillippes's, Mabbut's suggestion does not seem to have had much traction.

Leases for three lives and leases for 21 years, with a few exceptions, run hand in hand well into the eighteenth century. It was the sale of leases and other life-contingent products related to land, as exemplified by Thomas Clay's and John Kersey's practice problems, and not the life insurance or life annuity industry, that was the greatest motivation for Dodson's predecessors to work on the mathematics of life annuities.

Dodson wrote against the custom of making leases for lives equivalent to leases for years for the purpose of evaluation. There was another custom related to annuity valuations that is below the surface, one that Dodson participated in without reservation. What first broke the surface on annuity and lease valuations was a genre of books specializing in the single topic of interest and annuities, books such as Witt's *Arithmeticall Questions* and Clay's *Certaine Briefe and Necessarie Tables*. The commercial arithmetic books, which covered a wide range of topics, were slower to respond to the demand for information on the valuation of annuities. The same is true for the eighteenth century, when books on the valuation of life annuities first appeared.

3 Edmond Halley's Life Table

What is seen by modern actuaries and mathematicians as the foundational work in actuarial science is Edmond Halley's 1693 life table and its application to the valuation of life annuities and life insurance.[1] Just as there was a divide between traditional leases for lives and the development of life annuities separate from land, the insurance and annuity industries became established, and the valuation of leases for lives continued, without the use of Halley's table. What is the historical context for Halley's life table? And what, if any, impact did it have?

In 1688 there was a revolution in Britain. James II, the reigning monarch who had earlier converted to Catholicism, fled to France following the successful invasion of his Protestant son-in-law William of Orange. After a special parliament, known as the Convention Parliament, was called in February 1689, William and James's daughter Mary were declared co-regents and later crowned as joint monarchs William and Mary. Once on the throne, William pursued a vigorous military policy, against Louis XIV of France, that became known variously as the Nine Years' War, the War of the Grand Alliance or the War of the League of Augsburg. The valuation of leases for lives and the wars of King William III are, in an odd way, connected. The waging of war costs money; the connection between leases and war is in one of the financial instruments that the government used to finance William's wars.

Initially the war was financed by various taxes on property and estates. The only other source of revenue available to the government, an excise tax, was dismissed in view of the uncertainty about the amount that it would raise. The cost of war was mounting as the reign of William and Mary progressed. By mid-December 1692 Parliament was considering raising £2 million for the war effort by imposing a tax of 4 shillings in the pound (20%) on all personal estates other than household goods and stock on the land, and on all offices other than positions in the army or navy. The MP Thomas Neale, who was Newton's predecessor as Master of the Mint and hence the possessor of an office, suggested instead that the government take a loan of

£2 million and then raise £120,000 annually to pay the interest on the loan. The legal annual rate of interest at the time was 6%.[2] Another MP, Paul Foley, who later became Speaker of the House, objected to this mode of financing the war and countered with a novel proposal. He suggested a tontine. Whatever sum was raised (the intention was £1 million), the government would pay 6% of it annually to the surviving members of the pool of investors. Despite some opposition and much debate, the scheme was adopted.[3] The formal act of Parliament established the tontine as well as an alternative if the target of £1 million was not reached.[4] In that case the purchase of a life annuity would be offered, which would provide annual payments of 14% of the purchase price. This is approximately following the concept that the length of one life is equivalent to 7 years' purchase (1/7 reduces to 0.1429 approximately). Rather than using a land tax, the annual payments made to the tontine participants and the annuitants were financed by a tax on beer, ale, cider, vinegar, and brandy that was to continue for 99 years. Since the funds received from investors were paid into the Office of the Exchequer, these government life annuities came to be known as Exchequer annuities. Although new to England, tontines and life annuities were not new to public finance on the Continent. Both had been used in William's native United Provinces of the Netherlands to finance long-term public debt.[5] The general idea behind these financing schemes is that the debt would disappear once all the life annuitants and tontine participants died. Of course, the debt for William's wars did not disappear, but became the beginning of the English national debt.

Further details on the establishment and working of the English tontine and Exchequer annuity, as well as another Exchequer annuity made possible through an act of Parliament in 1693, are relevant to the development of life annuities in Britain.[6] The price of a share in the tontine was set at £100. A purchaser attached a name to each share that he purchased and the share was valid during the lifetime of the nominee. If the tontine was fully subscribed at 10,000 shares, the government promised to divide the sum of £100,000 annually among the surviving nominees until the year 1700 and then afterward to divide annually the sum of £70,000 among the survivors. When the pool of survivors fell to seven, then any survivor received £10,000 annually until his or her death. There was a deadline for entering into this tontine – May 1, 1693. By the deadline there were only 1,012 subscribers to the tontine at £100 each; the tontine payments were reduced in proportion to the number of subscribers to the fund relative to the projected 10,000. The ability to contribute to the fund by the purchase of a life annuity paying

£14 annually per £100 investment was then introduced and remained available until September 20, 1693. The sale of life annuities brought in an additional £780,293 14s 2d, so that when this combined with the amount raised by the tontine, there was a shortfall of £118,506 5s 10d.[7] In a subsequent act of Parliament more Exchequer annuities were offered to cover this shortfall, with a deadline of May 1, 1694 for buying an annuity.

As Foley's legislation was being put into practice, Halley published his life table, or more accurately a population table, that could be used for the proper valuation of the Exchequer annuities. His methods appear timely and it is tempting to say that they were motivated by the creation of the Exchequer annuities. On the other hand, Halley went well beyond the Exchequer annuities as they were offered in 1693.

The data for Halley's table came from Caspar Neumann, a Protestant pastor working in the city of Breslau (now Wrocław). Neumann had collected data on births and deaths from the city's church records for the 5 years 1687 through 1691.[8] He had one advantage over the English on vital statistics. The age of death was recorded in Breslau's parish registers; in the English registers it was not. What motivated Neumann to look at the mortality data was a scientific question. He was interested in physico-theology, the "theology based on the constitution of the natural world, esp[ecially] on evidences of design found there."[9] With respect to human mortality, the question that would arise for Neumann is whether there was a pattern to mortality. For Neumann the question was tied up in the concept of climacterics. This was a question of interest to English scientists as well.

The idea of climacteric years has its origins in the ancient world, but was very much "on the table" throughout the seventeenth century. Writing in 1645, David Person describes the concept as seen through the eyes of Roman authors:[10]

> Macrobius, Aulus Gellius and others observe, that every seventh yeare in the life of man there followeth some alteration either in estate, voyce, colour, hayre, complexion, or conditions: And Seneca, *Septimus quis{que} annus aetati notam imprimit*, wherefore the 7. 14. 21. 28. 35. 42. 49. 56. and 63. the great Climactericke yeare are counted dangerous for all. Firmian adviseth all to take great heede to themselves in these yeares: Octavianus Caesar having passed this date, writ to his Nephew Caius, to congratulate with him, that he had yet seven yeares more to live.

The possibility of climacteric effects reverberated at the highest levels of seventeenth-century society. In 1595 when Queen Elizabeth I fell ill, there was much concern in the court as she was 63 and thus in her grand climacteric, the most dangerous of years. In response to the perceived danger, vagrants were removed and sent abroad, the guard was increased at Westminster, and some military preparations were made.[11] When her death occurred in 1603 at the age of 70, another climacteric year, the playwright Thomas Dekker wrote that great changes quickly occurred, at one end of the spectrum the union of the Scottish and English crowns and at the other end an outbreak of the plague in London.[12] The idea of climacterics persisted throughout the seventeenth century and is mentioned as late as the 1720s by the historian Joseph Morgan when describing a sixteenth-century Ottoman admiral who died in his 63rd year.[13] In view of these generally held perceptions, the empirical investigation of climacterics was a reasonable avenue of inquiry for Neumann.

Neumann's work eventually reached the Royal Society by a circuitous route.[14] He wrote to Gottfried von Leibniz sending him a manuscript of his work. In May 1692, Leibniz wrote to Henri Justell, mentioning at the end of the letter that Neumann had made some good points about the births and deaths in Breslau, in particular that there was no substance to the notion of climacteric years. Leibniz's connection to Justell is that they were both librarians; Leibniz was the court librarian in Hanover and Justell was the royal librarian in England. On January 18, 1693, Justell presented the data to a meeting of the Royal Society. A record of the meeting states that:[15]

> The Climactericks are rigorously examined, to see if there be any thing worth remark which by these notes seem to argue to be a Groundless Conceit.

As it was for Leibniz, the main focus of the Society's fellows was on disproving the validity of climacterics. The raw data were brought to the Royal Society meeting of February 8. This meeting would probably have been the first time that Halley saw the data.

Halley saw potential in the data to answer questions beyond the issue of climacterics. As he wrote in his introductory remarks to the paper that he published on the data, there had previously been work done in England on mortality data by John Graunt and William Petty that had been "most judiciously considered." There were three problems with these earlier data, Halley said, that were limiting further analyses. These were lack of knowledge of the population size, lack of knowledge of the ages of deaths, and substantial immigration or lack of a stationary population. These problems are overcome, Halley claimed, in the Breslau data. Throughout the eighteenth century these three issues would continue to dog those in England trying to construct life tables relevant to the English experience.

Initially motivated almost certainly by Graunt's and Petty's work, Halley took the data presented at the February 8 meeting and returned a month later, on March 8, to read a paper on a first analysis of the data. A record of the meeting states:

> Halley read some considerations on the Bills of Mortality of Breslaw giving a Table of the ages of the whole peoples of that City, and thereby shewing the proportion of mortality in each age, and a rule to estimate how long any person may reasonably be supposed to live.

Presumably, this was the table that appears in the published paper as shown in Table 3.1. After the meeting, Halley took his table and made some further calculations. One week after his first analysis of the Breslau data, on March 15 Halley presented new work:

> Halley produced a paper wherein he shewed a method of computing the values of annuities for one, two, or three lives, with all the cases of the reversions of them, either after any one, or any two lives of three proposed which was ordered to be printed in the Transactions.

What also appears in the published paper in *Philosophical Transactions* is a table showing values of single life annuities at various ages. Halley's annuity table is reproduced in Table 3.2.

What inspired Halley to look again at the mortality data with a view to making annuity valuations is impossible to say from surviving contemporary sources. From one account there was also little initial reaction to Halley's paper. Robert Hooke attended the meetings of January 18, February 8, and March 8, and made no comment about the data in his diary.[16] He did mention that there were thirteen fellows, including himself, present at the March 8 meeting. His only comment on the March 15 meeting was that, "Hally read again his paper of burials," giving the impression that it was just a déjà vu for Hooke. There was no meeting of the Royal Society on March 22. Instead, a number of people met at Hooke's lodgings at Gresham College. There Halley seemed keen to discuss his work on the bills of mortality as well as his other scientific work. Hooke reported in his diary, "discourse of Hally on mort[ality] bills of Breslaw; of comets."[17]

Table 3.1, Halley's table, is a population table rather than a life table. The difference is subtle yet distinct. A population table shows the number in the population alive at each age. The abbreviation "Age. Curt." in the table stands for age current, or the year of life in which an individual is living. Halley's 1,000 individuals at "Age Curt." 1 is the number of people in the population who are in their first year of life or who will be age 1 on their next birthday. Adding all the entries in the table yields

Table 3.1. *Halley's Breslau table*

Age. Curt.	Persons	Age. Curt.	Persons	Age. Curt.	Persons	Age. Curt.	Persons	Age. Curt.	Persons	Age. Curt.	Persons	Age. Curt.	Persons
1	1 000	8	680	15	628	22	586	29	539	36	481	7	5 547
2	855	9	670	16	622	23	579	30	531	37	472	14	4 584
3	798	10	661	17	616	24	573	31	523	38	463	21	4 270
4	760	11	653	18	610	25	567	32	515	39	454	28	3 964
5	732	12	646	19	604	26	560	33	507	40	445	35	3 604
6	710	13	640	20	598	27	553	34	499	41	436	42	3 178
7	692	14	634	21	592	28	546	35	490	42	427	49	2 709
Age.		Age.		Age.		Age.		Age.		Age.		56	2 194
Curt.	Persons	Curt.	Persons	Curt.	Persons	Curt.	Persons	Curt.	Persons	Curt.	Persons	63	1 694
43	417	50	346	57	272	64	202	71	131	78	58	70	1 204
44	407	51	335	58	262	65	192	72	120	79	49	77	692
45	397	52	324	59	252	66	182	73	109	80	41	84	253
46	387	53	313	60	242	67	172	74	98	81	34	100	107
47	377	54	302	61	232	68	162	75	88	82	28		34 000
48	367	55	292	62	222	69	152	76	78	83	23	Sum	Total
49	357	56	282	63	212	70	142	77	68	84	20		

Table 3.2. *Halley's life annuity valuations at 6% interest*

Age	Years' purchase	Age	Years' purchase	Age	Years' purchase
1	10.28	25	12.17	50	9.21
5	13.40	30	11.72	55	8.51
10	13.44	35	11.12	60	7.60
15	13.33	40	10.57	65	6.54
20	12.78	45	9.91	70	5.32

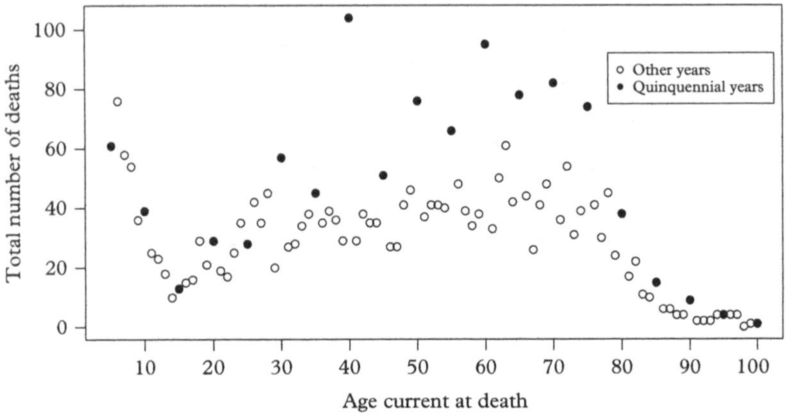

Figure 3.1. Number of deaths in Breslau for the period 1687–91

the population size of Breslau, which Halley estimates at 34,000. In a life table the first entry at age 0 is an arbitrary number, called the radix of the table. It is the size of some fictitious cohort of individuals at birth and is usually some power of 10 (modern British life tables use 100,000). For all his calculations Halley makes no explicit distinction between the two. To explain some of Halley's results it is useful to employ life table notation and to treat the table as a life table. In modern actuarial notation l_x denotes the number living at age x and $d_x = l_x - l_{x+1}$ denotes the number dying between ages x and $x + 1$. For example, in Halley's table $l_{21} = 592$ and $d_{21} = 592 - 586 = 6$.

Halley approached Neumann's data in a very pragmatic way. He tended to smooth out unusual variation. Figure 3.1 shows the total number of deaths in Breslau for the years 1687–91. The numbers behind the graph were collected by Jonas Graetzer, the medical officer in Breslau, who reconstructed Neumann's data in the early 1880s; what Neumann originally collected and what Halley used for his life table are no longer extant.[18] The points shown with solid dots are the total number of deaths at 5-year age intervals beginning at age five. What is apparent from the graph is that beginning around age 40 and continuing to about age 75, the number of deaths at these quinquennial ages is higher than at the surrounding ages. This probably reflects family members or friends reporting an approximate or rounded age at death to the parish clerk. Halley also provides a table showing the number of deaths by age that he had calculated from Neumann's data. At many of the quinquennial ages experiencing a higher than usual number of deaths, Halley takes an average of deaths for surrounding ages.

Halley tended to round his calculations both for clarity of presentation and for ease of calculation.[19] Rounding in two entries in Table 3.1 has led to some confusion and speculation in the past about how Halley constructed his table. The two entries, which are central to my interpretation of Halley's table construction, are the 1,000 people at age current 1 and the 34,000 people for the total population size. If I take these as rounded numbers rather than exact ones, then the construction of the table for early ages becomes a simple exercise in arithmetic that would have been obvious to Halley. The completion of the table requires only that the population size be approximately 34,000 and that the complete life table yields the annuity values that Halley obtained, shown in Table 3.2.

Halley states that in the years 1687–91 there were on average in Breslau 1,238 births and 348 deaths in the first year of life. Then 890 (1,238 − 348) individuals would attain their first birthday. On average, there would be (1,238 + 890)/2 or 1,064 persons who are age current 1 in the population. With Halley's penchant for rounding, I would speculate that he rounded the 1,064 to 1,000 and then distributed the "excess" lives into other age groups. This is illustrated in Table 3.3. The average number of deaths in the third column in the table is taken from Graezter's data, with the exception of the first entry of 348 deaths that was claimed by Halley.[20] The number of lives at any age in the table is found by subtracting the number of deaths in the previous year from lives in the previous year. The calculated number at each age current is the average of lives from column 2 at that age and at 1 year younger. When the calculated number at each age current is compared to Halley's values, the differences sum to −1, which I claim shows the distribution of the excess lives over Halley's 1,000 at age current 1.

Halley's table is incomplete. There are no entries for the number of persons at age current 85 and beyond; only the number 107 is given for the total number of people who are in their 85th year or higher. After all the people at all the ages are added up, the total comes to the nice round number, 34,000. When trying to reconstruct the number of

Table 3.3. *Halley's adjustments to the table at early ages*

Age in years	Number of lives	Average number of deaths	Age current	Calculated number at each age current	Halley's values at each age current	Difference
0	1238.0	348.0	1	1 064	1 000	64
1	890.0	93.6	2	843	855	−12
2	796.4	44.6	3	774	798	−24
3	751.8	23.6	4	740	760	−20
4	728.2	12.2	5	722	732	−10
5	716.0	15.2	6	708	710	−2
6	700.8	11.6	7	695	692	3
7	689.2				Sum	−1

persons at the individual ages beginning at 85, a useful tool is Halley's table of the value of life annuities at various ages given in Table 3.2. The value or fair price for a life annuity is the expected value of all future annual payments. The usual actuarial notation for the value of an annuity, given to the person aged x at the time the annuity is issued, of £1 paid at the end of every year until the person dies is a_x. The mathematical definition of a_x, in terms of the survivor function l_x and the interest rate i, is given in Appendix 1.

One strategy for obtaining the end-of-table values in Halley's table is to begin with a reasonably guessed reconstruction of the end of the table and check to see if the resulting annuity values agree with what is in Table 3.2. Then vary the end-of-table values and iterate until there is good agreement between the calculated values and Table 3.2. There is one twist. Halley's calculations were all done by hand and there may be errors in his arithmetic. A check on Halley's arithmetic can be made using a relationship between a_x and a_y, given in Appendix 1 where the relationship involves values of the survivor function l_x, for ages between x and y, and the interest rate i. Assuming that a_1 has been correctly computed by Halley, then the remaining a_5 to a_{70} can be calculated using a_1 and l_2 through l_{70} from Table 3.1. This exercise shows that the a_5 given in Table 3.2 should be 13.01, rather than 13.40, and that a_{15} should be 13.19, rather than 13.33. I published my guesses at l_x for x between 85 and 100 in 2011.[21] After I gave a talk about Halley's table, Jonathan Lee, a very enterprising and bright graduate student, used some statistical methods that produced results that fit the annuity values in Table 3.2 better than my guesses. I show his results in Table 3.4. The total number of persons in this age group is 167, not 107 given by Halley, so that the estimate of the population of Breslau is 34,060,

Table 3.4. *Reconstruction of Halley's table for ages 85 through 100*

Age. Curt.	Persons	Age. Curt.	Persons	Age. Curt.	Persons	Age. Curt.	Persons
85	19	89	15	93	10	97	5
86	18	90	13	94	9	98	4
87	17	91	12	95	8	99	3
88	16	92	11	96	6	100	1

Table 3.5. *Halley's treatment of intermediate ages – 8 to 25*

Age	Deaths (1)	Persons	Deaths (2)	Deaths (3)	Age	Deaths (1)	Persons	Deaths (2)	Deaths (3)
7	11	692	12	7	16	3½	622	6	6
8	11	680	10	7	17		616	6	6
9	6	670	9	7	18	5	610	6	6
10		661	8	7	19	6	604	6	6
11	5½	653	7	7	20		598	6	6
12		646	6	6	21	4½	592	6	6
13		640	6	6	22		586	6	6
14	2	634	6	6	23		579	6	6
15		628	6	6	24	6½	573	6	6

(1) Average number of deaths in Breslau in a year as reported by Halley.
(2) Number of deaths in a year computed from Halley's table.
(3) Number of deaths in a year computed from the Christ's Hospital experience (1% per year).

which rounds off to Halley's estimated population size. Now whenever I carry out calculations using Halley's table, I use the combined numbers in Tables 3.1 and 3.4. The complete table is reproduced in Appendix 2.

Halley obtained the intermediate ages in Table 3.1, ages 8 through 84, by a judicious massaging and smoothing of the deaths in each year of life. For example, with respect to early ages, the age group 9 to 25 approximately, Halley notes that from Neumann's Breslau data about 6 people die per annum in this group. This can be seen roughly in the column labeled "Deaths (1)" in Table 3.5, which appears in Halley's paper. He adds, "And by my own Experience in Christ-Church Hospital, I am informed that there die of the Young Lads about one per Cent. per Annum, they being of the aforesaid Ages." The column labeled "Deaths (2)" in Table 3.5 is the number of deaths at each age computed from Table 3.1. As seen from this column, Halley needs to get from 12 deaths in a year for persons aged 7 down to the 6 deaths that he says was the Breslau experience for this age group. He does this by decreasing the deaths by 2 to obtain 10 at age 8 and then by decreasing the deaths each year by 1 until he reaches 6 deaths in a year.

Essentially, Halley has arbitrarily smoothed the data to what he considers the stable average. Then he justifies what he has done by the experience at the boys' school Christ's Hospital of 1% mortality each year at each age. The column labeled "Deaths (3)" in Table 3.5 is 1% of the column labeled "Persons" rounded to the nearest integer. The Christ's Hospital school experience closely matches what Halley claims as the Breslau experience. Halley uses a mixture of the data and commentary to argue for smoothed data in the deaths in the remainder of the table.

After presenting his life table, Halley outlines seven uses of it in his 1693 paper. The table could be used: (1) to find how many men there might be in the population able to bear arms; (2) to find the differing degrees of mortality at various ages; (3) to find the median age at death; (4) to price 1-year term insurance; (5) to price a single life annuity; (6) to price an annuity on two lives; and (7) to price annuities on three lives as well as reversions. In a follow-up paper, Halley looks into another use of his table: (8) social planning. With respect to (8), from his table he estimates the number of women of child-bearing age and notes that only about one in six of them had a child in any 1 year. For what he said was the good of the state, Halley suggests methods to increase the birth rate such as a tax on celibacy and finding employment for the poor to reduce the financial burden on the general public. Halley's uses (1)–(3) might be associated with his March 8 presentation at the Royal Society and with building on Graunt and Petty's work. After that meeting new uses of the table, particularly insurance and annuities, occurred to him and by the next week he had the numerical work to back it up. Graunt's and Petty's concerns for the state were not forgotten and he returned to these issues in his follow-up paper. Halley's total of eight uses for his table may be reduced to three: questions of demography, the pricing of insurance, and the pricing of annuities.

All of Halley's demographical calculations are done in the spirit of Graunt's and Petty's study of political arithmetic. Of his applications to demography, the median age at death surfaces years later in some wrong-headed attempts at annuity valuations. Halley describes the median age at death as the number of years at which it is an "even lay" or a fair bet that a person of a given age will die. For a person aged x there are l_x in the population so that the median age at the death is that age y such that $l_y = \frac{1}{2} l_x$.

From the example Halley gives concerning the proper pricing of life insurance policies, it appears that what Halley had in mind was 1-year term insurance. For this kind of insurance an amount is paid to the insured if he or she dies within 1 year of the commencement of the insurance contract. The "fair" price, or value, of 1-year term insurance for an individual is the expected value of the possible future payment to the individual or the present value of an amount 1 paid at the end of the year times the probability of making the payment, which is the probability of death within a year.

At the time that Halley was writing there were no formally established life insurance companies; the first life insurance society was formed in 1696.[22] Contracts for life insurance were made prior to 1696, usually between individuals or between a group of individuals as insurers and the insured. The term for the insurance was typically 1 year or less. Normally, the policy would be registered at the Office of Assurance that had been established during the reign of Elizabeth I to deal mainly with the registration of marine insurance policies. The main group that took out life insurance appears to have been the merchants, including those involved in marine trade, needing funds to cover the repayment of outstanding short-term loans in the event of their deaths.[23] Early in his career, Halley had associations with various London trading companies, particularly the Levant Company,[24] and so it is likely that Halley came to know of the workings of life insurance in the early 1690s through these connections.

Halley's fifth use for his table is to find the value of a single-life annuity. He describes the method for obtaining the value a_x in words rather than the formula as given in Appendix 1. The value of a_x is not easy to calculate by hand and Halley gives a table of logarithms in an effort to ease the burden of calculation. After describing how to make the valuation, Halley gives a table of the values of single-life annuities at various ages, reproduced in Table 3.2. Immediately after the annuity table Halley comments:

> This shews the great Advantage of putting Money into the present Fund lately granted to their Majesties, giving 14 *per Cent. per Annum*, or at the rate of 7 years purchase for a Life; when young Lives, at the usual rate of Interest, are worth above 13 years Purchase. It shews likewise the Advantage of young Lives over those in Years; a Life of Ten Years being almost worth 13½ years purchase, whereas one of 36 is worth but 11.

This may have been an afterthought and a later insertion, and so it may not have been related to his initial research into the pricing of life annuities.

To support the quotation as an afterthought, it is necessary to look at the timeline of events. Halley initially saw the Breslau mortality data in raw form on February 8, 1693, when Henri Justell brought the data to a meeting of the Royal Society. His first presentation of the mortality table was at the meeting held on March 8, 1693. A week later he presented his annuity calculations based on his table.[25] The "Fund lately granted to their Majesties" was part of the bill, known later as the Million Act, given royal assent on January 26, 1693.[26] But the option of purchasing life annuities did not come into effect until May 1, 1693. Even on May 1, the Exchequer was not prepared to receive money for the purchase of life annuities for at least six weeks. Those who had requested life annuities prior to May 1 were to pay for them within 14 days after June 24, 1693.[27] Depending on the interpretation of "present Fund," Halley may have written the paragraph after May and inserted it in the paper when the manuscript was with the printer.

Halley's insight into the advantage of age was also noticed by the general public, but in a different context. Figure 3.2 shows the age distribution of those in the 1693 tontine, compared to the age distribution of the population of Breslau in Halley's table. Clearly there was a marked preference for younger ages for the beneficiaries of the tontine.

Halley's application of his table to joint life annuities, the sixth use of his table, begins to show, I believe, the real motivation for his annuity calculations. As with a single life, Halley describes in words the valuation of annuities on two lives. Implicit in his description is the valuation of a joint survivor annuity, or an annuity of £1 paid at the end of each year while both people are living. In standard actuarial notation this is denoted by a_{xy} for two lives aged x and y. Halley goes on to describe a reversionary annuity which he initially calls "the value of the remainder of one life after another." This is an annuity of £1 paid to a person currently aged x on the death of another currently aged y. In standard actuarial notation the value is given by $a_x - a_{xy}$, the value of lifetime payments made to the person currently aged x less the payments made while both (one aged x and the other aged y) are alive. The valuations of joint survivor and reversionary annuities are described in Appendix 1. After providing a geometric description with diagrams of his own method of valuation of this annuity, Halley concludes by saying, "whereby may be cast up what value ought to be paid for the Reversion of one Life after another, as in the case of providing for Clergy-mens Widows and others by such Reversions."

The reference to clergymen's widows is both interesting and revealing. A typical term for the financial support of a Church of England clergyman was that he held a benefice or a living. The living was financed by rents on lands held by the Church. When a clergyman resigned from his living or died, all financial support from the Church ceased and the living passed to the next incumbent. Some clergy held lands or had access to rents independently of the Church, and so could

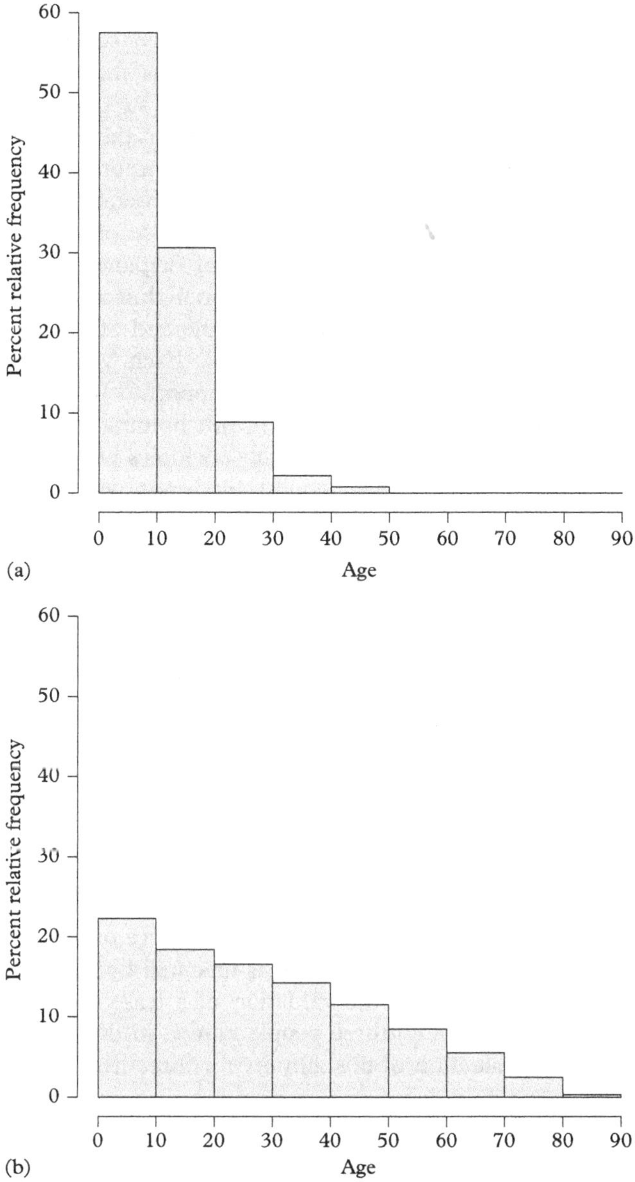

Figure 3.2. Age distributions

provide for their widows and children in the event of their death. Others did not, and there was no formal pension scheme for them. Instead, there were some charitable organizations that could provide assistance, including housing and some financial support. In terms of financial support, a major organization was Sons of the Clergy, a charitable group founded in 1655, during the Commonwealth, to help clergymen who remained loyal to the crown. Subsequently in 1678 it was given a royal charter with the express purpose of contributing to the relief of widows and children of Church of England clergymen who were poor. Money was raised during an annual church service held in London (settling in St. Paul's Cathedral by the end of the century), as well as from other donations and bequests. Each year widows and orphans might apply to the fund for some support.[28] In the early years of the charity, widows of clergy who died while holding a living typically received £3 in a year.[29] About forty of these widows were supported in any year. As early as 1697, the request for funds was outpacing the donations received. Early in the eighteenth century there was a suggestion that the Church set up a fund to provide widows of clergy with pensions or reversionary annuities, but nothing seems to have come of it.[30] Since such funds did not exist in 1693, Halley's comment on reversions for widows of clergymen seems to have been made in the same spirit as his suggestions regarding social planning (use number 8 for his table).

The final use that Halley gives for his table is for the evaluation of annuities on three lives. Like the accounts for single life annuities and annuities on two lives, the description is verbal, followed by a geometrical description. For three lives Halley concentrates not on various aspects of reversions or joint survivorship, but instead on finding "the value of an annuity during the continuance of any of those three lives." This is a last-survivor annuity in which payments are made while any of the three persons are alive. Though this is unstated by Halley, this kind of annuity applies directly to the valuation of a lease on three lives in which the term runs until all three people named in the lease are dead. A formula for the valuation of this annuity for three lives aged x, y, and z is given by:

$$a_{xyz} - a_{xy} - a_{xz} - a_{yz} + a_x + a_y + a_z$$

Even the briefest of glances at this formula reveals that many calculations are required to obtain the numerical values for it at any given set of ages. Halley noticed this difficulty in making so many calculations and suggested making them for every fourth or fifth year and interpolating to obtain the intermediate values.

In the follow-up paper to his life table, Halley acknowledged one of the great drawbacks in the application of his table. Regarding the calculations involved for annuities on two and three lives, Halley conceded that it "seems (as I am inform'd) a work of too much Difficulty for the ordinary Arithmetician to undertake."[31] The difficulty apparently also applied to single life annuities. Very few took the time to make annuity calculations directly from life tables. In the mathematical world, the first reasonable solution to the problem of reducing the onerous calculations behind proper life annuity valuations did not appear until 1725, when Abraham De Moivre published his *Annuities upon Lives.*[32]

4 Halley's Impact or Lack of It

Halley's published insights into the valuation of 1-year term insurance had no effect on the business of early eighteenth-century life insurance companies. England's first insurance society was the Friendly Society for Widows, established in 1696.[1] The death benefit paid by the Society was set at £500. On any notice of death each subscriber, of an intended 2,000 in number, was to pay 5 shillings to cover the benefit. This kind of scheme is known as a contributorship. Several subsequent societies offered a mortuary tontine; in any year the society set aside a fixed amount of money, which was divided among the beneficiaries of those who died during the year. Since insurance ran from year to year in both mortuary tontines and contributorships, their various schemes were all forms of 1-year term insurance. It was in 1721 that London Assurance Corporation offered insurance on a fixed premium, usually 1-year term insurance at a premium of about £5 per £100 of insurance irrespective of age.[2] In all these schemes, Halley was ignored.

Halley's work also had no impact on the price of life annuities offered by the Exchequer. The ideas and legislation behind the Exchequer annuities offered in 1693 had been enacted before Halley's work was in print. The Exchequer completely ignored Halley's work in later offerings of life annuities. In 1694, for example, the government offered life annuities on one, two, or three lives.[3] For a £100 investment the annual payments were £14, £12, and £10 for one, two, and three lives respectively. This is equivalent, approximately, to 7, 8½, and 10 years' purchase, respectively. Later, during the reign of Queen Anne, life annuities were offered at 9, 11, and 12 years' purchase on one, two, and three lives, respectively.[4] This was a much better bargain than George Mabbut suggested in 1686 (10, 19, and 27 years' purchase) or Henry Phillippes in 1653 (12, 23, and 33 years' purchase). It appears that, even if the legislators had read Halley's paper, the price of a life annuity was connected to the economics of supply and demand, as well as the risks associated with war, rather than representing a fair actuarial price.

Where impact was felt in the annuities market was in Paul Foley's decoupling of land and life annuities in the legislation to establish the Exchequer annuities. A very early scheme is William Assheton's reversionary annuity plan that was operated by the Mercers' Company, beginning in 1699.[5] Some land was set aside to provide partial backing for the scheme, but when an eventual shortfall did develop between income and expenses, the rents from the land were insufficient to meet that shortfall. Speculative projects were put forward that were financed by the sale of annuities. Only the success of the enterprise, not the stability of rents on land, was offered as security to the annuitants. Some were of dubious merit, such as a reversionary annuity scheme related to the English fisheries industry. It was floated in 1713 through a benefit society established by Daniel Cholmondeley of London.[6] I will examine the Mercers' Company scheme and Cholmondeley's scheme in more detail, especially through the lens of Halley's life table.

In the eighteenth century, and before, one form of a reversionary annuity was a marriage settlement. As part of a marriage contract, a landowner entering into marriage would agree to set aside some of his land with accompanying rents so that on his death his future bride would be provided for. On her death the land set aside for her would revert to the husband's estate. The attraction of Assheton's scheme through the Mercers' Company and of Cholmondeley's benefit society is that a man without land but with money (such men were called by one historian "men of movable property") or men with only a small amount of land and again some money, could make the same provisions for his wife.[7] Both Assheton and Cholmondeley made this attraction explicit in the descriptions of their schemes.[8]

Originally, Assheton's scheme was meant for the widows of clergymen. Halley had suggested such a scheme in 1693 as one of the uses of his mortality table. Assheton's idea for reversionary annuities for widows was probably independent of any thoughts Halley may have expressed, since the funding of his proposal was independent of any mortality table. By the time that the Mercers' Company decided to put this scheme into operation the possible clientele was expanded to all married men in good health under the age of 60 living in England who were neither seamen nor soldiers. The scheme was very simple. For whatever amount a husband invested, 30% of that amount was paid yearly to the widow for the rest of her life on the death of her husband. If she predeceased her husband, then nothing was paid. To enter the scheme, a minimum investment of £50 was required, with a maximum set at £300. To provide some security to the scheme, it was backed by land held by the Mercers' Company, which in 1698 brought in rents of £2,888.[9]

Table 4.1. *Cholmondeley's reversionary annuity scheme*

Scheme	Cost to P	Annuity payment to B	Duration of payments to B
1	£80	£20	B's lifetime
2	£40	£20	B's lifetime or 21 years, whichever is less
3	£20	£10	B's lifetime or 21 years, whichever is less

The reversionary annuity offered by Cholmondeley's benefit society was very similar to the one offered by the Mercers' Company. It was more restrictive about the amount to be invested – a maximum of £80. It was in a sense less restrictive, however, in that there were some options for the length of the reversionary payments. Cholmondeley offered three types of reversionary annuities, as laid out in Table 4.1. In the table P is the purchaser and B is the beneficiary who receives the annuity on P's death. It was his intention that there would be 3,000 participants in each annuity scheme, which would provide a total capital of £420,000. In contrast to the prospectuses for the Mercers' Company, Cholmondeley addressed the issue of expected mortality of the participants, albeit in a very simplistic way.

The intended £420,000 in capital that Cholmondeley wanted to raise was to be invested in the fisheries industry, at least in all the accoutrements of the industry: boats, docks, nets, salt, warehouses, and more. Cholmondeley was to make his money from the scheme by receiving a fee of £1 for every reversionary annuity purchased (intended to cover registration costs and advertising) and 5% of the first annuity payment when the reversion went into effect.

In his prospectus for the benefit society, Cholmondeley claimed that the funds invested would earn 12% per annum. After defending this claim at length, he says:[10]

> Moreover, it is well known that Subscriptions have of late years been taken for raising a Joint-Stock to Improve the Fishery, wherein Adventurers never received less than Twenty Pounds clear Gain for One Hundred Pounds for a year.

This passage points to the possible source of Cholmondeley's inspiration. Because of the long-standing dominance of the Dutch in the lucrative herring fishery, there was a desire in early eighteenth-century England to improve the country's fishing industry.[11] The company "of late years" that Cholmondeley may have had in mind is the South Sea Company; no other fishing companies were chartered around this time. This company was given its charter in 1711, and its full name is the "Corporation of the Governor and Company of Merchants of Great Britain Trading to the South-Seas, and other Parts of America, and for Encouraging the Fishery."[12] It was specified in the company charter that 1% of the capital stock was to be used in improving the British fishery. Very quickly the South Sea Company made its money buying up government debt and ignoring trade in the South Seas and the fisheries. Speculation in its stock eventually became so rife that there was a market crash in 1720, known as the South Sea Bubble.[13]

There were flaws on all sides of Cholmondeley's plan. There seems to have been no contingent business plan concerning what to do once all the matériel for the fishery was put in place. Would the benefit society run a fishing fleet? Or, instead, would the society rent out the equipment that it owned? Nothing was said in any of the published proposals or newspaper advertisements. The success of the scheme depended on making 12% per annum on capital, which seems high.[14] Success also depended on a fairly low mortality rate. Cholmondeley assumed a 3% mortality rate in the first year of operation among those buying into the society, or 90 deaths in each of the three schemes with 3,000 participants. He stayed with a constant number of 90 deaths per year for the whole length of the scheme, stating that "there is no manner of probability that above ninety of the annuitants nominees will die in each class every year." The 3% may have come from William Petty's investigations. Petty estimated the death rate in 1682 to be between 2% and 3.3%, with the lower percentage pertaining to an adult population living in healthy places and the higher percentage pertaining to the whole population.[15] A much better idea of the death rate that Cholmondeley's benefit society would have experienced comes from data published by the Amicable Society for a Perpetual Insurance Office, an insurance company that was founded in 1706. The Amicable's data, given in Table 4.2, shows the company's mortality experience over a 4-year period from 1706 to 1709.[16] On average the death rate among those insured was slightly less than 1 in 20.

Despite the flaws, at a 12% gain on capital and a 3% death rate among the participants, the society looked very profitable on paper, which in the prospectus is 5½ pages of simple arithmetic showing the profitability of Scheme 2. At a £40 cost for entering the scheme, with 3,000 participants, the initial fund would be £120,000. The fund would grow 12% every year and be reduced by £20 for every reversionary annuity payment. With a 3% death rate among the purchasers, there would be 90 annuitants to be paid in the first year, 180 in the second year, 270 in the third year, and so on. After 29 years the fund was projected to stand at £426,177.

Table 4.2. *Mortality experience among Amicable Society subscribers*

Year	Number of deaths	Numbers of subscribers	Proportion of deaths
1706	29	875	0.0331
1707	96	2 000	0.0480
1708	122	2 000	0.0610
1709	87	2 000	0.0435
Total	334	6 875	0.0486

Both the Mercers' Company and Cholmondeley's reversionary annuities were offered at a fixed cost, irrespective of the age of the purchaser or the annuitant. Did they set reasonable prices that would cover their costs? Using Halley's complete life table from Appendix 2, I evaluated three of the annuity schemes when the annuities are standardized to pay £1 per year. The three are the Mercers' Company annuity and Cholmondeley's annuities under his Schemes 1 and 2. For the Mercers' Company annuity the equivalent price would be £3⅓ (or £3 6s 8d). For his Scheme 1 Cholmondeley's equivalent price would be £4 and for his Scheme 2 it would be £2. I carried out the annuity valuations at ages from 21 up to 60 for the beneficiary (B) and in three cases for purchaser (P): P is at the same age as B, P is 10 years older than B (whose maximum age in this case is 50, since P must be at most 60 years of age), and P is 20 years older than B (whose maximum age is 40).

In Figure 4.1 I show a summary of the results, describing the valuations at each of the 40 ages under the three age differential assumptions for a reversionary life annuity, and under the Mercers' annuity, and under Cholmondeley's Scheme 1. The points in the plot are the values of the reversionary annuities at various ages of the wife. The horizontal line at 3⅓ is the cost to buy the annuity from the Mercers' Company and the line at 4 is the cost to buy from Cholmondeley. Under Halley's mortality assumptions, both the Mercers' Company and Cholmondeley's Scheme 1 annuities are financially viable (cost to buy is greater than the average benefits paid) unless the husband is 20 years older than his wife. Cholmondeley's Scheme 2, shown in Figure 4.2, is very much underpriced at £2 and gets worse as the age difference increases. The annuity valuations in Figures 4.1 and 4.2 are very similar, the former only slightly more than the latter; the present value of future benefits more than 21 years in the future is small.

Cholmondeley's benefit society probably died with him in 1716. The last reference to the scheme in the London newspapers is from April 1716, after an approximate 2-year gap in advertisements.[17] He wrote a

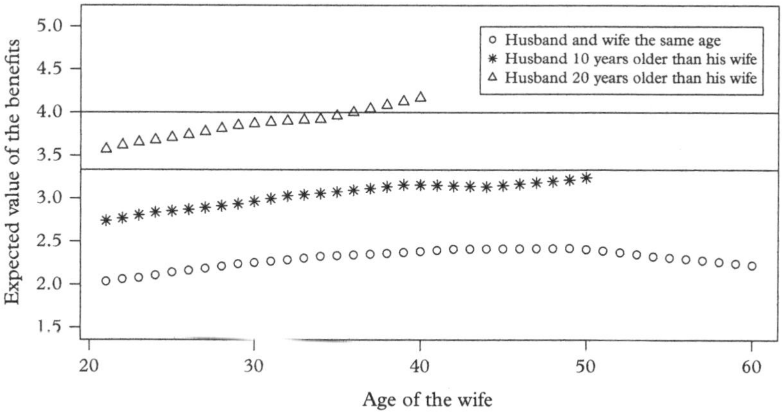

Figure 4.1. Valuations of the Mercers' Company and Cholmondeley's scheme 1 annuities

Figure 4.2. Valuations of Cholmondeley's scheme 2 annuities

one-sentence will, signed May 6, 1716, in which he left his entire estate to his wife Anne and made her executor of his will.[18] Cholmondeley's approach to business might parallel his approach to marriage. His will was contested.[19] Apparently, he had married another woman named Anne in about 1700. She had brought a large sum of money to the marriage. Cholmondeley had a number of creditors and did not want to bring attention to this newfound money, and so his first wedding took place quietly in a public house near the Fleet Prison, the debtors' prison. In 1712 Cholmondeley left this Anne and was married, bigamously apparently, to another woman named Anne, the woman to whom he left his estate.

Assheton's scheme, as run by the Mercers' Company, continued until 1745, when the annuity payments were stopped by the Company.[20] In the next year, the Company offered 10 shillings in the pound (50%) for annuity payments in arrears. Shortly thereafter, some of the annuitants organized themselves to launch a lawsuit. A month later the Company petitioned Parliament for help in paying these annuities and other debts, reporting that many annuitants had been reduced to poverty.[21] With no income from subscribers, the Mercers' Company reported that the annuity payments for 1747 totaled £7,534. The income from rent on lands they had set aside to back the scheme had grown to only £4,148 from the £2,888 in 1698. In order to pay the annuitants, the majority of whom were clergymen's widows, Parliament passed an act providing the Mercers' Company with £3,000 a year for 55 years from money raised on duties levied on coal for the City of London.[22]

As seen in Figure 4.1, the expected stress on Assheton's scheme would come from men who married much younger women. At the end of the first decade of this scheme's operation the Mercers' Company partially recognized this source of stress by restricting policies on husbands over the age of 45. In that category, no policy would be issued when the wife was more than 15 years younger than the husband. This did not provide a long-term solution. When men and women have the same mortality experience, and when the husband and wife are of the same age, then about half of the policies would result in no payment to a widow, since she would have predeceased her husband. The experience of the Mercers' Company was that this happened for only about 20% of the policies, a much lower figure than so predicted.[23] Using Halley's life table, I examined the 20% figure further. At each age of a husband from 21 to 60 years, I calculated the probability that the wife would die before the husband. This was done for cases when the husband is 10 years older than his wife and when he is 20 years older. In the case when the husband is 10 years older than his wife then, depending on the age of his wife, between about 32% and 40% of the wives will predecease their husbands. When the age differential is changed to 20 years, then between about 21% and 31% of wives will follow that pattern.

At 20%, the proportion of policies where this situation prevailed for the Mercers' Company was below both ranges. There could be several explanations for this. The mortality experience in Breslau, as expressed in Halley's table, is much different from that for London, or more generally for England. Another possible factor is that the age difference for many policies was even greater than 20 years. The most likely explanation is the age differential, combined with what may be an early example of adverse selection. Men who took out these policies may have been healthy, but below the average health of the general population, and their wives above average in health. With a significant age differential, these men would have had the highest motivation to buy the Mercers' Company annuities. Adverse selection was first seen and documented in the early nineteenth century with the issuance of government life annuities that were valued using the Northampton life table from the 1780s.[24]

Prior to the 1720s, Halley's greatest impact was on mathematical writers. What may have intensified this impact was that Halley's 1693 paper was twice reprinted in its entirety in *Miscellanea Curiosa*, initially in 1705 and later in 1708. The volumes of *Miscellanea Curiosa* contain reprints of papers in the *Philosophical Transactions*. To paraphrase the preface to the first volume of *Miscellanea Curiosa*, there was a recognition that important results in mathematics and other areas of science were buried among a number of other articles in the *Philosophical Transactions*, making it difficult for most people to access the results. The intention was to bring the major related mathematical and scientific results to the public together in one place.

There were two types of books that referenced and described Halley's work on annuities. The first is a direct descendant of the genre of books from the seventeenth century that specialized in annuities and compound interest. The second is a genre of general mathematics books different from commercial arithmetic books. These books were intended for the instruction of young gentlemen. Some of them show up on mathematics curricula at Oxford and Cambridge universities and at dissenting academies run by ministers outside the Church of England.[25] These books treat arithmetic, algebra, geometry, and sometimes conic sections and other material, in preparation for learning about the then rapidly developing subject that was called natural philosophy. They may also contain material on interest and annuities related to rents and leases to prepare the young scholar in areas useful to a future landlord.

The first book that I can find that was influenced by Halley's work on life annuities is John Ward's 1707 *The Young Mathematician's Guide*. Ward was a mathematics teacher who had worked in the Excise Office. In the section on algebra there is a treatment of the topic of interest and annuities.[26] It is a scholarly treatment and the examples used deal mainly with rents, pensions, and leases. Near the end of the section, Ward discusses probabilities of life, referring to a work by Petty of 1674 and to Halley's 1693 paper.[27] Ward follows this with a short précis of Halley's results on annuities, including a reprint of Halley's annuity table, shown in Table 3.2. Ward prefaces this material with remarks that directly connect Halley's work to leases for lives:[28]

> Thus far concerning such *Annuities* or *Leases*, &c. that are *Limitted* by any Assigned *Time*; and 'tis only such that can be computed by *Theorems* or certain *Rules*. However, it may not perhaps be *Unexceptable*, to insert a brief Account of some *Estimates* that have been Reasonably made, by *Two* very Ingenious *Persons*, about the Proportions, or Difference of *Mens Lives*, according to their several *Ages*; which may be of good Use in Computing the *Values* of *Annuities*, or taking of *Leases* for *Lives*, &c.

The book was fairly popular. Up to the 1770s, it went through twelve editions. Despite the fact that the legal annual rate of interest changed from 6% (used by Halley) to 5% in 1714, the material on Halley's work in *The Young Mathematician's Guide* was repeated verbatim through to the eleventh edition in 1762, and was only changed in the twelfth and final edition.

In their treatment of Halley's work, at least two other books are derivative from *The Young Mathematician's Guide*. In 1717 Philip Ronayne published a book on arithmetic, algebra, and geometry meant for young gentlemen. As Ronayne admits, much of his material on interest and annuities was merely transcribed from *The Young Mathematician's Guide*.[29] This includes what Ward had written on Halley's work.[30] Gideon Royer, a writer of commercial arithmetic books, also transcribed Ward's material on Halley in his 1721 *Arithmetick*. It was a late afterthought. He inserted the transcribed material into a scholium at the very end of his book, over 200 pages after his own treatment of interest and annuities.[31]

Three years after the first edition of *The Young Mathematician's Guide*, Ward wrote another book, *Clavis Usurae*. This was devoted to interest and annuities, and follows in the genre of seventeenth-century books written on that topic. In this book, Ward goes into more detail about Halley's work on life annuities than he did in *The Young Mathematician's Guide*, giving what might be called an extended synopsis of it rather than a short précis.[32] Both Halley's life table (Table 3.1) and his annuity table (Table 3.2) appear in *Clavis Usurae*. Where Halley's work is placed in the book is revealing. It appears in a section entitled "Of purchasing free-hold or real estates, and how to estimate the value of annuities and leases for lives &c." The same material with the same title appears in Ward's *A Compendium of Algebra*, published in 1724.[33] Once again, I take this as evidence that Halley's work on annuities, and the interpreters of his work, were motivated by issues related to land rather than the newly developing annuity and insurance industries.

Just as Ward had prefaced Halley's work in *The Young Mathematician's Guide* with a reference to William Petty, he did the same in *Clavis Usurae*, but with a difference.[34] He went further in *Clavis Usurae* by trying to simplify the arithmetic in life annuity valuations, noting later in his discussion that Halley's calculations are "troublesome to perform." Ward uses Petty's method of duplicate proportion to try to find an easy way to calculate the present value of a life annuity. Petty had argued that there are more people living that are between 16 and 26 years of age than at any other 10-year age interval.[35] He then formulated a "law" for the proportion living at various ages. Take 16 as the standard age and find the square root of 16, or 4. Then the fraction of people, relative to those aged 16, living at age x is $\sqrt{x}/4$ when $x < 16$ and $4/\sqrt{x}$ when $x > 16$. Assuming that an annuity, or lease, on one life is worth 9 years purchase, which according to Ward had been recently legislated by Parliament, then Ward's value of the life annuity at age x is $9\sqrt{x}/4$ or $36/\sqrt{x}$ as appropriate. Ward provides a table of values, with a few minor numerical errors, for ages 1 to 71 in intervals of 5 years.

The author of another book coming out of the seventeenth century annuity genre also tried to grapple with the arithmetical difficulties facing those evaluating life annuities when using brute force calculation from a life table. This was Edward Hatton's *An Index to Interest*, first published in 1711 with a second edition in 1714 and a third by 1718.[36] At the end of the 1714 edition (it may also be in the first edition, but no copy was available to me), Hatton gives a brief introduction to Halley's work on annuities and reproduces Halley's annuity table (Table 3.2). This is followed by a novel approach for an approximation to the valuation of annuities on two and three lives that simplifies the arithmetic substantially by using the values of annuities at fixed terms. With this approach published annuity tables for fixed terms can be used. For two lives Hatton uses the example of two people aged 40 and 45. Take the older age (45) and find the value of the single life annuity (9.91 from Table 3.2). For an annuity that runs for a fixed term of n years, the formula $a_{\overline{n}|}$ for the present value, as given in Appendix 1, is a function of n and the interest rate i. Equate $a_{\overline{n}|}$ to 9.91 and solve for n, which is 15.5 approximately at 6% interest per annum. Using annuity tables Hatton settles on 16. Add the difference in ages, which is 5, to the solution for n to obtain 21. Then find the present value (Hatton uses tables) of a 21-year annuity, which is 11.76 at 6% interest. Hatton takes 11.76 as the value of the last survivor life annuity for two lives aged 40 and 45. For three lives, make the same type of calculation for the last survivor annuity based on the youngest and oldest of the three. To account for the middle person, add 1 to the value of the annuity. If, in the example of the last survivor annuity for two lives aged 40 and 45, a third is added who is aged 43, then the value of the last survivor life annuity is 12.76. When there are three lives, Hatton claims that the approximation works best when the difference in ages between the oldest and youngest is at most 7 years. Like Ward's in *Clavis Usurae*, Hatton's application of his results is to the valuation of a lease for lives. When the third edition of the book appeared, the advertisement for it was accompanied by a testimonial from the mathematician William Whiston, who wrote, "I do not know of any Book of this kind so easy, and particular and useful as this."[37] Whiston had been Lucasian professor of mathematics at Cambridge University, but in 1710 was expelled from Cambridge for his unorthodox religious beliefs.

Hatton's one calculated approximation to the value of a last survivor annuity on two lives is 11.76. Using Halley's life table, the "correct" value is 12.62; this means that Hatton's approximation underestimates the true value by 0.86 years' purchase, or about 6.8%. For three lives Hatton's approximation is 12.76, while the "correct" value is 13.54. Again there is an underestimation, in this case 0.78 years' purchase, but it is smaller than in the case of two lives. This observation holds at other ages. To examine the approximation further, I found the differences between Hatton's approximation and the value calculated from Halley's complete life table at ages 21 through 65 for the younger ages and when the difference between the older and the younger ages is 5 years for annuities on both two and three lives. The errors in the approximation to the number of years' purchase (approximated value of the annuity minus the true value) are shown in Figure 4.3. There is a distinct relationship to age. The error values generally increase with age. Until about age 60 the errors are negative, showing an underestimation of the true value.

For annuities on three lives, as previously stated Hatton claims that the approximation works best when the difference in ages between the oldest and youngest is at most 7 years. This is an interesting claim because, if it holds up, it indicates that Hatton probably did a few intense calculations to study his approximation. Consequently, I carried out the approximations at ages 21 through 65 for the youngest life when the age differences between the oldest and the youngest of the three lives are 5, 10, and 15 years. I arbitrarily chose the age of the middle life to be 3, 5 and 7 years, respectively, older than the youngest life. The errors in these approximations are shown in Figure 4.4. Generally,

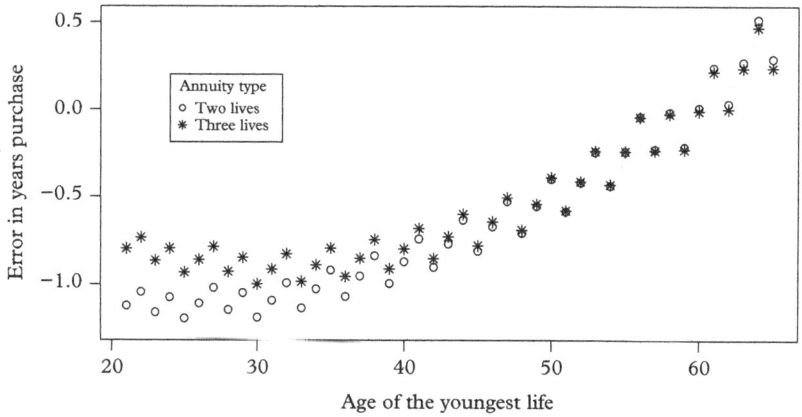

Figure 4.3. Annuities on two and three lives, five-year age differential differences between Hatton's approximation and the calculated values from Halley's table

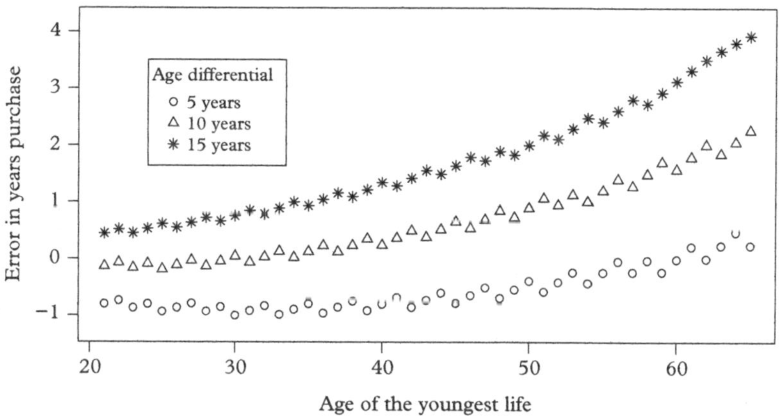

Figure 4.4. Annuities on three lives with different age differentials differences between Hatton's approximation and the calculated values from Halley's table

the errors increase with age at each age differential. The rate at which the errors increase also increases with the size of the age differential, confirming Hatton's more vague statement about the virtue of the approximation.

Because they take into account new mathematical results, Ward's and Hatton's books are a natural outgrowth of what appears in seventeenth-century annuity books. There is a further connection to the genre.

Some of the seventeenth-century writers of annuity books were surveyors. As surveyors these writers would both have been knowledgeable in issues around property and the related traditional methods for property valuation. John Ward was a mathematics teacher who had previously worked in the Excise Office, where he had held the position of surveyor and gauger (measurer of the capacity of barrels).[38] Edward Hatton was probably a surveyor for a fire insurance company; he also authored other mathematical books, as well as a book giving a detailed general description of London.[39] The fact that both Ward and Hatton tried to apply Halley's methods to the valuation of leases for lives is evidence of a budding interest in the use of the new mathematical results to value leases. There is, however, no known surviving manuscript evidence to show that anyone took any action on Halley's new methodology in the marketplace. The situation with respect to manuscript evidence does change in the 1730s.

The worlds of finance and property were changing rapidly in the late seventeenth century and continued to do so well into the next century. A number of men were growing wealthy in the emerging financial markets. In the words of one historian:[40]

> The country was growing richer more or less continuously, and few would dispute that there were more wealthy men around in 1750 than at the beginning of the century, and many more yet at the end of it; or that the average size of their fortunes was greater.

Many of those with newly created wealth had aspirations to become landowners and invested some of their funds into land. By the 1720s this was true of some London merchants who bought estates in Essex and Surrey near London.[41] The price of land had remained relatively stable during the last half of the seventeenth century, with a modest increase by the end of the century. As the War of the Spanish Succession came to an end in 1714, the price of land began a more or less steady rise over the eighteenth century. The time when the price of land was rising most rapidly was in the period spanning the mid-1710s to the 1730s. This coincided with Abraham De Moivre's major publication on the pricing of life annuities, published in 1725. As we shall see, the topics that De Moivre covered are intimately connected to land.

Moreover, in 1714 the official annual interest rate fell to 5%. This had a continuing impact on the cost of renewing a lease based on lives. The level of the renewal charge or fine changed in the early part of the eighteenth century. As I have indicated in the discussion of Mabbut's lease tables in Chapter 2, the renewal fine is evaluated by $a_{\overline{n}|} - a_{\overline{m}|}$

Table 4.3. *Present values for the renewal fine at various interest rates*

Annual rate of interest (%)	Value of the fine
11½	1.010
11	1.093
10	1.282
9	1.506
8	1.773
7	2.090
6	2.469
5	2.923

when the length of the initial *n*-year lease is extended by $n - m$ years. For a lease on three lives with a single life equated to 7 years, when one life drops the fine is $a_{\overline{21}|} - a_{\overline{14}|}$. As the legal rate of interest declines, then the amount of the fine should rise, since money discounted at a high rate of interest is worth less than money discounted at a low rate of interest. Table 4.3 shows the present value, at various rates of interest, of the fine $a_{\overline{21}|} - a_{\overline{14}|}$.

Initially, the fine was set at 1 year's purchase corresponding to an annual rate of interest of approximately 11½%, slightly above the legal rate of 10%. The 10% rate remained in place as the legal rate until 1624, when it changed to 8%. It was reduced to 6% in 1651 and then, in 1714, to 5%.[42] Many landowners moved with the times and adjusted their fines. Churches and colleges, as well as other charitable organizations such as hospitals, did not. There is evidence that the fine for church and college leases remained at 1 year's purchase into the eighteenth century. By the first third of the eighteenth century, college and church fines were set at at most 1½ years' purchase corresponding to an approximate 9% rate of interest per annum, one percentage point above the legal rate in effect between 1624 and 1651. In 1730 the typical fine for all other landowners was 2½ years' purchase, corresponding to an approximate 6% rate of interest, again one percentage point above the legal rate set in 1714. The two groups had diverged substantially. One of the reasons for the gap in the values of fines between church and lay landlords comes from the way in which church and college lands were leased. Large holdings of church lands were often leased to one person who sublet smaller areas to tenant farmers. Essentially, with the payment of the fine, the single lessee was a middle man buying an annuity with some management responsibilities as part of the cost. The lessees of church and college lands were often landed gentry or titled noblemen; and they were powerful enough to keep their fines low when it was time to bargain for the renewal of their leases.[43]

In view of the changing economic times, many landowners in the 1720s and 1730s were interested in the valuation of property. This is apparent in a pamphlet from 1730 entitled *A Dissertation on Estates upon Lives and Years, Whether in Lay or Church-Hands*, written by Edward Laurence.[44] Like many of the authors of annuity books in the seventeenth century, Laurence was well qualified to write his pamphlet. He was originally a teacher of mathematics. Early in his career, he began working as a land surveyor and became very prominent in his field, working for several aristocrats and other landowners. Laurence also had literary and scientific interests that ranged from history and antiquities to practical astronomy.[45]

Laurence spends most of his pamphlet providing practical advice on the kind of leases that should be offered and how they should be renewed, as well as issues surrounding the low level of the fines in church and college leases. In an earlier book, *The Duty of a Steward to His Lord*, written in 1727, Laurence gives several examples of accounts kept by stewards. One particular example shows the results of a tenant bargaining with the landlord on the value of a fine in 1725. The example entry in the account book reads:[46]

> Receiv'd from the aforesaid *John Todd*, a Fine for his being admitted Tenant to his Father's Estate Mr. *Thomas Todd*. The Fine formerly accepted by the Lord of the Manor for this Estate used to be but 80 Pounds; but, in consideration that the value of Money is decreas'd very much of late years, the said *John Todd* agrees to pay ... 110 *l.*

This is an increase of 37½% in the fine. Other examples that Laurence gives are similar, with percentage increases as low as 33⅓%. From Table 4.2, the increase in the fine when using a 6% annual rate of interest, compared to an 8% rate of interest, is 39.3%.

Laurence appeals to Halley when discussing life annuities or leases for lives. In the middle of his advice on leases and fines in his 1730 pamphlet, Laurence inserts a discussion of Halley's work related to life annuities. Initially, he reproduces Halley's population table for Breslau (the column showing the number of persons in Table 3.1). Then he copies many of the uses of the table almost word for word from what Halley has written, including the same numerical examples, finishing with a reproduction of Halley's table of life annuity values calculated at a 6% annual rate of interest (Table 3.2). What is new in Laurence's pamphlet is the discussion that follows the annuity table.

After noting the differences in the values of life annuities at different ages (12.78 at age 20 and 10.57 at age 40, from Table 3.2, for example), Laurence says:[47]

It also plainly appears by this Table, that an Annuity or Lease of 100*l. per Annum* for a Life of 20 Years old, is worth 1278 Pounds; and for a life of 40, is worth but 1057 Pounds. From these Examples, the *Lessor* may justly argue for a reasonable Allowance in the Fine, on Account of the plain Difference betwixt a *young* and an *old Life*.

Rather than a hard and fast rule or calculation to determine a fine, Laurence uses Halley's table, now out of date because of the 6% interest rate, to give the landlord some additional strong arguments with solid backing to bargain with his tenant over the level of the fine.

Three years prior to the publication of Laurence's pamphlet, Richard Hayes published *A New Method for Valuing of Annuities upon Lives.*[48] Like Laurence on estates, Hayes was well qualified to write about life annuities. He was a London teacher who described himself as an "accomptant and writing master."[49] During the height of his career in the 1720s and 1730s he ran his own boarding school, which prepared a variety of people to work in business: merchants, traders, agents, and gentlemen. The subjects most often taught in his school were handwriting for business, arithmetic, and accounting. Hayes published several books which show he had a wide knowledge of business practices as well as the financial and property markets. His *New Method for Valuing of Annuities upon Lives* followed very quickly on De Moivre's *Annuities Upon Lives* (the former published in 1727, the latter in 1725). Despite the closeness in dates of publication, Hayes seems to have been influenced by Halley, not De Moivre.

In his book, Hayes provides extensive tables showing the value of a life annuity offered at ages 30 through 73 and at annual interest rates from 4% to 8%, but does not say what method he used to make his annuity calculations. Possibly the earliest, and perhaps the only, conjecture as to Hayes's method of calculation is from the actuary, Edwin Farren. Writing in 1844, he says:[50]

Mr. Hayes does not state how he computed his Tables otherwise than by saying at the commencement, that he calculated them 'according to the chance of Annuitants living to the extremity of the common oldest age of Life,' and this upon suppositions of 'the various degrees of probability which Lives of different ages have to continue in being.' As, however, this last description also occurs in the Preface of De Moivre's Treatise, it is probable that Mr. Hayes adopted some arithmetical version of the Hypothesis [the chances of survival decrease linearly with age] originated by that author.

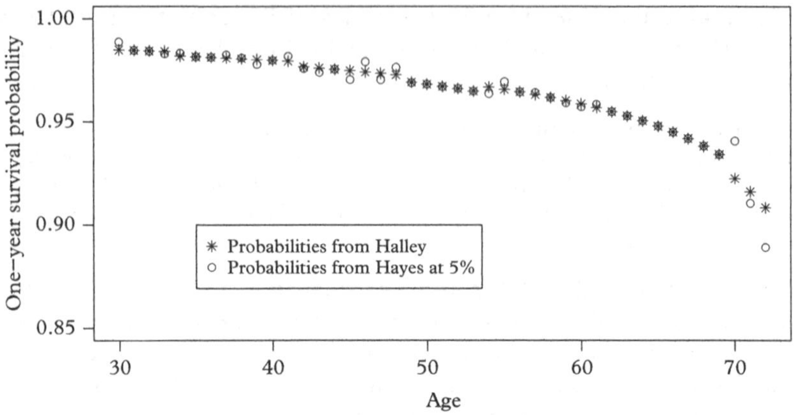

Figure 4.5. One-year survival probabilities from Halley's table and Hayes's annuity valuations at 5%

I checked a number of entries in Hayes's tables against De Moivre's usual approximation and they do not agree. The phrase "the various degrees of probability which lives of different ages have to continue in being" does appear in the preface to De Moivre's *Annuities Upon Lives*, but that is the only phrase of any length that is common to the introductory material in the two publications. Hayes claims to have worked on his book "for many years" prior to its publication, and so the work going into his book probably predates De Moivre's book. Hayes's claim is probably true. There are several other tables in the book in addition to the life annuity valuations. As John Ward remarked, life annuity calculations done by hand from first principles are "troublesome to perform," so that even though Hayes's book is relatively short (44 pages of text and 84 pages of tables), the work required to produce the tables is long and arduous.

There is evidence that Hayes based his work on Halley's 1693 Breslau table, rather than on De Moivre, as Farren had conjectured. This can be seen by using the annuity values to calculate a person's 1-year survival probability to age $x + 1$, given that the person has reached the age of x. The method for obtaining these probabilities from the annuity values is given in Appendix 1. From 1714 the legal rate of interest was 5% per annum. This seems to be a logical place to start if one is using Halley's life table and Halley's method of life annuity valuation. In Figure 4.5, I compare the 1-year survival probability from Halley's life table to the 1-year survival probability calculated from Hayes's annuity values at 5% interest. Except at the higher ages there is

Table 4.4. *Comparison of Hayes's life annuity values to Halley's values from his table to age 84*

Age x	Hayes a_x	Halley a_x	Age x	Hayes a_x	Halley a_x	Age x	Hayes a_x	Halley a_x
30	13.13	13.07	45	10.79	10.79	60	7.97	7.97
35	12.36	12.36	50	9.93	9.93	65	6.69	6.69
40	11.61	11.61	55	9.11	9.07	70	5.19	5.19

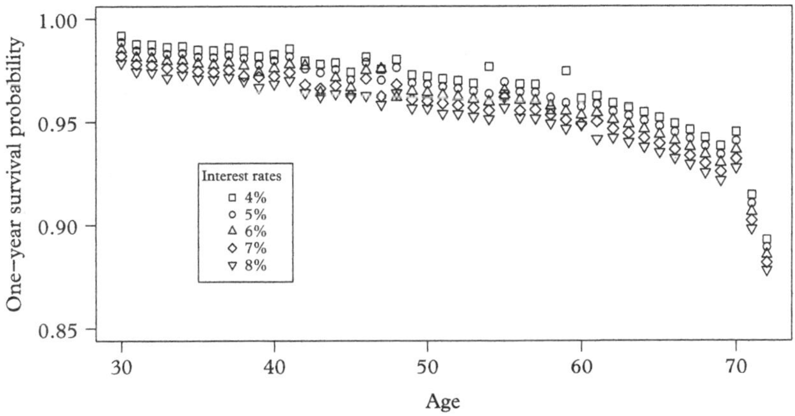

Figure 4.6. One-year survival probabilities from Hayes's annuity valuations at various rates of interest

fairly close agreement between Hayes's and Halley's probabilities. Based on this table we might conclude that Hayes used Halley's table. The question that now arises is: Did Hayes use Halley's truncated table as printed (the table for 1-year increments in age ends at age 84) or did Hayes construct the end of the table to account for the 107 lives that Halley reports between the ages of 85 and 100, as I did in Chapter 3? I calculated a_x, the present value of the life annuity issued at age x, using Halley's table as printed in 1693. This assumes that no one survives to age 85. My calculations are compared to Hayes's calculations in Table 4.4. Except in two places where the differences are very small, my calculations agree with those of Hayes. From this it may be concluded that, at least at a 5% rate of interest, Hayes made his life annuity calculations from Halley's table and ignored the end-of-the-table problem.

These simple insights do not easily carry over to other rates of interest. The 1-year survival probabilities calculated from the annuity values at other rates are related, but different from the one calculated from the table at 5% interest per annum, as shown in Figure 4.6. At each age,

Table 4.5. *Comparison of Hayes's life annuity values for a_x to (1) Halley's original values and (2) values calculated from the table truncated at age 84*

Age x	Hayes a_x	Halley (1)	Halley (2)	Age x	Hayes a_x	Halley (1)	Halley (2)	Age x	Hayes a_x	Halley (1)	Halley (2)
30	11.28	11.72	11.70	45	9.48	9.91	9.85	60	7.25	7.60	7.46
35	10.69	11.12	11.13	50	8.81	9.21	9.14	65	6.17	6.54	6.32
40	10.11	10.57	10.53	55	8.17	8.51	8.42	70	4.88	5.32	4.97

the calculated survival probabilities decrease as the interest rate increases, rather than remaining constant at Halley's life table values. At the same time, the survival probabilities are highly correlated between interest rates, the smallest correlation being 0.98. I investigated this further for an interest rate of 6%, since this is the rate that Halley used and for which he published values of a_x based on his complete, rather than truncated, table. In Table 4.5 I show the values of a_x that Halley gave in 1693 and compare these values to Hayes's published value at 6% and values calculated from Halley's truncated table. As expected, but with one exception, the values of a_x based on the truncated table are less than what Halley published. The values that Hayes provides for a_x are consistently lower than those based on the truncated table. Consequently, I can get a little closer than Farren to how Hayes calculated his life annuities at the legal rate of interest in his day. At other rates of interest his method is probably based on Halley's table, but the fine details of his calculations are at the moment shrouded in mystery.

Hayes's treatment of last survivor annuities on two and three lives is closely related to Edward Hatton's work described earlier in the chapter. For two lives aged x and y Hayes first sets $a_x = a_{\overline{m}|}$ and $a_y = a_{\overline{n}|}$. He solves for m and n and rounds them to the nearest integer. In other words, he finds the terms of fixed-term annuities that are equivalent to the two life annuities. Hayes approximates the required last survivor annuity value, which should be valued at $a_x + a_y - a_{xy}$, by $a_{\overline{m+n}|}$. Hatton's approach is slightly different. Suppose x is less than y. Like Hayes, Hatton sets $a_y = a_{\overline{n}|}$ and solves for n. Where they differ is that Hatton's approximated last survivor annuity value is $a_{\overline{n+y-x}|}$. The difference between Hayes's and Hatton's methods seems minor, but it is major when the difference in ages between the two lives is small. When $y - x$ is small, Hayes's life annuity valuations will be much greater than Hatton's valuations.

This is shown in Figure 4.7, which shows the errors in years' purchase for Hayes's and Hatton's methods. For the purposes of illustration, the 5% legal rate of interest is used in the calculations. It is also

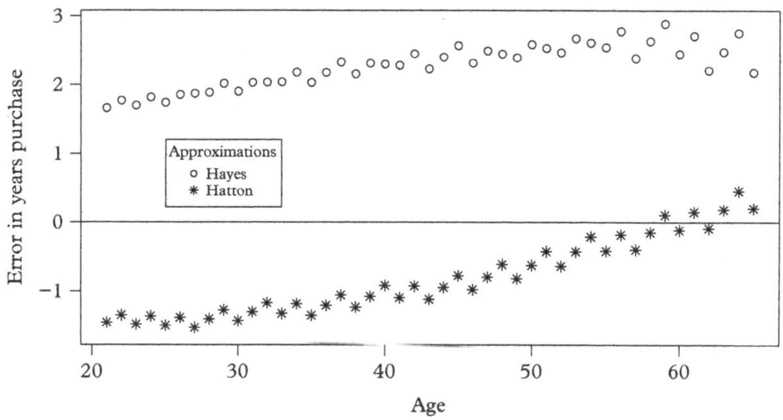

Figure 4.7. Annuities on two lives, five-year age differential differences between the approximations and the calculated values from Halley's table

the rate of interest at which Hayes's valuations of a single life annuity most closely follow Halley's 1693 table. From Figure 4.7, it can be seen that not only are Hayes's valuations larger than Hatton's, but also that Hayes's method provides approximations that are much larger than Halley's valuations, while Hatton's approximations are smaller, at least at lower ages.

Early in his book, Hayes indicates the existence of a market in life annuities in London. All that he says about pricing is:[51]

It is the practice of some companies and corporations, who grant annuities upon lives, to give some certain ages more, and others again less; ...

After this initial description, the rest is a little vague, but it appears that a person with £100 could bargain to obtain annual payments between £6 and £12, depending on age and health. Later in the book, Hayes addresses the valuation of estates and reversions, showing the ties of life annuities to land. Apart from property, as one specific example he uses the Mercers' Company reversionary annuity. In doing so he makes two errors, one serious and the other less so. The less serious error is that for £100 investment the widow receives £20 per annum on the death of her husband, instead of £30, as advertised by the Mercers' Company. Hayes correctly evaluates the reversionary annuity as the difference between the value of the annuity on the joint lives of the husband and wife less the value of the annuity on the life of the husband. Although questionable, he uses his method of approximating the value of the joint life annuity. Where he errs seriously is in his statement,[52] "And the Company [Mercers' Company] has near 2 chances to 1 on their side, if the wife will ever enjoy the said annuity."

I believe that the 2 to 1 comes from Hayes's annuity valuations. He says that the value of a single life annuity on the husband is worth 10 years' and 5 months' purchase, while the value of the wife's reversion is only 5 years' and 4 months' purchase. What Hayes has done is to equate ratios of expected values to ratios of probabilities.

Although surveyors and lesser mathematicians continued to produce books on the valuation of annuities for lives as they relate to property, there was a distinct shift in the 1720s to some of the leading mathematicians in England taking on the problem of life annuity valuations. These mathematicians would have a significant influence on the subject, initially within the mathematical community and then beyond, into the marketplace. The first of these is Abraham De Moivre and his *Annuities Upon Lives*, which De Moivre dedicated to Thomas Parker, 1st Earl of Macclesfield – Whig politician, prominent judge, fellow of the Royal Society, friend of Newton, and great landowner.

5 De Moivre and His Early Influence

A methodology that would ease the burden of calculation in the valuation of life annuities eluded Halley as well as those who followed in his wake, such as John Ward and Edward Hatton. It was Abraham De Moivre, a Huguenot refugee and fellow of the Royal Society, who made a significant breakthrough on this problem in 1725.[1] With this breakthrough and the subsequent publication of his *Annuities upon Lives* in 1725, the amount of calculation was reduced from several hours to a fraction of an hour. Despite his insights, as Lorraine Daston and others have pointed out, De Moivre's work was initially ignored by the budding insurance and life annuity industry. There was a small but growing uptake of his work in life-contingent contracts related to property in the 1730s and 1740s.

It is evident from Halley's work that the valuation of life annuities is through probability arguments. As the author of a pioneering work in probability published as a paper in 1711 in the *Philosophical Transactions* and substantially expanded into the book *The Doctrine of Chances* in 1718, De Moivre was well versed in the subject.[2] He was also familiar with the valuation of fixed-term annuities; in 1706 Halley sought De Moivre's opinion on approximating the interest rate in an annuity when the term and value of the annuity were given.

Halley and De Moivre were friends. It was Halley who first brought De Moivre's mathematical work to the attention of the Royal Society. It was Halley who suggested to De Moivre that he work on problems in astronomy to take his mind off an academic fight over the calculus in which he was hotly engaged with the physician George Cheyne. It was De Moivre who examined Halley's Breslau table and formulated a model for the data that allowed easy calculations for the value of a life annuity.

After examining Halley's table and making several life annuity calculations, De Moivre argued that life annuity values could be reasonably approximated from age 12 onward by assuming that a person's chances of survival decrease linearly with age. The comparison of this assumption

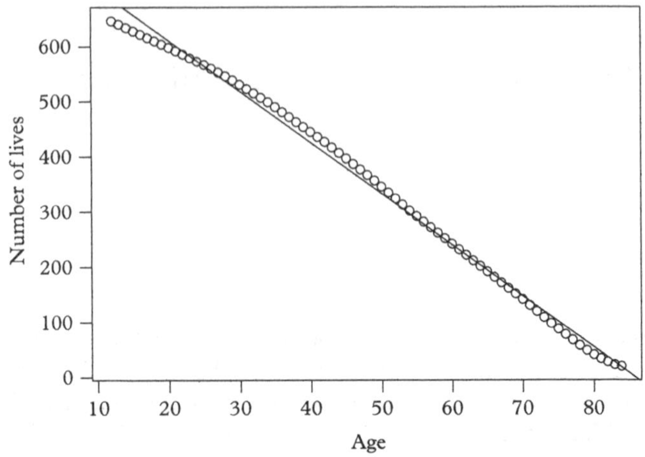

Figure 5.1. Halley's survivor function approximated by a straight line

to the reality of Halley's table is shown in Figure 5.1 where the data from Halley's table and a fitted line are displayed. In the graph the line crosses the axis for age at about age 86. With a little algebra, De Moivre showed that the value of a life annuity for someone currently aged x could be obtained from the given interest rate, the difference between 86 and the current age x, and the value of a fixed-term annuity for a term of $86 - x$ years. Several fixed-term annuity tables had been published, so that what had been a laborious and tedious process, to obtain the value of a life annuity, was reduced to looking up a number in a table and then carrying out four simple arithmetical operations involving multiplication, division, and subtraction. Without the fixed-term annuity table there would be some additional calculations to find the value of that annuity; and that most likely would involve using tables of logarithms. The accuracy of De Moivre's approximation to a_x is explored in Figure 5.2, where I have found the differences between the values of a_x using Halley's life table and its values using De Moivre's approximation, i.e. the error in the approximation. What is plotted is the relative error (the difference divided by Halley's value) expressed as a percentage. I did these calculations at a 6% annual rate of interest, the legal rate used by Halley in 1693 and at 3%, a rate often in use in the mid-eighteenth century. What is evident from Figure 5.2 is that De Moivre's approximation tends to underestimate a_x up until x is 31 or 32 and then to overestimate it.[3]

De Moivre also introduced the assumption that the chances of survival decrease exponentially, rather than linearly, with age. This was done

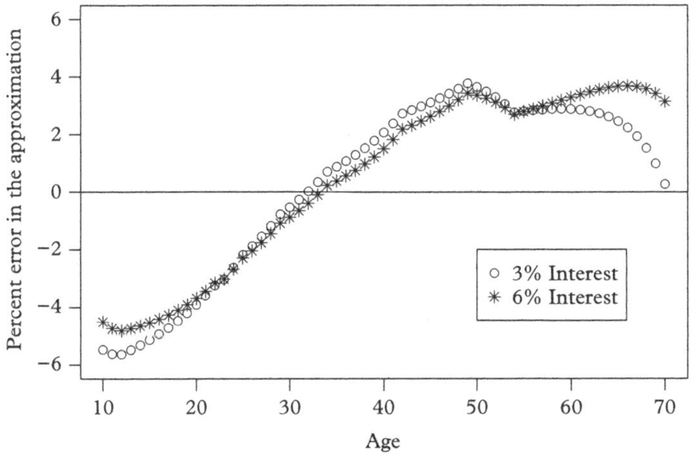

Figure 5.2. The accuracy of De Moivre's approximation to a_x

to make the valuation of joint life annuities easier to carry out. Under this assumption joint life annuities could be expressed as simple functions of single-life annuities and the rate of interest. Although De Moivre's simple assumptions of linear and exponential survival are contradictory, De Moivre would make the exponential assumption to get an algebraic expression for the value of a joint life annuity in terms of single-life annuities, and then would proceed to make the linear assumption to evaluate single-life annuities. De Moivre's two basic results in the valuation of life annuities are shown in Appendix 1.

With those two conflicting assumptions in place, De Moivre proceeded to obtain all the results concerning life annuities that appear in Halley's paper dealing with the Breslau data. He went beyond what Halley had done by showing how several additional, and complex, annuity contracts could be valued in a relatively easy way. De Moivre finished his book by considering various scenarios related to expected future lifetimes: the average lifetime of a single individual and the average lifetimes of the shortest or the longest of the lives among a group of two or three people, as well as the probability that a given individual will outlive one or two other individuals. These are all concerns related to joint survivor and last survivor annuities. This was well beyond what Halley had done; he had calculated only the median future lifetime of a single individual, a much easier calculation to make. All but one of the annuity contracts that De Moivre considered are shown in Table 5.1. As seen in the table, De Moivre misnumbered his problems; he labeled two of them Problem VII. The one problem that I left out seems to me

Table 5.1. *A catalog of the annuity contracts that De Moivre considers*

Type	Find the cost of the contract in the following situations	Problem number
Joint survivor	1. A and B receive payments until the first one dies.	IV
	2. A, B, and C receive payments until the first one dies.	VI
Last survivor	1. A and B receive payments until the last one dies.	V
	2. A, B, and C receive payments until the last one dies.	VII (a)
	3. A, B, and C each receive ⅓ of the payments while they all live, then the survivors each receive ½ of the payments on the death of one of them, and finally the last survivor receives the entire payment.	XII
Reversion	1. B receives payments on the death of A.	VII (b)
	2. C receives payments on the death of the last survivor of A and B.	VIII
	3. On the death of A, then B and C receive payments until they both die.	IX
	4. C receives payments on the death of A or B, whichever comes first.	X
	5. On the death of A, then B and C receive payments until the first one dies.	XI
	6. On the death of A, then B and C each receive ½ of the payments until one of them dies, and then the survivor receives the whole payment thereafter.	XIII
	7. On the death of A, C receives payments only if A survives B.	XXVII
Succession	1. A receives payments and then B receives the payments on the death of A.	XIV
	2. A receives payments, then B receives the payments on the death of A, and then C receives the payments on the death of B.	XV
Renewal	1. An estate is to receive a payment when any of A, B, or C dies.	XVI
	2. A life annuity is purchased on the lives of A, B, and C on three conditions: (1) when one of A, B, and C dies, the annuity is renewed for a fee; (2) when two of A, B, and C die in a single year, the annuity is renewed for another fee; and (3) when all three die in a single year, the annuity is renewed for a third fee.	XVII

to be of a more theoretical, rather than a practical, interest. The contracts in Table 5.1 involve up to three people, whom I call generically A, B, and C. The standard actuarial (or shorthand) notation for the value of the joint life annuities in Table 3.1 is a_{xy} for two lives (Problem IV) and a_{xyz} for three lives (Problem VI) where x, y, and z are the ages of the three lives.

De Moivre made a quick check on the use of the incompatible assumptions that he made to calculate a_{xy}. Rather than the calculation of a_{xy} for Problem IV he calculated the value of the annuity for the last survivor of the two lives (Problem V). The value of this annuity is $a_x + a_y - a_{xy}$, which has a straightforward interpretation; each person receives £1 annually during their lifetime and a value of 1 is subtracted while they are both alive so that a payment of £1 annually is made until the last one dies. De Moivre calculated a_x and a_y under the assumption that the chances of survival decrease linearly with age. He also calculated a_{xy} under the same assumption and calculated it again with his approximation that uses the exponential assumption. He made the two calculations when the ages are 26 and 36 and found that the difference in the values of a_{xy} is only 0.02. He stopped there without any further calculation, seemingly satisfied that the incompatible assumptions provide a reasonable approximation. De Moivre made a numerical error somewhere. The difference between the two values of a_{xy} is 0.67.

In *Annuities upon Lives*, De Moivre gives no specific examples put in a practical setting that would provide the reader with a motivation for writing the book. Most of the annuity contracts that De Moivre considers could be interpreted as types of annuities that could be obtained in the budding life annuities industry. Today, that would be the common interpretation, especially when considering pensions. William Assheton's pension scheme meant for widows, the reversionary annuity operated by the Mercers' Company, was still in operation in 1725, although in some distress.[4] Cholmondeley's annuity scheme was long gone by 1725. On applying the results of his Problem VII (b) to reversionary annuities, De Moivre could have provided the Mercers' Company with approximate individual costing for each of their policyholders as Richard Hayes did. De Moivre did not, and the Mercers Company apparently did not request it; Assheton's scheme continued in the way it had been set up until the 1740s.

There are three hints in *Annuities upon Lives* that point to land and property as De Moivre's motivation to write his book. First, although De Moivre speaks of annuities generally throughout the book, he usually refers to the annuity payments as "rents." The common interpretation of "rents," even in the eighteenth century, is "income from land or property." The second hint is in the dedication of the book to Thomas Parker, 1st Earl of Macclesfield. The dedication begins:

> My Lord, I should not presume to inscribe the following piece to your Lordship, were it not that the subject it treats of has been made the entertainment of some of your leisure hours.

Macclesfield was a landowner and also Lord Chancellor in the High Court of Chancery from 1718 to early 1725, just before the publication of *Annuities upon Lives*. In both capacities he would have seen many situations involving life-contingent contracts. The third hint is that the treatment of problems related to the renewal of annuities is only applicable to renewable leases in which a fine is paid by the tenant to the landlord on renewal. Problems XVI and XVII in *Annuities upon Lives* speak to the situation in which a life named on the lease dies and is replaced by another on payment of a fine. In these two problems, De Moivre finds the present value of future possible fines, so that the estate could be valued based on the money coming from the combination of rents and fines. This situation does not apply to life annuities bought in the marketplace. The annuity payments would end at the death of the last survivor and would not be renewed by someone else on payment of a fine.

Like all landowners, Macclesfield would have been interested in maximizing his rental income; Macclesfield, in particular, was a man eager for more money. For a landowner leasing his lands on lives, this would mean increasing the fines, a reasonable thing to do as interest rates fall. From Table 4.3 the fine for renewing a lease at the legal interest rate of 5% per annum when one life drops is nearly triple the traditional amount from a century or more before. The amount could be more or less than triple if the fine is calculated as the difference between the values of a last survivor annuity on three lives and a last survivor on two lives. Suppose there are three lives on a lease who are 70, 60, and 50 years of age. The oldest life drops and is replaced by another aged 20. Without replacing the life, the value of the lease is the present value of a last survivor annuity on the two remaining lives, aged 60 and 50. When the life aged 20 is added, the value of the lease is now the value of a last survivor annuity on the three lives aged 60, 50, and 20. The difference in the two values is the fine, which at 5% interest is 3.57. When the middle life is 45 or 40, the fine is 3.17 or 2.80, respectively; the latter is below 2.92, the amount based on a traditional calculation.

On the legal side, Macclesfield dealt with some interesting life-contingent contracts while he was Lord Chancellor. Here are two Chancery cases heard by Macclesfield that could have led him to think about the valuation of life-contingent contracts.[5] The first given here was heard in 1724 and the second the previous year.

1. *Coventry* v. *Coventry*: Gilbert Coventry, 4th Earl of Coventry, married Anne Master in 1715. This was Coventry's second marriage; he had a daughter by his first marriage but no male heirs. Anne brought

a large dowry to the marriage on condition that she would receive a marriage settlement of £500 per year. Coventry had a draft for the settlement written but it lay among his papers unexecuted. He died suddenly in 1719 and a distant relative, William Coventry, ascended to the earldom. The new earl did not recognize the marriage settlement, and so Anne, the dowager countess, sued the new earl. She won.

2. *Hobson* v. *Trevor*: Edward Trevor's relationship with his father, Sir John Trevor, was so bad that he was not allowed to be in the presence of his father. Consequently, although he was the eldest son, Edward's inheritance was uncertain. Even in these circumstances Edward wanted a good marriage for his daughter Elizabeth. For her marriage to Richard Hobson to take place without the knowledge of Richard's mother, Lady Hobson (Richard was also under age and could not make a marriage settlement on his own), Trevor pledged on a bond of £5,000 that one third of any of his inheritance from his father would go to Hobson within 3 months of Sir John's death and one third to his daughter Elizabeth after Edward's death. If Edward died before his father or if his father cut Edward out of his will, then the £5,000 would go to Richard. Sir John Trevor died intestate and all of his estate went to Edward as eldest son. Edward wanted to keep the estate intact for himself and was willing to pay his son-in-law the £5,000 only. Richard Hobson sued his father-in-law and won.

The first case is an example of a reversionary life annuity. Without the legal glitch of the unexecuted document, the value to the countess of the marriage settlement is an example of De Moivre's Problem VII (b). The second case is a little more complex since it relies on the order of the deaths. In order for Elizabeth to inherit, Sir John must die before Edward Trevor and she must outlive her father. There is also the added twist of the risk of Sir John Trevor dying intestate, or of his making a will disinheriting his son Edward, or of his leaving all or part of his estate to Edward. Ignoring the added twist, the value of the estate to Edward, of which ⅓ would go to Richard Hobson, is given in the second edition of De Moivre's annuity book, slightly retitled *Annuities on Lives* and published in 1743 (Problem XV).[6] The value to Elizabeth is similar to, but not the same as, another problem in De Moivre's second edition (Problem XVII).

The final problem in the first edition of *Annuities upon Lives* (Problem XXVII) is similar to, but not exactly the same as, a case regarding a reversion that came before the High Court of Chancery in

1751, with a judgment rendered in 1752. The case shows the extent of the penetration of De Moivre's ideas by mid-century into the valuation of life-contingent contracts related to property. Problem XXVII reads:

Supposing three persons A, B, C, whereof first A is in possession of an annuity for his life; the second B to stand next in reversion exclusive of C, and C to have the expectation of the reversion for him and his heirs forever, in case A survives B, to find the value of the expectation of C.

In the Chancery case, a cavalry officer named John Nichols owned the reversion to a small estate. Title to the estate was meant to pass from the current owner (the "tenant for life") to his son or sons. If they all died without offspring then the reversion was to go to Nichols. The current owner had no children nor was he married. The report of the case describes Nichols as "poor." He was not exactly poor in the usual sense. He had held the entry rank of cornet or ensign in the Royal Irish Regiment of Dragoons since the beginning of 1750.[7] It was probably a purchased commission (the going rate was about £400).[8] Either it was purchased for him to provide an income or he went into debt to purchase the commission himself. To advance to the rank of lieutenant, which he did in 1756, he would need additional purchase money.[9] Hence Nichols's need for money. He sold his reversion to a gentleman with the surname Gould and within a month the tenant for life died leaving no children. Nichols sued Gould, claiming the sale price was an undervaluation. In terms of Problem XXVII, A is the tenant for life, B is his son, who is nonexistent, at A's death, and C is Nichols. The Lord Chancellor in the High Court, Lord Hardwicke, considered and rejected probability arguments to determine the value of the reversion, and included a reference to De Moivre in his ruling:[10]

There is no proof of any fraud or imposition on the plaintiff; nothing but suspicion; and therefore it is too much to set aside this purchase merely on the value. Every purchase of this kind must be on the foot of great uncertainty as to the value. The first of this kind, which may be purchased, is a reversion after an estate-tail; which the law does not consider of any value: and yet by accident it may be a most valuable thing, and will take place in possession, if tenant in tail dies without suffering a recovery: nor can the court say, it must be computed how much it was worth on all the contingencies, as of the health of tenant in tail, &c. according to *Demoivre*'s rule. The next interest to that is the purchase of a reversion after an estate for life with contingent remainders to the children of tenant for life; which is a better reversion than the other; as it cannot be barred by tenant for life, until the contingent remainder comes *in esse*, and attains twenty-one, to join in the conveyance. But still this is liable to uncertainty and difficulty in computation as to the value, which depends on such a number of chances; as whether tenant for life is healthy and likely to have children, (in which case the reversion would be worth but little) that it is impossible to compute it: and though they have rules in *London* to make such a computation, still there must be strict evidence as to it; for no general rule can be laid down, it depending on the particular circumstances of every person.

Nichols lost the case. There was no evidence of fraud in the determination of the purchase price of the reversion that he reached with the purchaser. The reference to De Moivre seems to have come from the Chancellor himself or was made in court by the counsel for Nichols. I found no reference to De Moivre in the surviving depositions in the case.[11]

A report of a similar, yet more complex, case than John Nichols's reversion makes reference to De Moivre and his work. This was a lawsuit that began in about 1730 over a disputed reversion and was not settled until a judgment was made in the House of Lords in 1744. De Moivre's involvement may be apocryphal; other than an anecdote reported in 1812, there is no known surviving evidence that De Moivre's opinion was sought or offered. The origin of the lawsuit is in a will drawn up in 1674 for Oliver Neve by John Norris, a lawyer and Neve's distant relative by marriage. Neve had property in Witchingham, Norfolk, worth £1,500 a year in rents. Neve's will specified a number of contingent reversions. Initially the property was willed to a distant cousin, Oliver Le Neve and his legal heirs (Le Neve's sons and their sons). Should Oliver Le Neve die without legal heirs, the property would then go to Oliver's elder brother Peter Le Neve and his legal heirs. Third in line was another distant cousin, Francis Neve. Finally, if all three died without a legal heir, the property would go to Oliver Neve's closest male relative, who turns out to be a cousin named John Neve, a blacksmith. Oliver Neve died in 1678, whereupon the distant cousin Oliver Le Neve took his inheritance. Since Le Neve was underage, John Norris acted as the trustee for the estate. Shortly after the elder Oliver Neve's death, John Norris purchased John Neve's reversion for £30. Francis Neve died in 1708 leaving no offspring and Oliver Le Neve died in 1711 leaving only daughters. Peter Le Neve then inherited the estate. When he died without offspring in 1729, Peter Le Neve had intended to leave the estate to his brother's daughters and their sons. At this point the great-grandson of John Norris, another John Norris, who was a minor at the time, claimed the estate and his trustees applied to have Oliver Le Neve's daughters ejected from the estate. Lawsuits ensued. The Le Neve side of the case claimed that the elder John Norris's purchase of the reversion was fraudulent because he was in a conflict of interest while he was acting as a trustee to Oliver Le Neve.

They argued that such an action more generally is undesirable from anyone in such a position of trust, saying:

And they will be seduced to discover titles or reversions, standing out, for the sake of getting them for their own use, which otherwise might never be known, or be incapable of being proved; which therefore they will always be able to pick up for meer trifles; as in the present case, an estate of one thousand five hundred pounds a year, is got in consideration of thirty pounds.

The Norris side denied the allegation of fraud, but seemed to acknowledge that the reversion that the elder John Norris purchased was undervalued. It is at this point that the anecdote involving De Moivre is reported:

The purchase-money was only 30 *l.* which it was contended was no valuable consideration; but, on the evidence of Demoivre, and others well versed in calculations, it was adjudged to be full price for the chance at the time; there being so many remainders over.

Whether or not De Moivre actually carried out the calculation (which at the moment seems impossible according to the Lord Chancellor's decision in the Nichols case), what is important is the general perception that these kinds of calculations were relevant to property valuations.

De Moivre's work may have stirred interest in annuity valuations, but it did not cause an immediate revolution. Just as the proprietors and managers of insurance and annuity companies continued to go their own way independent of the mathematicians, some of the mathematical community either were not aware of, or ignored, De Moivre's work. Publishing his own work on life annuities 2 years after the publication of *Annuities upon Lives*, Richard Hayes could have benefited from De Moivre's insights into the calculation of last survivor annuities. Although De Moivre's approximation to obtain the value of a last survivor annuity on two lives overestimates the true value of the years' purchase as shown in Figure 5.3, Hayes's overestimates seen in the previous chapter are much worse. Edward Laurence the surveyor also ignored, or was unaware of, De Moivre's work. Both were influenced by Halley instead.

There were at least three lesser mathematicians who knew of De Moivre's work in the decade and a half after the publication of *Annuities upon Lives*. What is common to their work is property. There were also some differences. One followed De Moivre's approach to annuity valuations to the letter. The two others tried their own approaches, one based on Hayes's and Hatton's method of approximation to a life annuity and

Figure 5.3. Annuities on two lives, 5-year age differential errors in De Moivre's and Hayes's approximations to joint life annuities

the other with his own unique and incorrect approach. The latter provides an example of the general lack of understanding of the mathematical issues in the valuation of life-contingent contracts. A brief description of the careers of the three mathematicians provides insight into their commonalities as well as the target audiences for their books.

1. Gael Morris (d. 1772) was a stockbroker licensed in the city of London and an adept calculator with scientific interests in astronomy.[12] He was investing in the market for government annuities as early as 1722 and at his death in 1772 he owned a government annuity jointly with two others. He was also a small landowner with an estate near the village of Cuddington in Buckinghamshire. As a broker he provided investment advice to others, including the composer Georg Friedrich Händel. As an astronomer, Morris worked with Astronomer Royal James Bradley, making several computations for astronomical tables.
2. Weyman Lee (ca 1680–1765) spent his entire career as a barrister at the Inner Temple in London.[13] He entered the Inner Temple in 1703 and was called to the Bar in 1709. He became a Master of the Bench in 1743 and briefly served as treasurer of the Inner Temple in the period 1751–2. Lee's will shows that he had landed interests. He had leases to estates in Southwark and in Raunds, Northamptonshire.
3. John Richards (1690–1778) was a land surveyor working mainly in Exeter and mapping estates for various landowners in the county

of Devon.[14] He also worked at times as a builder (he was responsible for designing the Devon and Exeter Hospital in 1741), as an accountant, and as an instrument maker. In addition to his books related to life annuities, he also wrote a book on measuring the ullage in a cask, or the difference between the volume of a cask and the volume of the liquid in it. Richards was also interested in recreational mathematics, submitting solutions to problems in the *Ladies Diary* and reporting in the *Diary* on an eclipse of the sun in 1724.

The three mathematicians also have commonalities with their forebears who wrote books on annuities and leases during the seventeenth century. Most of these earlier authors were surveyors or teachers of mathematics. All were adept in the mathematics of their day, but at the same time were not the leading mathematicians of the day.

For a little more than a decade, it seems that the farther one gets in time from De Moivre's 1725 *Annuities upon Lives*, the farther the early writers on life annuities get from the correct mathematical results. John Richards published *The Gentleman's Steward and Tenants of Manors Instructed* in 1730. Based on De Moivre's methodology, Richards provides extensive numerical tables of annuity values for single and joint lives. Writing in 1735 and 1737, respectively, both Gael Morris and Weyman Lee acknowledged De Moivre's work. Morris used some of De Moivre's results, and yet ignored him on important points related to life annuities for single lives. Lee seems to have taken issue, incorrectly, with almost everything De Moivre wrote.

Richards shows explicitly, and in detail, how the valuation of life annuities and joint life annuities applies to the valuation of estates and to the purchase of leases. The rents coming in from an estate are a life annuity for the person or persons holding the estate for their lives. There are also expenses such as repairs, rent to the lord who owns the land, and tithes to the Church. Depending on how the estate is held (last survivor or joint survivor, for example), the value of the estate is the present value of the appropriate life annuity related to the rents minus the present value of the same life annuity related to the expenses. Richards uses a higher rate of interest for the present value of the rents compared to expenses, usually a 1% to 2% differential, which results in giving a higher value to the expenses compared to income. The difference in the rates, Richards says, is due to the different risks involved; there is a higher risk in actually receiving a rent than the risk in actually paying the expenses, and the interest rate rises with the risk. The valuation of a lease to be purchased follows the same recipe: take into account the basis on which the lease is granted – joint survivor or last survivor; then consider the rents and expenses as annuity payments valued at different rates of interest.

Morris's method for valuing life annuities for a single life may have been inspired by the writings of Richard Hayes or Edward Hatton on life annuity valuations.[15] Morris begins with Halley's table for values of a_x determined at a 6% annual rate of interest (Table 3.2). For each of Halley's values, Morris sets $a_x = a_{\overline{n}|}$ and solves for n using a 6% rate of interest. For a given value of n Morris determines $a_{\overline{n}|}$ at 4%, the then current rate on government securities. Morris substitutes these values for Halley's values at 6%.

For his part, Lee railed at length against De Moivre's methods as well as the work of John Richards, De Moivre's disciple as Lee saw it. His arguments were lengthy and mostly fallacious. After a long diatribe, Lee tried his own approach to the valuation of a_x based on a misinterpretation of what Halley had written about the valuation of life annuities. Halley says:[16]

> for it is plain that the Purchaser ought to pay for only such a part of the value of the Annuity, as he has chances that he is living; and this ought to be computed yearly, and the Sum of all those yearly Values being added together, will amount to the value of the Annuity for the Life of the Person proposed.

Lee interpreted this differently from how Halley actually performed the calculations:[17]

> But then the latter Part of the Rule, where it directs that this Operation must be repeated for every Year of the Nominee's Life, does not distinctly and expressly say for what Number of Years this Computation must be made: But I cannot find out that 'tis capable of any other Meaning than one of these two, either that it must be made for so many years as the Nominee has an even Chance to live, or for so many years as he has any Chance at all, or a Possibility to live.

In the end, Lee went the route of an even chance to live. The age to which a person has an even chance to live is the median age at death. Halley had found this value as one of the examples for the use of the Breslau table. Calling the median age at death y for a person aged x, Lee went to great lengths to argue that a good value for a_x could be determined from the median future lifetime $m = y - x$. For any given rate of interest, he sets $a_x = a_{\overline{m}|}$.

Lee's preference for the median age at death may have come from his legal training. In law there is a concept, called "semi-plena probatio," that is medieval in origin. A modern derivative of it is in the phrase "balance of probabilities," which is used in civil law rather than "beyond a reasonable doubt" as in criminal law.

I came up against "balance of probabilities" once in a legal consultation as a statistician. It was a suit for malpractice against a doctor whose patient had died before receiving surgery. The patient had been in an automobile accident and was brought to the emergency room of a hospital. After the examination the doctor booked an operating room for an hour later and then left the hospital. On returning within the hour the doctor found the patient dead. The case hung on whether the patient had had a better than 50–50 chance of surviving had the surgery been done immediately (a finding of malpractice) or a less than 50–50 chance (no malpractice). It was settled out of court since the numerical value of the probability could not be accurately determined to be greater or less than ½.

Returning to the eighteenth century, an interpretation of semi-plena probatio in a 1717 legal case comes close to this notion of "balance of probability":[18]

> *Semiplena* probatio therefore they concluded to be, that degree of evidence which would incline a reasonable man to either side of the question; and implies in the notion of it, that a positive witness has not deposed to the principal fact.

As had been done by custom in leases for lives, Lee wanted to reduce a lease for lives to a fixed-term annuity where the term is estimated to what he says is a "tolerable degree of probability" or a "reasonable degree of probability."[19] On using the concept of semi-plena probatio, the median future lifetime is the tipping point for deciding on the probable length of the term for a life annuity.

To see how well Morris's and Lee's approximations perform, take the 4% annual interest rate that Morris used. For this interest rate, I calculated the values of a_x using Halley's complete life table in Appendix 2. This value is subtracted from each of the two approximations of a_x. The resulting differences are shown in Figure 5.4. Morris's method tends to underestimate a_x and Lee's tends to overestimate it; at all ages Morris's approximation is better than Lee's in terms of being closer in absolute value to a_x. In both cases the approximation improves with age.

Beginning in 1728, information related to the age at death was published in the Bills of Mortality for London. Based on this new information, Morris seems to have dismissed his own approximate valuations of a_x as values that should be used in the market. Both his table for values of a_x and Halley's table (Table 3.2) show that, with the exception of ages 5 and under, the value of a_x decreases as the age at issue increases – buying a life annuity at an earlier age is more expensive than it is at a later age. On the other hand, Morris claims that the Bills of Mortality

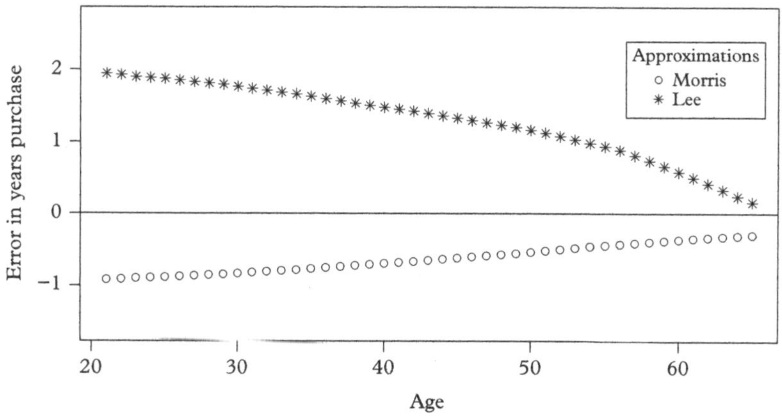

Figure 5.4. Errors in approximations to a_x using the methods of Morris and Lee

show an elevated risk of death between the ages of 15 and 25. He implies that life annuities for those in this age group can be obtained in the marketplace for less than life annuities for older people. Consequently, to dismiss what follows Morris's approximation to a_x misses what other insights can be gained from his work. After recalculating Halley's values of a_x from a 6% annual interest rate to 4%, Morris goes on to copy Problems IV, V, VI, and VII (a) directly from De Moivre, along with his solutions. These are problems related to joint survivor and last survivor life annuities on two and three lives. Nothing new, but at least it is correct. Where Morris possibly breaks new ground is in the renewal of a lease, a problem related to, but not the same as, De Moivre's Problem XVII. An annuity or lease is held on three lives. When one life drops, De Moivre considers that there is a given renewal fee and finds the present value of the fee. For the same situation Morris considers how to determine the fee. He makes the following argument. At the time when the life drops, the value of the lease is the present value of a last survivor life annuity on the two remaining lives. With the addition of the third life, the value of the lease is the present value of a last survivor annuity on all three lives. The renewal fee should be the difference in the two lease values, he says.

As expected from his use of median future lifetime to evaluate a single life annuity, Lee extended these concepts to annuities on two lives. He spent most of his time discussing last survivor annuities for two lives and complaining that De Moivre's calculations in this area were wrong. To apply his median future lifetime concept to last survivor annuities,

Lee needed to find the probability that both lives expire within a certain number of years or the complementary probability that at least one, or the last survivor, is alive within the time period. Then the median future lifetime *m* is the number of years such that the two probabilities are the same and equal to ½. The value of the last survivor annuity is given by $a_{\overline{m}|}$.[20]

De Moivre ignored Weyman Lee's criticisms and errors. It was the surveyor John Richards who responded in writing to Lee. To confuse matters a little, Richards mixed up the concepts of median future lifetime, which Lee used, and expected future lifetime, which De Moivre used. The two are the same when, as De Moivre assumed, the chances of survival decrease linearly with age, so that the argument that De Moivre made can apply in the criticism of Lee's work made by Richards. The nub of the criticism is based on the practice of taking the value of a life annuity, equating it to an annuity with a fixed term, and solving for the term as Hatton, Hayes, and Morris had done. A life annuity is a weighted sum of the future payments of value 1 discounted to the present time where the weights are the survival probabilities. Put in the same terms, expected lifetime is the weighted sum of amounts of value 1 (not discounted) where, again, the weights are the survival probabilities. Setting the value of expected future lifetime equal to the value of an annuity of fixed term is equivalent to setting the value of a life annuity without interest equal to the value of the annuity of fixed term at some given rate of interest. De Moivre argued that since the value of life annuities should depend on interest and mortality, making expected future lifetime and an annuity of fixed term equivalent in value is not valid. Richards repeated De Moivre's argument and concluded in the same vituperative spirit in which Lee originally wrote:[21]

> I am not at all surprized that the Author denounced War with every body that hath treated of this Subject; for as he set out on such fallacious Principles, no wonder that his Computations would not agree with any others. Error is very prolifick, and the Performance I am considering is a flagrant Instance of it: For, in short, this single Blunder influences and quite invalidates the whole Work; And yet the Gentleman is so full of his Abilities, and on the Success of having, as he thinks, discover'd an Inconsistency in Mr. de Moivre's Rules, that his Vanity becomes as intolerable as his Ignorance.

James Dodson's great-grandson, Augustus De Morgan, included Weyman Lee's method of valuing a life annuity in his *A Budget of Paradoxes* published in 1872.[22] He demolished Lee's method much more succinctly than Richards' reference to De Moivre by showing how Lee's method breaks down when considering the extreme case of 1,000 prospective annuitants, of whom 500 will die within a year and the other 500 are immortal. Using median future lifetime, according to Lee the price for the life annuity for each individual is the present value of a single payment made in 1 year, a price which would quickly bankrupt the scheme.

Richards criticized Lee not only for his incorrect assumptions about life annuity valuations but also for his approach to lease renewal and valuations. As Richards had done, the usual approach to valuing an estate is to take the present value of future rents and to deduct the present value, at a lower interest rate, of regular expenses such as repairs, tithes, and rent to the person who owns the land. Lee proposed valuing these expenses as a fixed proportion of the rent. He also thought that other expenses should be considered as a fixed proportion of rent. These expenses include compensation for the tenant's trouble in managing and looking after the estate as well as what amounts to an insurance premium that would cover losses and damage that might come about from working the estate. Richards mocked Lee's ideas. Others did consider Lee's ideas seriously and rejected them. In the Canterbury Cathedral Archives there is a handwritten critique of Lee's proposals regarding the treatment of expenses.[23] The writer, whose identity is not disclosed, calculated the fines for renewing some leases under Lee's proposal and compared them to the Church's traditional method. He found that Lee's fines were typically larger, often considerably larger, than what the Church calculated. The writer concluded that adopting Lee's proposals would cause unrest among the tenants and so the only use of Lee's book was to demonstrate that Church fines were low, should a tenant complain about the fine.

De Moivre's work marks a change in the genre of annuity books. Many leading mathematicians of the eighteenth century subsequently took an interest in the valuation of life annuities and most of the mathematical advances were due to them.

In addition to writing a book on life annuities or perhaps subsequent to writing it, De Moivre was a consultant for the valuation of life-contingent contracts often related to property. When he started as a consultant is unknown. It could have been as early as 1706, when Edmond Halley sought De Moivre's opinion about an issue related to fixed-term annuities. De Moivre's response shows that at that time he had knowledge of, and facility in, annuity calculations. It was a fairly difficult problem. Halley had written a chapter on interest and fixed-term annuities that appeared in Edwin Sherwin's *Mathematical Tables*. One of Halley's problems was to find the rate of interest, given the term and value of the annuity. De Moivre wrote to Halley verifying the approximation Halley had used to determine the rate of interest.

The approximation that appears in *Mathematical Tables* is the same as what is in De Moivre's letter, down to the notation that is used.[24] Based on this sliver of evidence, all that can be said is that before the publication of *Annuities upon Lives* in 1725, De Moivre almost certainly had the knowledge to consult on the traditional valuation of leases using fixed-term annuities, or other related problems. There is no surviving evidence that he did.

Whenever De Moivre did begin work as a consultant on annuity valuations, by the 1730s and 1740s he was joined by some other mathematicians. Consulting work became a small cottage industry for mathematicians knowledgeable in the mathematics of life annuities and in the calculation of their values. This activity continued until the end of the eighteenth century, even as mathematicians became more prominent in the life annuity and insurance industries.

6 Mathematicians as Consultants

Up to about 1760, the number of mathematicians who are known to have acted as consultants on the valuation of life annuities and related contracts can be counted on the fingers of one hand: Abraham De Moivre, James Dodson, William Jones, and Thomas Simpson. To complete the hand, there is one other, William Chapple, who did his calculations for one person only. Chapple was the estate steward for Sir William Courtenay, a landowner in Devon who was elevated from a baronetcy to viscount in 1762. There were other mathematicians who showed interest in the valuation of life annuities through their published books containing sections on annuities, but with no manuscript evidence of carrying out consultations for clients. There was one mathematician, Brook Taylor, with manuscript evidence of interest in life annuities but with no known work as a consultant.

The bulk of the surviving letters are requests for valuations for a variety of life-contingent contracts or the responses providing the valuations. There is one letter from De Moivre held in a branch of the Berlin State Library; the remaining letters, held either in Cambridge University Library or Columbia University Library, are to or from Jones (in Cambridge) or Simpson (in Columbia). They cover a range of situations.

There are many interconnections between De Moivre, Dodson, Jones, Simpson, and Taylor, who were all fellows of the Royal Society. Dodson studied mathematics with De Moivre. De Moivre and Jones were both tutors to George Parker in his youth, before he became 2nd Earl of Macclesfield. Simpson had disputes over annuity valuations with both De Moivre and Dodson. John Rowe, whose activity in consulting surfaced later in the century, was a friend of Simpson when both Rowe and Simpson resided in London. It was through Rowe, who had moved to Exeter and close to Chapple, that Chapple corresponded with Simpson about life annuities. The connections of this trio are illustrated in the beginning of a letter from Chapple to Simpson shown in Figure 6.1.[1] Taylor and De Moivre were friends, De Moivre at times

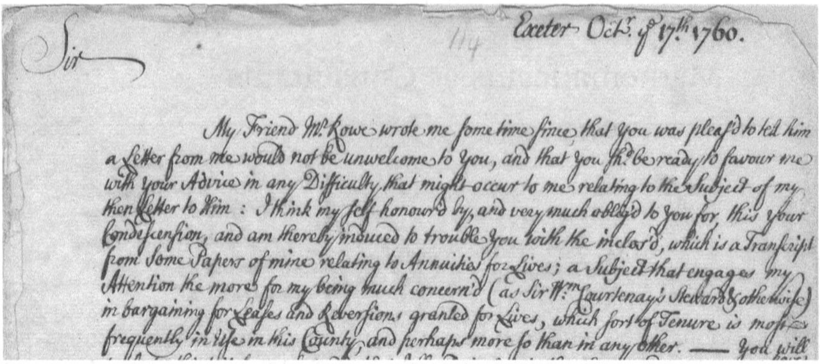

Exeter Octr. ye 17th 1760.

Sir

My Friend Mr. Rowe wrote me some time since that you was pleas'd to tell him a Letter from me would not be unwelcome to you, and that you shd. be ready to favour me with your Advice in any Difficulty that might occur to me relating to the Subject of my then Letter to him: I think my self honour'd by, and very much oblig'd to you for, this your Condescension, and am thereby induced to trouble you with the inclos'd, which is a Transcript from Some Papers of mine relating to Annuities for Lives; a Subject that engages my Attention the more for my being much concern'd (as Sir Wm. Courtenay's Steward & otherwise) in bargaining for Leases and Reversions granted for Lives, which sort of Tenure is most frequently in Use in this County, and perhaps more so than in any other. — You will

Figure 6.1. Excerpt of the letter from William Chapple to Thomas Simpson. *Source*: Photo by Columbia University Library

translating material into French for Taylor and Taylor putting De Moivre in touch with an artist who designed the engraving that is the frontispiece for De Moivre's *Doctrine of Chances*.[2]

Working as a consultant requires finding clients. Finding clients requires some kind of advertising. Today the most common types of advertising are word of mouth, referral work based on work for previous clients, or mass media, which include newspapers, magazines, radio, television, and the Internet. In the eighteenth century, word of mouth, referral work, and newspapers were the only options.

After trawling through the online Burney Collection of Newspapers in the British Library using several different keyword searches, it appears that newspaper advertisements for consulting work were few and far between. And they all involve De Moivre. Figure 6.2 shows the only three advertisements that I could find up to 1760.[3] The third advertisement is from a newspaper published about 2 weeks after De Moivre's death on November 27, 1754. The person who helped De Moivre with his consulting during his old age is unnamed in the advertisement, but was probably James Dodson. At the time Dodson was looking for a teaching position and probably wanted to maintain the cash flow he had enjoyed for a few years. The reason that I believe it was Dodson is that about 9 months later, in September 1755, shortly after he was appointed to a teaching position in the Royal Mathematical School, he placed an advertisement in the newspapers announcing his ability and availability to carry out accounting work.[4] In December 1754 letters were to be left at the bar of Pons Coffeehouse, a place frequented by De Moivre and several of his Huguenot friends. In September 1755 letters could be left at the bar of Pons Coffeehouse, as well as the Bank Coffeehouse behind the Royal Exchange, or at the

July 11, 1739.

Mr. DE MOIVRE,

HAVING in the Beginning of January, 1737-8, publiſhed his Second Edition of *The* DOCTRINE *of* CHANCES, And having ſoon after advertiſed it, deſires ſuch of his Subſcribers, as have not already received their Books, that they would be pleaſed to ſend for them to Slaughter's Coffee-houſe in St. Martin's-Lane, any Time before the firſt of January next. He alſo takes this Opportunity of making it his Requeſt to thoſe, who are pleaſed to conſult him by Letter about any Caſe relating to Leaſes, for a Number of Years certain, or to Annuities upon Lives, to mention what the Rate of Intereſt is, which is agreed on between the contracting Parties.

March 12, 1740-1.

IF the Gentleman who Yeſterday ſpoke to Mr. A. DE MOIVRE, upon the Pavement in St. Martin's-Lane, about a Queſtion relating to Annuities on Lives, will come to Slaughter's Coffee-houſe, he ſhall receive entire Satisfaction about the ſame; and his Pardon aſked for the Anſwer he received, it being not immediately recollected, by Reaſon of different Dreſs and other Circumſtances, that he was the ſame Perſon who ſome Days before had propoſed the Queſtion.

MR. ABRAHAM DE MOIVRE, who has been juſtly celebrated for his Knowledge in, and Treatiſes concerning the Doctrine of Chances, Annuities for Lives, Survivorſhips, and other Branches of Mathematical Learning, having lately died in a very advanced Age it is thought proper to inform the Publick, That the Perſon who has for ſeveral Years laſt paſt, during which his Sight was greatly impair'd, aſſiſted him in the Solution of thoſe Problems in the above Sciences, which have been referred to him during that Time, will continue to give Anſwers to ſuch Queſtions, of thoſe Kinds, as ſhall be left for that Purpoſe at the Bar of Pons's Coffee-houſe in Caſtle-Street, near Leiceſter-Fields.

Note, The Mathematical Sciences, are taught, Eſtates ſurvey'd, and Accounts audited or adjuſted, by the abovementioned Perſon.

Figure 6.2. Advertisements in London newspapers for consulting on annuity and lease valuations. *Source*: Reproduced with permission from the British Library

Royal Mathematical School. The Bank Coffeehouse was near the Royal Mathematical School; Pons Coffeehouse was a walk of at least half an hour. Dodson would have had no reason to go to Pons Coffeehouse unless he had already established a reputation there.

If the newspapers were not used to obtain clients, then the advertising must have been done through referrals or by word of mouth. It is very difficult to find written sources for this kind of information and one can only speculate. In the surviving correspondence there is only one example of a referral. After seeking help from Simpson regarding a valuation of his property in London, Edward Dickinson told Simpson that he had passed Simpson's name and address to Lionel Pilkington, who wanted some calculations done.[5] Pilkington was a baronet and the Member of Parliament for Horsham, and so the issue for Pilkington was probably also land-based. Another possibility for getting publicity is via the reputation gained through their books on life annuities. This could account for De Moivre and Simpson. Dodson's consulting work occurred before he published his major book on life annuities, although during the first half of the 1750s he published some articles on life annuities in the *Philosophical Transactions* and he helped De Moivre with his consulting activities.[6] Publications probably do not account for William Jones's work as a consultant. He had no book devoted entirely to life annuities. His one book, *Synopsis palmariorum matheseos*, published in 1706, treats only interest and annuities for fixed terms.[7] Several of Jones's mathematical manuscript notebooks related to his work as a tutor are in the Macclesfield Collection held by Cambridge University Library. Among them are notebooks containing notes on simple and compound interest, written neatly in a fine hand, probably meant for the student to copy into his own notebook.[8] Mixed in with this are notes on purchasing freehold estates. This opens the possibility of a reputation gained through teaching, which would apply not only to Jones but also to De Moivre, Simpson, and Dodson.

The topic of interest and annuities for a fixed term was a common one, taught by private tutors and in various institutions of learning.[9] The only information we have about Abraham De Moivre's career as a tutor is a set of notes for his lessons in algebra given over the 2 years 1742 and 1743, for a student visiting London from Hanover. The notes contain a very short and simple treatment of interest and annuities.[10] A 1745 advertisement for a private academy in the village of Heath near Wakefield, Yorkshire describes the mathematics curriculum for young gentlemen in the school:[11] A course of mathematics and philosophy, viz. geometry, geography, astronomy, and natural philosophy; the valuation of estates, annuities and reversions. Depending on the instructor, the mathematics curriculum at Cambridge may have included topics on interest and annuities. Robert Green's 1707 curriculum in arithmetic and algebra at Clare College, Cambridge includes William Jones's *Synopsis palmariorum matheseos*, as well as John Ward's 1707 *The Young Mathematician's Guide*, on the reading list. Both Jones and Ward treat similar topics in interest and annuities, with the difference being Ward's addition of a discussion of Halley's work on life annuities. Of course, although the books were on the reading list, there is no guarantee that Green actually taught any of the material on interest and annuities. The reason that the topics of annuities and interest seem to permeate the curricula of various places is that it was a topic of importance to a young gentleman, especially one whose father had landed interests. Should a young gentleman inherit his father's estate it would be useful for him to have at least a smattering of knowledge regarding interest and annuities in order to talk intelligently to his steward or estate agent.

Some of the better students might have been able to solve moderately complicated problems, but once the problem became complex enough only the more accomplished mathematicians could solve it. At this point a mathematician might be called upon to provide a solution, perhaps for a fee. Such is the case for a consultation requested by a Church of England clergyman. The vast majority of these clergymen attended Oxford or Cambridge, where they would have studied some mathematics. It is reasonable to assume that many would be able to use the various eighteenth-century editions of George Mabbut's *Tables for Renewing & Purchasing of the Leases* for the standard property issues facing the Church of England and its land holdings. One clergyman, representing an unnamed cathedral in England, was faced with a non-standard case. He wrote to Thomas Simpson in 1756. All that survives of the correspondence is the reply he received from Simpson:[12]

Rev^{d} sir,

In order to form a just Calculation of ye purchase und[er] consideration and to determine ye advantage or disadvantage of ye Dean and Chapter in accepting of ye Terms proposed, I find it necessary to desire your answer to the following Queries.

1. What is the present annual produce, to the Dean and Chapter, of the Lands and Tenements in Question? Or what has been received as their sum (at a medium) for some years past? N.B. The Advantage arising from future Improvements must be considered apart as that cannot be subject to strict or regular calculation.
2. Have ye present Occupiers of ye said Lands and Tenements continued to renew regularly, at ye end of every 14 Years? Or have any considerable part of them suffered their Leases to run nearly out?
3. Whether, at ye expiration of 99 years ye absolute property of y^{e} (improved) Estate is to revert to y^{e}, then, Dean and Chapter to lett out in new Leases for any Term of years (not exceeding 40) as they shall think proper? Or whether they are then only permitted to receive Fines for Renewing of Leases in which there are 26 years to come (according to ye present custom)?
4. What are ye sums respectively, offered to ye Dean and Chapter, as Equivalents for ye Premises and Right of Possession of ye Estate for ye Term of 40 years, and for ye Reversion of 59 years?

When I have received your answer to the above Queries I shall endeavour to lay before you as exact a calculation of this intricate matter as ye Nature of ye subject will admit of. I am

Rev^d^ sir,

Royal Academy
Woolwich, Jan 21, 1756

your most obedient
Humble Servant

Tho. Simpson

This is not the case of a simple table lookup; the necessary calculations to provide a valuation are not straightforward. In view of his reputation in life annuities, well established before the 1750s, Simpson was a good choice as a consultant.

There is one undated letter by De Moivre that is a "consulting report." There are some clues in the handwriting that suggest a date in the 1730s, or earlier, in the 1720s. The chief clue is in De Moivre's rendering of the letter "I." There is a flourish to it that appears in two other known letters of De Moivre that are definitely from the 1720s or 1730s. In a series of letters to Philip Stanhope, 2nd Earl Stanhope, written in the mid-1740s, the florid "I" is a little more muted. Earlier, in a 1705 note, De Moivre writes "I" in a much plainer fashion quite different from his later style. Here is De Moivre's report in its entirety:[13]

Monday Morning
Sr
According to your desire, I send you the solutions of the three Questions you ask'd me,

1 what is the value of the reversion of an Estate, after 21 years, supposing the Estate worth 25 years purchase.
Answer ... 11 years purchase

2 ye value of the reversion of the same after 14 years
Answer. 14½ years purchase

3 ye value of the reversion of the same after 7 years.
Answer 19 years purchase. I am

Sr
your most humble
and obedient servant
A. De Moivre

De Moivre is not talking about a reversionary annuity, but rather the reversion of an estate. Whatever the annual rent was, the estate was valued at 25 times the rent. The client wanted to know what would be the present value of this estate to the person who would obtain the estate, by reversion, in any of 21, 14, or 7 years. I tried the present value calculations at various annual rates of interest near the 1714 legal rate of 5% and found that at a 4% interest rate the present value of 25 payable at 21, 14, and 7 years in the future is 10.971, 14.437, and 18.998, respectively, which are all close to De Moivre's answers. The 25 years' purchase is then the value of a perpetuity at 4% interest. What gives further support to a dating of the document to the 1720s or 1730s is that around 1730 the interest rate in the market for leases was 4% or 5% at the most.[14] It is impossible to know the client's motivation in asking his three questions. A reasonable speculation is that the estate was leased on lives, since the numbers that were used – 7, 14, and 21 – are the traditional numbers of years in leases for lives with one, two, and three lives, respectively.

Simpson's letter illustrates a complex problem, beyond the capability of someone who may have had a basic training in mathematics. De Moivre's letter addresses a much simpler problem that could easily have been solved by someone with a smattering of mathematics and access to some tables of interest. From this meager evidence I conclude that the range of problems presented to consulting mathematicians was quite broad. The nature of the request depended on the mathematical abilities of the consultee.

There is one other aspect of this consulting work. As I have experienced in my own consulting activities, confidentiality is a key issue. In the eighteenth century this is illustrated by the 1741 advertisement that De Moivre placed in a London newspaper, shown in Figure 6.2.[15] De Moivre was unwilling to provide his opinion on a requested valuation to someone whom he did not know (thereby breaking confidentiality with his client) and apologized when it turned out to be a case of mistaken identity.

De Moivre's consulting activities during the 1730s and 1740s may be conjectured from some of the additional problems he inserted in the second edition of his *Doctrine of Chances*, published in 1738 and the second edition of his book on annuities, slightly retitled *Annuities on Lives*, and published in 1743.[16] The second edition of *Doctrine of Chances* is a compendium of all the results he had obtained on probability to that date and so it contained his work on life annuities from 1725, as well as new work since that time. The material on life annuities appears near the end of the book, after De Moivre had devoted 200 pages to a thorough treatment of his major, and minor, results in probability theory. De Moivre did not reproduce all the results from 1725 in the 1738 *Doctrine of Chances*; rather, he gave representative results from each of the annuity types given in Table 5.1. Following the material on life annuities, De Moivre inserted a number of miscellaneous probability problems, some of which had been suggested to him by his friends while he was writing the book. In the middle of this grab bag of problems are two very practical problems related to life annuities that may have come about as a result of De Moivre's consulting activities. The 1743 edition of *Annuities on Lives* contains all the new material on annuities that appears in *Doctrine of Chances* and a few additional annuity problems, many of which can be construed as illustrations of consulting problems that De Moivre had worked on. What supports my conjectures is a phrase taken from what De Moivre wrote in his dedication to George Parker, 2nd Earl of Macclesfield, for the 1743 *Annuities on Lives*. He says that the new edition "I conceive has received many considerable Improvements, owing to Study and Experience ..." I interpret "Experience" as his consulting experience.

The first problem that De Moivre considers in the second edition of his *Doctrine of Chances* is the valuation of an advowson. This is a custom in the Church of England whereby an individual can purchase the right to appoint a clergyman to a living. The right could be purchased for the next appointment only or in perpetuity. With the practice of primogeniture the eldest son inherited the estate. The younger sons were provided for by having them enter the army, the navy, or the Church. Commissions, such as the one held by John Nichols or the promotion that he desired, could be purchased in the army or navy. For the Church, it would be useful for the parent or relative to purchase an advowson so that the son obtained a reasonable income; not all parishes could provide their clergy with good financial support. De Moivre provides a valuation based on the practical situation in which there is an incumbent in the living so that the purchaser would have the right of appointing the successor.

The second problem was directly related to land. It is a problem related to the valuation of copyhold estates where a tenant typically paid a large fine to enter into the lease and then nominal annual rents thereafter. In De Moivre's example the lease ran for the life of the tenant, and when this ended another fine would be paid by the new tenant taking on the lease with the landlord. De Moivre simplified the problem by assuming that every incoming tenant was the same age at entry as the previous one so that the value of the life annuity associated with each tenant was the same. Following in the tradition established by Edward Hatton, Richard Hayes, and Gael Morris, De Moivre equated the life annuity to an annuity certain and solved for the term, say n, of the annuity certain. This gives the approximate time between renewals so that the present value of the fines is a perpetuity with payments made every n years.

De Moivre's method can be extended to a copyhold estate with a lease on three lives. In De Moivre's solution, he uses as a given the value of a single life annuity. What could be easily substituted into De Moivre's solution is the value of a joint survivor annuity on three lives. When one of the lives drops, the lease is renewed with three lives, two existing and one new, on the payment of a fine. This minor change provides the approximate value of an estate that is rented on three lives rather than one. Following De Moivre, the solution is based on the assumption that on any renewal the age distribution of the three lives is always the same.

De Moivre's approach to copyhold estates is different from the one given in Gael Morris's 1735 *Tables for Renewing and Purchasing of Leases* (discussed in Chapter 5). Morris estimates the value of the fine when renewing a lease on three lives after one of the lives drops; given the fine, De Moivre finds the value of the estate. From Edward Laurence's *A Dissertation on Estates upon Lives and Years, Whether in Lay or Church-Hands* (and Laurence appears to have had vast experience in property and leases), it is apparent that the amount of the fine was determined in a bargaining process between tenant and landlord. There could be a difference between the calculated value and the price agreed through bargaining. Morris's approach might be useful when bargaining for the fine; in his letter to Thomas Simpson (Figure 6.1) William Chapple makes allusion to this. Both Morris and De Moivre address practical questions, although when Dodson's complaints about custom over calculation are recalled it would appear that the question that De Moivre answered was probably more frequently asked.

Two more problems appear in *Annuities on Lives* in 1743. Both are directly related to problems involving property. In 1725 De Moivre addresses the problem of a reversionary life annuity (Problem VII (b) in Table 5.1) in which B receives a life annuity on the death of A. The same problem appears in the 1743 edition prefaced by a related and easier one: B and his heirs receive a perpetuity on the death of A.[17] This is the situation of an estate in which the heir and his heirs receive the rental payments from the estate successively during their lives after the death of the possessor. Finally, in the 1725 edition all life annuities are paid at the end of each year that the person is alive. For life annuities that are from rents on land, when the landlord dies his estate could receive as a final rent payment an amount that is proportional to the fraction of the year from the last rental payment to the death of the landlord. De Moivre provides the valuation without proof in the 1743 edition and five pages later makes a vague comment about how this "is better fitted to Annuities paid by a Grant of Lands."[18] A year later De Moivre provides a proof for his valuation in the *Philosophical Transactions*.[19] Eleven or twelve years later, at the very beginning of the third volume of his *Mathematical Repository*, Dodson makes a distinction in his valuations between life annuities paid at the end of the year (considered in the second volume of the same work) and life annuities secured by land (considered in the third volume).[20]

The final problem that takes into account rental payments to the moment of death also illustrates the level of friendship among some of the members of this network of mathematicians. De Moivre's publication of the proof of this type of annuity valuation was done at the urging of William Jones, who was also the one who placed the paper before a meeting of the Royal Society.[21] By this time De Moivre was 77 years of age and his health was beginning to decline, so that he was probably an infrequent attendee at Royal Society meetings.

In the 1739 advertisement for the second edition of *The Doctrine of Chances* (Figure 6.2) De Moivre says that clients could "consult him by Letter about any Case relating to Leases, for a Number of Years certain." This kind of work is also mentioned in the second edition of *Annuities on Lives*. De Moivre provides a table of the renewal fines for various years remaining on leases issued by colleges for 20 and 21 years where interest has been calculated at 8% per annum (lower than the 11% that was used at the beginning of the century for college and church leases). He prefaces his tables by saying that although the work seems unrelated to annuities on lives, the tables can provide some useful information. In particular, suppose a person purchases a 21-year lease from a college where by custom he should be paying about £10.02 at the calculated 8% interest to obtain a yearly rent of £1 through sublets. Paying more than £10.02 for the lease will lower the rate of interest that he earns on the yearly rent of £1. In particular, he earns 6.75%, 5.8%, or 4.8% on his money if he pays £11, £12, or £13, respectively, for the lease. In view of the one surviving letter reproduced earlier that shows De Moivre's consulting activities in the related area of a valuation of a reversion, this table with the suggestion proffered was probably a handy piece of advice that might attract future business.

Among the surviving letters of Jones and Simpson, there are about ten that deal with queries or answers regarding aspects of life annuities.[22] All but one are concerned with valuations of property. The letters deal with reversions, including one encumbered by a debt, as well as renewals of leases for lives and the value of the fine on entering a lease. One of the queries about property, from Moses Williams to William Jones, concerning the value of a reversion, shines another light on one of the aspects of consulting that still holds true today. It is common for people to want answers to their questions immediately if not sooner! At least Williams asked to have his valuation by the next evening. I wonder if

Jones thought that the request was an imposition on their friendship. They were good friends. They had other connections, too: both were Welsh and fellows of the Royal Society.

Among these surviving consulting cases, my favorite is the one that Jones attributes to Sir William Heathcote.[23] In its most general form the problem is:

It is agreed among three persons, A of 50, B of 40, and C of 22 years of age; that C is to have an estate of *a*£ p an on the demise of A; and another estate of *b*£ on the longest liver A or B: What is the present worth of C's expectation, supposing mony to be at 4£ p C^t p an?

The statement is accompanied by several solutions written on different pieces of paper in different hands. Not many arithmetical details accompany the solutions, typically just a few intermediate and final numerical answers. Often *a* and *b* are given the same numerical value, £1,200. What interests me about this problem are the cryptic puzzles in it for which some solutions (perhaps not always definitive) can be put forward. Here are the puzzles:

1. Is this an easy problem to solve or a difficult one in the mathematics of life annuities?
2. The problem is undated. When was it posed?
3. Why was it posed?
4. There are several solutions to the problem. Do the solutions agree with one another?
5. Why are there several solutions?

The answer to the first question is that the solution at first glance seems easy, provided that De Moivre's annuity book is in hand. There are two reversionary annuities. One is the reversion to *C* on the death of *A* and the second is the reversion to *C* after the deaths of *A* and *B*. These are Problems VII and VIII given in De Moivre's 1725 *Annuities upon Lives* or VII (b) and VIII in Table 5.1.

Since Heathcote is given the honorific "Sir," the problem was definitely posed after 1733 when he was made a baronet. Sir William Heathcote was born in 1693 and his son Thomas in 1721, which would make them about 50 and 22 years of age in 1743.[24] I have been unable to track down the date of birth of Sir William's wife, Elizabeth Heathcote, who was the daughter of Thomas Parker, 1st Earl of Macclesfield, but I would suspect it was about 1702 or 1703, which would make her 40 years of age in 1743.[25] The problem then has the appearance of being the valuing of the son's inheritance when he has come of age where part of the inheritance of £*a* per annum is coming from the father's estate and the £*b* per annum is the result of a marriage settlement in which Elizabeth receives £*b* per annum for her life on the death of William. This is perhaps why the problem was posed.

Among Jones's papers there are nine solutions to the problem, with three different answers.[26] Assuming $a = b =$ £1,200, the most common answer is £19,134.65, with some variation in the last two decimal places. Following De Moivre's solution given in Problems VII and VIII of the 1725 *Annuities upon Lives* and using his linear survivor function to obtain the values of all the life annuities, single and joint life, I computed £10,949.91 for the total value of the two reversions, which is not even close to the most common answer given. Either these people were not very good as mathematicians or there is more to the problem that meets the eye. The latter turns out to be the case. The key word in the problem is "estate." What *C* gets in reversion is not a life annuity but a perpetuity; he obtains the income from the estate for himself and his heirs forever, provided that he survives *A* and *B*. The first step in the valuation is to obtain the value of the reversion to the perpetuity. This is the value of the perpetuity of £1,200 minus those payments made during the lifetime of *A* and the perpetuity of £1,200 minus those payments made until *A* and *B* are both dead. The sum of the two provides a value for the estate. The second step is to find *C*'s expectation with respect to the estate, which would take into account *C*'s "early" death. What is calculated as the final answer is the value of the reversions on the perpetuities times the probability that *C* survives *A*; the status of *B* is left out of the calculation. My calculations along these lines agree with the most common answer of £19,134.65. What supports the conjecture that there is a marriage settlement behind the problem is the calculation of the probability of *C*'s "early" death. Putting names to the letters, Thomas Heathcote inherits an estate of £1,200 per annum on his father's death. In addition his mother, Elizabeth Heathcote, has a marriage settlement that gives her £1,200 per annum on the death of her husband, Sir William Heathcote; until he dies Sir William keeps this income. If Elizabeth Heathcote survives Sir William, her £1,200 per annum goes into the estate on Elizabeth's death. If Thomas dies before Sir William, then Thomas gets nothing and a younger son or the closest male heir inherits; if Thomas dies after Sir William but before his mother, Thomas's heirs through his estate receive the funds from the marriage settlement. It is in this situation that the single chance of Thomas predeceasing his father is the only relevant probability.

There are two possibilities for why there are several solutions to the problem. The first is that Heathcote set it as a challenge problem, which

Jones distributed to people whom he thought knowledgeable in these kinds of calculations. The second is that Jones used this problem as a teaching tool for his students. The solutions are the homework answers that Jones saved. The solutions, to the challenge or to the homework, were done in 1743 or later. The calculation of joint life annuities (a_{xy}) in the most common solution follows the approximation put forward by De Moivre in his 1743 edition of *Annuities on Lives*. Because of the lack of detail in the solutions, I tend to favor these solutions as answers to a challenge problem.

Brook Taylor is the odd man out in this group of mathematicians interested in life annuity valuations. He had enough interest in life annuities to make some extensive calculations of the values of a_x at 4% and 5% interest annually for a wide range of ages (values of x from 1 to 89). There is no surviving evidence that says he put his calculations to any use in a consulting context. Despite this, there are a few things of interest about his four manuscript pages devoted to life annuities.[27] The manuscript was written between 1725 and his death in 1731. Taylor's calculations of a_{xy} for joint life annuities follow De Moivre's method, which appears in his 1725 *Annuities upon Lives*. Taylor used Halley's life table, but as I have discussed in Chapter 3 Halley's published values of l_x stop at $x = 84$, so that the table is incomplete. Taylor completed the table in his own way, taking the maximum value for x as 91. For some reason in the middle of the table he also adjusted downward by one person some of Halley's published values of l_x. Halley had given the total population size of Breslau as 34,000; Taylor's table reduces that number to 33,938.

A few other authors completed Halley's table in their own ways. One was Thomas Watkins. One of the four manuscript pages, with "Watkins" written at the top of the page, has a list of various values of a_x at 5% for x up to 90. At younger ages Taylor's and Watkins's values for a_x are the same. At age 30 they begin to diverge; Taylor's value of a_{30} is 13.07 and Watkins's is 13.084. The values diverge further as the age increases, so that at age 85 Taylor's value of a_{85} is 1.97 and Watkins's is 3.196. The reason for this is that Watkins has added more lives than Taylor to the end of Halley's table in order to complete it. This has little effect on the valuation of a_x at younger ages but a substantial effect at older ages. The reason I have picked Thomas Watkins as the Watkins who calculated the table is that this Watkins and Taylor were on the Royal Society's council together in 1718 and both were freemasons. Further, Watkins published a paper in 1714 on interest and annuities for a fixed term in the *Philosophical Transactions*.[28] Watkins is described as a "gentleman" and so would probably have had an "academic" interest in the valuation of life annuities rather than looking at them as a way of earning money.

While Brook Taylor's calculations for a_x were accurate to two decimal places (I checked them by recalculating them on the computer), the same cannot be said for some of James Dodson's calculations. In 1755, William Brakenridge published a life table based on the Bills of Mortality for London.[29] It was one of a series of five letters by Brakenridge published in the *Philosophical Transactions* examining the size of, and changes in, the population of England. The publication of the life table showing l_x for x from 1 to 87 inspired Dodson to make a table of life annuity values for ages 1 through 88 at 4% interest.[30] Brakenridge's table is incomplete; it ends at age 87 with 7 people left alive. Like Halley's table and the life annuity values he calculated from it, exactly what Dodson did is difficult to reconstruct, especially when a_{88} is not based on any data that Brakenridge published. The difficulty is compounded by the fact that some of Dodson's calculations do not make any sense to me. When I checked Halley's annuity valuations, I used the mathematical relationship between a_x and a_y where y is an age greater than x (given in Appendix 1). I tried something similar for Dodson's calculations. In this case I used the values of a_x and a_{x+1} along with the annual interest rate of 4% to calculate the probability that a person aged x will survive a year to age $x + 1$ for x ranging from 1 to 86. This same concept was applied in Chapter 4 to examine Richard Hayes's annuity calculations. I can also use Brakenridge's table to calculate the same probabilities. The results of this exercise are shown in Figure 6.3. If the two 1-year survival probabilities are in complete agreement, then when one is plotted against the other the points should all fall on the straight line shown in the graph. They do not. About one quarter of the points fall off the line. The largest differences between the two calculations are at the youngest and oldest ages. The worst case is the 1-year survival probability for a life aged 1; it is 0.677 calculated from Brakenridge's table and 0.813 calculated from Dodson's annuity values. At the moment, my only explanation for the differences is that Dodson was using some approximation unknown to me that was not very good, especially at the younger and older ages.

Simpson's calculations for life annuities given in his tables in *Doctrine of Annuities and Reversions* published in 1742 were also inaccurate, but in a different way from those of Dodson.[31] Where Dodson's appear to be inconsistently inaccurate, Simpson's were consistently inaccurate. The deviations from what Simpson published and what I calculated by computer are shown in Figure 6.4. The solid line is for a_x, a single life annuity, and the dotted line is for a_{xx}, a joint life annuity when the two

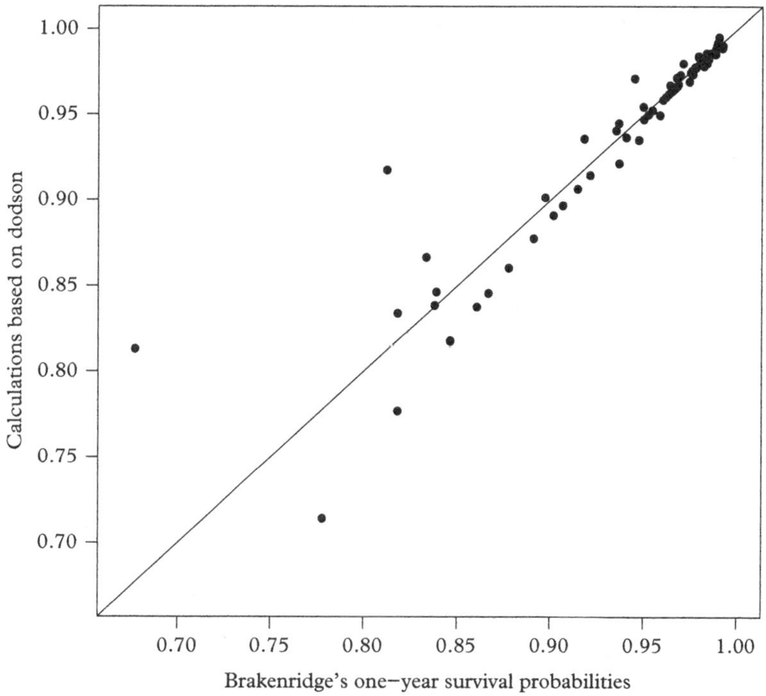

Figure 6.3. Comparison of the 1-year survival probabilities determined from Dodson's life annuity values to those from Brakenridge's table

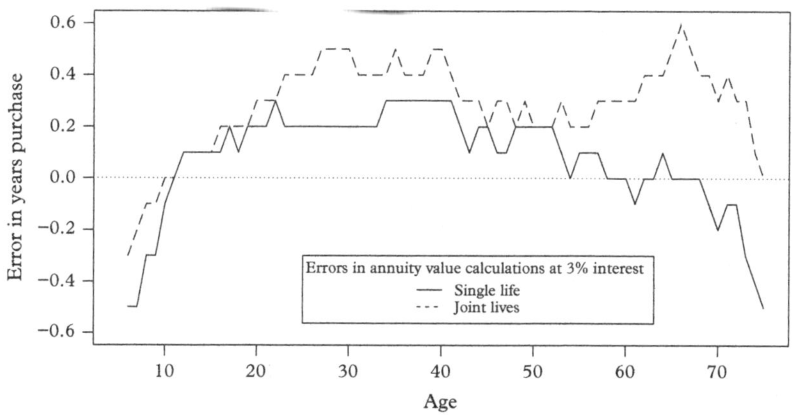

Figure 6.4. Accuracy of Simpson's calculations for a_x and a_{xx} at 3% interest

lives are of the same age. Simpson's calculations were made to one decimal place, rather than two or three like those of other authors, and so his errors in calculation are quite substantial even though they are close to zero (in terms of the one decimal place). On examining the trends in the errors, I think that Simpson's calculations suffer from an accumulation of round-off errors. He probably began by calculating a middle value such as a_{45} or $a_{45,45}$. Then using a formula that, for example, connects a_{45} to a_{44} or to a_{46}, any small error such as 0.1 or 0.2 in a_{45} would carry over into the valuation of a_{44} or a_{46}, and then to younger and older ages as the formula is reapplied to these ages. Any new errors would either accumulate or cancel one another out. This may account for the upside down U-shaped patterns of the trend lines in Figure 6.4.

Simpson was the first to base his annuity calculations on a life table other than Halley's 1693 table. The life table that Simpson chose was one constructed by John Smart in 1738. The table is specific to the City of London, to which Smart had strong ties; he was clerk to the Commission of Lieutenancy for the City of London, the organization in charge of London's militia.[32] Smart's table was presented to a meeting of the Royal Society on May 11, 1738 and published that same year in a broadside.[33] Smart was able to construct his table because the Company of Parish Clerks, which published the Bills of Mortality for London, began collecting the age at death and publishing deaths by age in the yearly bills, beginning in 1728. This move was probably based on recommendations made by Smart in his 1726 book *Tables of Interest, Discount, Annuities, &c.*[34] The minute taker at the Royal Society meeting in 1738 recorded that Smart's table would be better for annuity valuations "than from the Bills of Mortality in Breslaw, that small inland City of Germany." In his letter that came before the Royal Society, Smart did not quite make the same strong claim. He compared his table to Halley's and found that mortality in London was higher than in Breslau at early ages. He reasoned that the difference was because:

> Breslaw is an inland City in Germany, inhabited chiefly by sober, industrious Peoples, Strangers to Luxury that Parent of all Vices: whereas London is a City, abounding with Luxury amongst the Rich, and Debauchery amongst too many both of the Rich and Poor.

He made no claim in his letter that one table was better than the other. It was the minute taker who made the claim, quoting only part of what Smart had written in his letter.

Smart's table was constructed on the same principles as Halley's and its construction is much more transparent than Halley's. He assumed

Table 6.1. *Deaths by age group for the London bills of mortality 1728–37*

Age group	Total number of deaths	Deaths per thousand
Under 2 years of age	103 159	386
Between 2 and 5	23 505	88
Between 5 and 10	9 775	36
Between 10 and 20	8 242	31
Between 20 and 30	19 776	74
Between 30 and 40	24 302	91
Between 40 and 50	23 989	90
Between 50 and 60	19 693	74
Between 60 and 70	16 309	61
Between 70 and 80	10 684	40
Between 80 and 90	6 450	24
90 and above	1 266	5
Total	267 150	1 000

that the population is stationary, that is, that the number of births equals the number of deaths and that there is no migration. The total number of deaths recorded is then the number of births. As shown in the second column of Table 6.1 the total number of deaths for each of the years 1728–37 inclusive was recorded for the age intervals of under 2, 2 to 5, 5 to 10, 10 to 20, 20 to 30, and so on. For his table construction Smart arbitrarily set the number of births as equal to 1,000 and prorated the deaths accordingly, as shown in the third column of Table 6.1. The life table begins at $l_0 = 1{,}000$ and the number alive in each of the age groups is obtained by subtracting the number of deaths up to that age. Since the deaths were recorded for only the age intervals shown in Table 6.1, Smart needed to fill in the number of lives at the intermediate ages, with the restriction that the sum of the deaths within each age group should equal the entry in Table 6.1 for that group (for example, $d_0 + d_1 = 386$). This he seems to have done by eye, while trying to keep the number of deaths per year of age in each age interval nearly constant, with the exception of those up to 10 years of age. For the years 1728 through 1737 there were 171,667 christenings and 267,150 burials, which is definitely an indication of a nonstationary population. The only argument that could be made for stationarity is that the christenings include only those performed in the Church of England. Christenings at Baptist, Presbyterian, Congregationalist, and Quaker churches or chapels would not be included, although many from these denominations were buried in Church of England cemeteries. This argument also still ignores migration into London, which was significant.

Simpson made amendments to Smart's table, hoping to correct for the problem of migration into London, but did not explain his methods clearly. His table begins with 1,280 births. In the last century, prominent statisticians and actuaries, including Karl Pearson, Harald Westergaard, and Anders Hald, have examined Simpson's modifications to Smart's table.[35] For example, using christenings and deaths from the London Bills of Mortality for the years 1728 to 1737 and making some manipulations to Halley's and Smart's tables, Pearson tried without success to reproduce Simpson's l_0 value of 1,280.[36] He concludes:

> The whole of his account of what he has done is so vague that one cannot find out how he produced his Table, and it is equally certain that his method for allowing for migration before 25 years is fallacious. I do not think therefore, although he recognized the importance of immigration, that he overcame the difficulty.

Simpson did not completely rework Smart's table. Rather he forced his and Smart's table to conform by age 25; beginning at age 25 the values of l_x are the same for both tables. Smart's table with Simpson's amendments is given in Appendix 2.

It is useful to see what Simpson actually says about how he amended Smart's table, which is indeed a little obscure:[37]

> I have supposed the number of persons coming to live in town, after 25 years of age, to be inconsiderable, with respect to the whole number of inhabitants; and therefore the probabilities of life for all ages above 25 years, the same as this author [Smart] has made them; but then having increased the numbers of the living, corresponding to all ages below 25; so that they may, as near as possible, be in the same proportion to one another, as they would be, were they deduced from observations of mortality of those *only*, that are born within the bills. Which was done, by comparing together the number of christenings and burials, and observing, by help of Dr. *Halley's* table, the proportion which there is between the degrees of mortality at *London* and *Breslau*, in the other parts of life where the ages are greater than 25.

I tried to see if I could outdo Pearson, but could reproduce Simpson's l_0 value of 1,280 only by ignoring Simpson's phrase "by comparing together the number of christenings and burials" as it relates to London and applying it instead to comparing only the births in London and Breslau. Here is what I did. Generally, we want to find the size of the population of Breslau that is 25 years of age and under, and compare it to London's population (standardized to 1,000 births) of 25 years of age and under. The problem with the comparison is that Halley's table is given by age current, beginning with 1,000 lives at age current 1, while Smart's table begins with 1,000 births. The lives in Halley's table are approximately a half year older than the lives in Smart's table. As a first stab at the 1,280 I calculated the ratio of the sum of the first 25 entries in Halley's table to the first 25 entries in Smart's table and got 1.288049. Since Halley's population is one half year older than Smart's, this ratio is slightly too high. A simple adjustment is to reduce the first entry in Halley's table in a reasonable way and get an underestimate of the ratio. Halley reported that, on average, there were 1,238 births per annum in Breslau. On reducing Halley's first entry of 1,000 by the fraction 1,000/1,238 the ratio changes to 1.273277. The average of the two ratios is 1.280638. After multiplying by 1,000 and rounding to the nearest 10 this provides a new l_0 of 1,280, which agrees with Simpson's result. I admit that I may have obtained the correct answer with the wrong method; this often happens with students in examinations when they have a number of techniques learned but no clue as to which applies to the problem at hand.

There is more to Simpson's *Doctrine of Annuities and Reversions* than the use of a new life table. It starts with motivation. The book is a bit deceptive to the casual reader trying to decipher motivation; the great bulk of it is devoted to the calculation of various kinds of life annuities without giving any context for the calculations. Some context is provided much later in the book, when some example problems are solved. This is all very similar to Abraham De Moivre's *Annuities upon Lives*. The motivation is better seen through the eyes of Simpson's publisher, John Nourse. Advertisements for the book placed by Nourse begin to appear in newspapers late in 1741. The early advertisements start by stating that the material in the book is explained "in an easy and simple manner" and that the book is accompanied by tables that show the values of single and joint life annuities at various rates of interest. This is followed with:[38]

> Likewise the Value that ought to be paid for renewing of Leases upon any Number of Lives, and also how much the Rent Roll of an Estate ought to be increased upon account of such Renewals. To which is added, A Method of investigating the Value of Annuities by Approximation, without the Help of Tables.

This material on leases and estates is buried much further on in the book among some examples. It is not up front as suggested in the advertisement. The publisher was trying to appeal to landowners and their stewards, not to proprietors and managers of companies offering life annuities.

What appears in the newspaper advertisements as "a method of investigating the value of annuities by approximation, without the help of

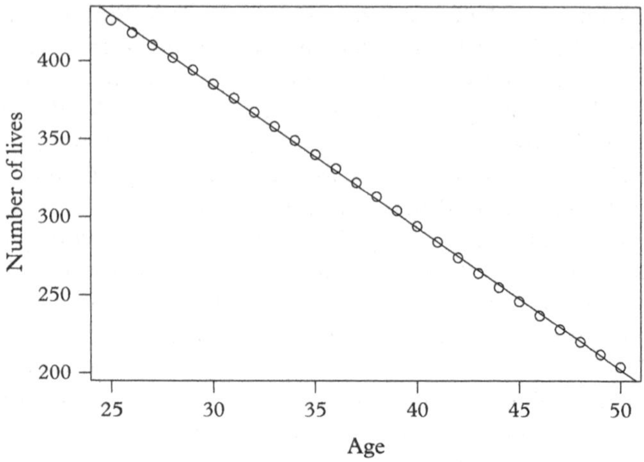

Figure 6.5. Simpson's survivor function between ages 25 and 50

tables" is the major item that differentiates Simpson's book from De Moivre's. Based on the life table massaged out of Smart's table, Simpson provides tables of annuity values for a single life (a_x) and for two and three joint lives when the ages of the joint lives are the same (a_{xx} and a_{xxx}). When the ages are not the same for the joint lives, Simpson provides approximations to the values of the joint life annuities. His simplest approximation is for the situation when the two ages x and y are not equal but are both between the ages of 25 and 50. The approximation is to take the average age $w = (x + y)/2$ and find from the tables the value of the joint life annuity when both are age w, i.e. a_{xy} is approximately a_{ww}. In his *Select Exercises for Young Proficients in the Mathematicks*, published in 1752, which contains several annuity problems, Simpson even gives an approximation to the value of a single life annuity a_x. Anders Hald comments on these approximations, "Clearly, these formulae have no theoretical foundation; they are presumably found by trial and error."[39] I do think there is method behind the seeming "approximation madness" of Simpson. I admit that many of the approximations are, or will be, difficult to crack. And I can crack only the simplest one at the moment, the case when a_{xy} is approximated by a_{ww}. Using a little mathematics (given in Appendix 1) this approximation works when the survivor function is linear (l_x is linear in x as in Figure 6.5), the number alive at x and y is relatively large, and the number of deaths between x and y is relatively small. All this occurs in the age interval 25–50.

De Moivre's incompatible assumptions of a linear survivor function to obtain the value of a_x and of an exponential survivor function to

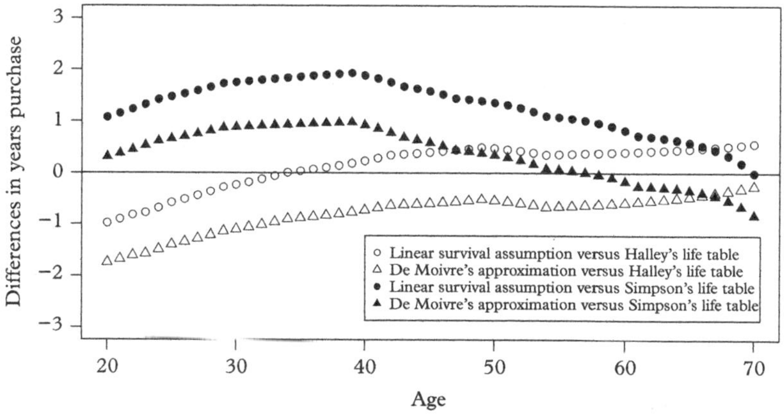

Figure 6.6. Differences between approximated and true values of a_{xx} for Halley's and Simpson's life tables

reduce a_{xy} to an expression in a_x and a_y came under attack in Simpson's 1742 *Doctrine of Annuities and Reversions*. Simpson calculated a_{xx} from his own life table, and under the linear survivor function as well as De Moivre's approximation. On comparing these values numerically Simpson concluded:[40]

Hence we may infer, that the probabilities of life, as given in the table of observations, do not come so near a geometric progression, as to an arithmetic one (which, in some measure, appears from the table itself) and consequently that the value of an annuity upon real lives, whether equal or unequal, will differ little from the value derived from the last hypothesis, but something more from the former.

De Moivre completely ignored this criticism. In his 1743 *Annuities on Lives*, he proceeded to give a second approximation to a_{xy} that applies to rental payments on land, when the final payment is prorated to the fraction of the last year lived by the first of the two lives to die. This was the approximation used by those solving Sir William Heathcote's problem.

In one sense Simpson's criticisms are unfair. De Moivre based his linear survivor model on Halley's life table. Simpson used his own life table to make the comparisons. Later in 1752 Simpson admitted that the linear assumption for survival fit the Breslau data better than the London data.[41] Also, when Figure 6.4 is examined, Simpson's calculations of a_{xx} contain some errors. I redid the calculations using both Halley's and Simpson's life tables and calculated a_{xx} under the linear survivor model and with De Moivre's approximation. The results appear in Figure 6.6, where I show the differences in years' purchase between a_{xx} calculated under the different assumptions and a_{xx} calculated directly from the appropriate life table using a 4% rate of interest. As Simpson noticed, De Moivre's approximation provides consistently smaller values for a_{xx} than those based on the linear assumption, whether his life table is used or Halley's. What Simpson missed is that De Moivre's approximation at most ages works better than the linear assumption for Simpson's table. In the second volume of his *Mathematical Repository*, Dodson comments that De Moivre's approximation to a_{xy} is much easier to calculate than the "exact" expression using the linear survivor function. If anyone had any objections to the accuracy of De Moivre's approximation, then Dodson had another approximation that follows from the linear assumption.[42]

De Moivre and Simpson fell into violent disagreement after the publication of Simpson's *Doctrine of Annuities and Reversions*.[43] Before that they had been on good terms. Simpson was a newcomer, having arrived in London in 1736. Soon thereafter he began publishing several mathematics books, including in 1740 a book on probability, his *Nature and Laws of Chance*. Compared to De Moivre's *Doctrine of Chances*, there are no new results in Simpson's probability book; rather he provides some alternate, and sometimes easier, proofs for some of the theorems than those De Moivre had obtained.

De Moivre may have seen Simpson's *Doctrine of Annuities and Reversions* as a threat to his own work, his consulting work included. Simpson had also found simple, but different (from De Moivre's), ways to make annuity calculations for two or more lives, which avoided onerous calculation. Simpson had based his calculations on mortality experience in London, De Moivre on that in a faraway German town. To potential clients Simpson's approach might have seemed more relevant, although 20 years later it was recognized that Halley's life table might apply to any place in the English countryside and Simpson's or Smart's table to any large city, because of the high mortality at younger ages in this table. What we do know is that De Moivre reacted strongly to Simpson's book and severely criticized it. The criticisms appear in 1743 in the preface to the second of De Moivre's *Annuities on Lives.* De Moivre objected to Simpson's complicated rules to value joint life annuities and objected to the fact that the price of Simpson's book undercut that of his own. Simpson responded to De Moivre in a pamphlet pointing out several errors that he had found in De Moivre's work on annuities. The dispute became a bit ugly. At some point, possibly in a private conversation, De Moivre referred to Simpson as a "beggarly fellow," which the reporter of this anecdote, Joseph-Jérôme Lalande, said he was ashamed to translate into French.[44] By "beggarly,"

De Moivre probably meant not Simpson's lack of material wealth but instead his intellectual poverty, and this was a serious slight by one esteemed mathematician of another.[45] By 1750, when the third edition of De Moivre's *Annuities on Lives* was published, De Moivre and Simpson seemed to have patched things up, at least in public.

A few years after the dispute and only 2 years before De Moivre's death in 1754, Simpson published his *Select Exercises*. The dispute may have simmered below the surface. Simpson had mentioned De Moivre in a positive way in both his *Nature and Laws of Chance* and his *Doctrine of Annuities and Reversions*. De Moivre's name does not appear anywhere in Simpson's *Select Exercises*, although Simpson treats De Moivre's result on annuities with the final payment prorated to the time of death. Ignoring De Moivre, Simpson refers only to his own work on fluxions to make the valuation of this annuity.[46]

The last quarter of *Select Exercises* is devoted to life annuity problems. Many of the problems are generic, such as Problem V: "To find the Value of an Annuity for an assigned Life." When specifics are given to the problem some key words that appear are "estate," "legacy," and "lease for lives," all issues related to land. Like De Moivre, Simpson's approach to a lease for lives is to find the value of the estate given the rent and the fine, rather than the value of the fine, as Gael Morris had done. Some of the problems expressed generically come with specific examples and this hints that a problem was motivated by a question posed to a consultant. The example attached to Problem XXXVII, a complicated variation on a reversion, reads:[47]

> A young Gentleman (A) aged Twenty-five, having greatly disobliged his Father (B) a Gentleman of Sixty, to whom he is sole Heir, is forced to contract with a certain Person (C) aged 35, for an Annuity of 200 *l.* (in order to [have] a Support) which he engages to repay, after his Father's Decease, with another of 300 *l.* to continue during the Life of C; *according to the Conditions specified in the Problem.*

The conditions specified in the general version of the problem are that A gets his annuity from C as long as they are both alive and that if C or A dies before B then C gets nothing. The object of the exercise is to find C's expected advantage or profit from entering into this contract. Though the problem is different, the relationship of the young gentleman and his father is similar to that of Edward Trevor and his father described in Chapter 5 in the case of *Hobson* v. *Trevor*.

The last major publication on life annuities from this group of mathematicians is James Dodson's *Mathematical Repository*. The second volume, published in 1753, contains several solved problems related to

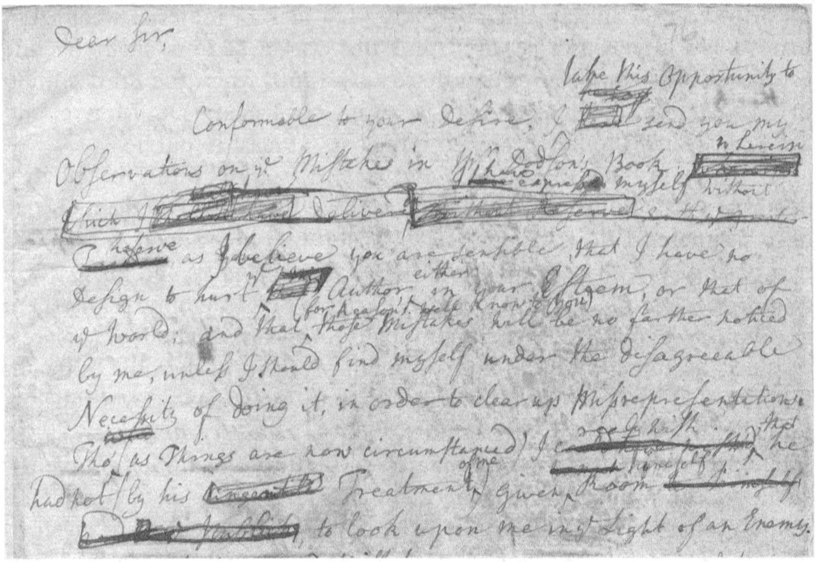
Dear Sir,

take this Opportunity to

Conformable to your Desire, I send you my

Observations on ye Mistakes in Mr Dodson's Book

as I believe you are sensible, that I have no

Design to hurt Author either in your Esteem, or that of

ye World; and that those Mistakes shall be no farther noticed

by me, unless I should find myself under the Disagreeable

Necessity of doing it, in order to clear up Misrepresentations.

Tho' (as Things are now circumstanced) he

had not (by his Treatment of me) given room

to look upon me in ye Light of an Enemy.

Figure 6.7. Letter from Simpson to an unknown recipient, April 4, 1755. *Source*: Photo by Columbia University Library

life annuities and the third volume, published in 1755, is almost entirely devoted to life annuity problems and their solutions.[48] The second volume contains a mixture of the use of life tables and the linear assumption for survival to calculate life annuity values, as well as De Moivre's approximation to joint life annuity valuations. Almost all of the third volume deals with life-contingent issues concerning property. Key words used throughout the book are annuities "secured by land," leases for lives including leases based on single and joint lives, and legacies equated to estates. Since Dodson worked with De Moivre as a consultant during De Moivre's declining years, I would not be surprised to find that many of the problems in the third volume of the *Mathematical Repository* originated as consulting problems posed by clients with landed interests.

Simpson also took issue, incorrectly, with some probability calculations done by Dodson as they relate to life annuities in the third volume of *Mathematical Repository*. Advertisements for the book appear in the London newspapers by mid-February 1755.[49] By April Simpson had seen the book and objected to some of Dodson's published results. In a letter to an unknown recipient dated April 4, 1755, shown in part in Figure 6.7,

Simpson claims that the solution to Question XIX in volume 3 is incorrect.[50] The problem as Dodson states it is:[51]

> The probability p that the lives of two persons of different ages, will both be extinct in a given space of time, being known; to find the probability that either of them will, within that space of time, die before the other?

The solution to this question can be applied to Sir William Heathcote's problem where what is required is the probability that Thomas Heathcote, the son aged 22, predeceases Sir William Heathcote, the father aged 50. Dodson solved the problem assuming a linear survivor function. When the younger age is x and the older age is y then the probability that the older survives the younger is in general $(\omega - y)/[2(\omega - x)]$ where ω is the oldest age in the life table (De Moivre, as well as Dodson, assume $\omega = 86$). Simpson thought that the probability should be ½. Simpson's solution applies when the probabilities are calculated from birth. The required solution is a conditional probability that the ages are x and y where x is less than y (shown in Appendix 1).

As can be seen in Figure 6.7, many of Simpson's letters are not easy to read. The surviving letters that he wrote to others are often in draft form with many changes and crossings out. Several pages are worn in places and there are some instances where the previous use of some clear adhesive tape has stained the paper.

7 Mathematicians and Early Life Insurance Companies

After Edmond Halley suggested that his life table could be used to price 1-year term insurance back in 1693, no other writer on life-contingent contracts approached the subject until James Dodson treated it in 1755. The last three problems (Questions XCVI, XCVII, and XCVIII) in the third volume of Dodson's *Mathematical Repository* deal with questions of pricing life insurance.[1] The first two of these questions are basic problems in life insurance – the cost of 1-year term insurance and the annual premium for whole-life insurance. The valuations were done assuming the linear survivor function as Dodson had done throughout the book. The third problem shows what Dodson thought would be one potential use for life insurance. He states the problem in terms of collateral security for a loan. Person A, who has a life income of some kind, borrows a sum of money from person B. A pays to B annually the interest on the loan as well as the premiums on the life insurance that would cover the debt to B on A's death.

Until Dodson, the mathematicians ignored the proprietors of insurance companies. There are only two instances that I can find before 1750 of mathematicians trying to apply their skills in the insurance and annuities markets. Of the 60 or more insurance and annuity societies that were formed between 1696 and 1721, only one of the proprietors had evidence of good mathematical training, and the proprietors of another society were given mathematical advice but chose to ignore it.[2] The proprietor with mathematical abilities was Richard Carter, who established the short-lived Friendly Society for Widows in 1696 in London. The proprietors who ignored mathematical advice ran the Amicable Society for a Perpetual Insurance Office, founded in 1706 and in a sense, still in operation today, having been acquired by Norwich Union Life Insurance Society in 1866, which became Aviva plc in 2009.

Carter's main business interests were in lotteries. There are hints in Carter's lottery work that he was a good mathematician. The drawing of tickets in English lotteries was quite cumbersome. There were two wheels, one containing the tickets and the other containing the blanks and prizes. One ticket was drawn without replacement from each wheel and either a blank or a prize from one wheel was matched to the ticket drawn from the other wheel. The draws often took weeks. For a 1711 lottery with 100,000 tickets, Carter suggested a time-saving procedure. Winning ticket numbers only would be determined using five 20-sided dice (icosahedra) with triangular sides cut from large ivory balls, along with a contraption for rolling the dice.[3] Opposite sides of each die carried the same digit, one of 0 through 9. Constructing such a die is an advanced problem in geometry, so Carter must have had some facility in mathematics.[4]

At the time that Carter was in business, state-run lotteries and annuities were closely connected. State lotteries with an annuity component were designed to entice people to lend money to the government. An example is a lottery from 1694. Through the issue of 100,000 tickets at £10 per ticket, the lottery was designed to raise £1 million to help finance the wars of William III against the French.[5] Over the course of the draw there would be 97,500 blanks and 2,500 prizes. Anyone holding a ticket with a blank was given a 16-year annuity with annual payments of £1. At the legal rate of interest of 6% per annum, the present value of the payments is slightly more than £10, the price of the ticket. The prizes were also 16-year annuities with annual payments ranging in value from £10 to £1,000. In contrast to what happens in a modern-day lottery more money was paid back to the ticketholders than paid in.

Once the lottery was drawn, some individuals sold their blank tickets to others; the going rate was £6 5s. This gave the new owner of the blank ticket an interest rate of slightly more than 14% per annum, the rate associated with the life annuity floated by the government in 1693. Entrepreneurs like Carter saw business potential in this.[6] While they had insufficient capital at hand to purchase several thousand blanks, they could see profit if the purchases were amortized in some way. So they encouraged holders of blank tickets to surrender their tickets and enter them into another draw. The entrepreneurs would use the income from the surrendered blank tickets to make staggered lump sum payments, determined by random draw, to the holders of blank tickets submitted for the draw. The payment plans were designed to make the entrepreneurs a tidy sum each year. One such scheme was operated by Thomas Neale and Dalby Thomas. Neale was already making money from the original draw; he held the lucrative government appointment of organizer of the 1695 state lottery. Carter offered a competing scheme similar to that of Neale and Thomas.[7]

Carter's lottery and insurance interests fused in an insurance scheme he offered in 1712, called the "Most Advantageous Insurers, upon the Lives of Men, Women, and Children." The state ran a lottery that year to raise £1.8 million, with tickets selling at £10 each.[8] As in the 1694 lottery, the holders of blank tickets were provided with fixed-term annuities which gave them back the price of their tickets on maturity of the annuity. Entry into Carter's insurance scheme was through the transfer of blank tickets to the company. There were three ways in which this could be done, resulting in three classes of policyholders. All required an initial payment of two tickets. The definition of the classes was in how the balance was paid: (1) eight tickets, one per year, could be submitted after the initial payment; (2) an additional seven tickets could be submitted with the initial payment; or (3) the company would lend the policyholder the £10 per year for 8 years, with the policyholder paying 6% interest annually on this loan. In this third class, any dividends paid by the company would be deducted from the principal of the loan. The death benefits in each class were the same – a fixed sum of money in a year divided by the total number of claims in the year. The three classes were equalized financially by the deduction, at the time of a death claim, of any outstanding lottery ticket payments from the death benefit. The total death benefits were set at £1,500 for 1714 and were to rise annually until they reached £16,000 in 1729. Carter's scheme is a form of a mortuary tontine; the death benefits in any year are a fixed sum divided by the number of deaths in the year.

Among the papers in the Macclesfield Collection held at Cambridge University Library there is a mathematical manuscript, probably originating with Carter, addressing the fairness of this insurance scheme.[9] What is shown in this manuscript is that the scheme is fair only when the sums paid in are all the same. When the sums paid in are different, for the scheme to be fair different payment classes should be set up according to the amounts paid in. I was a little confused when I first saw the manuscript at Cambridge. The library catalog (named Janus after the Roman god with two faces who looks to the future and to the past) attributes the manuscript to Henry Oldenburg, Secretary of the Royal Society from its inception, and gives the date range for the creation of the manuscript as 1650–77. The dates are well before the establishment of any life insurance company, so that it was an exciting find. When I looked at the watermarks in the paper, I found that the paper on which the manuscript is written dates from the 1720s. With a little further exploration I found that going by the description of the insurance scheme in the manuscript, it conforms to Carter's 1712 scheme. My stab at the provenance of the manuscript is that William Jones, whose manuscripts form the bulk of the Macclesfield Collection, saw Carter's original, possibly at Carter's office, and copied it. This copy, now in the Macclesfield Collection, is entitled "Solution to a Question relating to the Chances of lives which may serve as a caution to be observed by such as form or are like to be concerned in projects for Insurance of Lives."[10]

The proprietors of the Amicable Society for a Perpetual Insurance Office did not really need mathematical advice to ensure the success of their business, which is probably why they ignored it when offered. The Amicable Society offered a mortuary tontine. The subscribers, restricted to those between the ages of 12 and 55 at the time of admission, paid annual insurance fees of £6 4s regardless of age, £6 earmarked for benefits and 4 shillings for administrative expenses. With an intended 2,000 subscribers, the sum fixed for the total death benefit was set at £10,000, with the surplus £2,000 to be invested in the capital of the company with the hope that the capital would grow large enough so that the annual payments would be eliminated.[11]

Despite what looked like a workable plan, by the 1730s the Amicable Society was in some financial difficulty. There were several reasons for this, none of them related to the mathematics of premium calculations. The stock market crash of 1720, the South Sea Bubble, had reduced the company's capital; several members had not paid their annual dues, with the result that their policies were dormant and the total revenue of the company was down; and since 1719 the company had been insuring "bad" lives, thus increasing the number of claims, which reduces the death benefit.

In 1732, William Whiston, the mathematician who had been ejected from his position as Lucasian Professor of Mathematics at Cambridge because of his heterodox religious views, wrote a tract on what he considered to be the sorry state of the Amicable Society. Whiston was living in London and had been a subscriber to the Amicable Society since at least 1721.[12] At the time that he wrote his tract he was one of the directors of the Society. In addition to the issues mentioned above and a few others, Whiston suggested an "actuarial" reason for the Society's woes:[13]

> The Refusal now for these last 10 Years, or since the South Sea Year 1720, to sell the Society's Policies at any salable Price; and thereby sinking all that have been excluded, contrary to the former Practice; and, I think, contrary to the real Interest of the Society also.

One has the impression that Whiston had been agitating for the "proper" pricing of the Society's insurance policies for some time after he became a subscriber. Whiston suggests a pricing based on the age of

Table 7.1. *Table of values of 1-year term insurance*

Age range	Whiston's value	Probability of death	Age range	Whiston's value	Probability of death
7–14	15	0.0125	54–57	35	0.0342
14–20	16	0.0097	57–59	37	0.0375
20–25	18	0.0106	59–61	39	0.0405
25–29	20	0.0126	61–62	41	0.0431
29–33	21	0.0152	62–63	43	0.0450
33–37	23	0.0177	63–65	45	0.0483
37–41	25	0.0196	65–66	47	0.0521
41–45	27	0.0231	66–67	49	0.0549
45–48	29	0.0258	67–68	51	0.0581
48–51	31	0.0299	68–69	53	0.0617
51–54	33	0.0340	69–70	55	0.0658

the insured. The suggested prices are shown in Table 7.1 and are given, according to Whiston, "in round numbers only." To guard against the drawing up of policies on "bad" lives, Whiston suggests a differential pricing scheme. He uses the age group 41–45 as an example, where the price given in the table is £27. For an insured person in good health in this age group, the policyholder should pay the Amicable Society £30. When the policyholder sells his policy, if it is on someone else's life the selling price is £27 as given in the table, while if it is on his own life the price is £28 10s. Despite Whiston's pleas and arguments, the fixed annual payment remained in place until 1807, when a new charter for the company was obtained that allowed for premiums tied to the age of the insured.[14]

Whiston's values, which appear in Table 7.1, are not arbitrary or guessed-at numbers. They were based on Halley's life table. Figure 7.1 shows Whiston's premiums plotted against Halley's probabilities of death in each age group. Considering that Whiston gave his values in round numbers, there is a very close straight-line agreement between his values and Halley's probabilities of death. There is one small discrepant value and that is in the age group 7–14. If the earliest age range is taken to be 12–14, where 12 is the youngest age acceptable to the Amicable Society, then the probability of death is 0.0093 instead of 0.0125. The 0.0093 value, shown with the black dot in the bottom left of Figure 7.1, is closer to the straight-line relationship that is shown in the graph. Perhaps Whiston made a transcription error in his original manuscript regarding the age range.

Clearly the insurers were not interested in the work of the mathematicians. At the same time, it seems that the mathematicians as a group

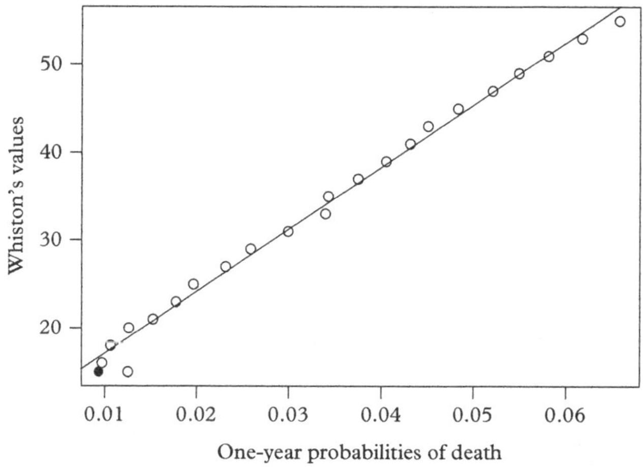

Figure 7.1. Relationship of Whiston's calculations to Halley's life table

were not particularly interested in life insurance. Rather, their interests lay in life annuities, their bread and butter in consulting activities up to the 1760s. This is exemplified by a letter to *Gentleman's Magazine* in January 1760, with a critique of it 2 months later in the same magazine.[15] The unknown author of the January letter based his arguments on a table showing the median duration of life for each of the ages from birth to 85 years. Expressed as Halley might have expressed it, the median duration of life or median future lifetime is the number of years at which it is an "even lay" (a 50–50 chance in modern terms) that a person of a given age will die within that duration. The table that appears in the article is taken from the 1749 volume of Buffon's *Histoire naturelle*.[16] The entries in the table are used to criticize unnamed life insurance companies that charge a yearly premium of £5 for a policy that pays £100 as a death benefit. Based on the calculation that the premiums invested every year at 3% interest will accumulate to just over £100 in 16 years, the author argues that the company will benefit when the median duration of life is at least 16 years. According to Buffon's table this occurs when the policy is issued at any of the ages 1 through 51. The author goes on to use the table to value a life annuity at any particular age by setting the term of a fixed-term annuity equal to the median future lifetime at that age. This is Weyman Lee's method of valuing a life annuity, and so the author of the letter may have been Weyman Lee himself or someone influenced by the latest edition of

Lee's book on the valuation of annuities and leases, published in 1754.[17] It was William Chapple who responded to the original letter. He demolishes the arguments for the valuation of life insurance in one short paragraph and proceeds to spill much more ink over the rest of the article on the shortcomings and inaccuracies of the proposed method for valuing life annuities. What leads me to believe that neither author was particularly informed about, or interested in, life insurance is that no company at the time offered what seems to be a whole-life policy with a death benefit of £100 for an annual premium of £5. The London Assurance Corporation, which began operation in 1721, typically offered 1-year term insurance, not whole-life insurance, at a single premium, not an annual one. As in the description of the insurance policy in the article, the premium was usually set at about £5 or slightly more for every £100 of insurance, and the amount charged was independent of the age of the applicant.

A whole-life policy is one that pays on the death of the person, at whatever age death occurs. A term insurance policy for a term of n years is one that pays the death benefit if the person dies within n years and pays nothing after that time. Standard actuarial notation, or shorthand, for the value, or the lump sum purchase price, of a whole-life policy with a death benefit of £1 to a person aged x at the time the policy is issued is A_x. For n-year term insurance the shorthand is $A^1_{x:\overline{n}|}$. The numeral 1 over the x indicates that death must occur before the n years are up. Leave out the 1 and the resulting notation is for endowment insurance; this is term insurance plus a payment of £1 if the person survives the n years. If annual premiums are paid throughout the length of the policy, the value of the premium is denoted by P_x for whole-life insurance and $P^1_{x:\overline{n}|}$ for term insurance. Mathematical descriptions of all these functions are given in Appendix 1. Like the shorthand symbols for the values of life annuities, I did not invent all this shorthand. It was agreed upon by a group of actuaries in 1898 and 1900 at the Second and Third International Actuarial Congresses, respectively.[18] A full list of this standard actuarial notation is given in an appendix of 7½ pages in length, appearing in the standard actuarial textbook I used when I was a student in the 1960s.[19]

With only two or three seemingly random blips of mathematical activity over a 60-year period, the life insurance and annuity industries remained relatively mathematics-free (life-contingently speaking at least) until the 1750s, when James Dodson initiated a proposal that led to the formation of the Society for Equitable Assurances on Lives and Survivorships. The accepted account of Dodson's motivation first appears in the proceedings of the Equitable Society in 1769, 12 years after Dodson's death:[20]

In the year 1756, Mr. James Dodson having been refused admission into the *Amicable Society*, on account of his age, determined to form a new society, upon a plan of assurances on more equitable terms that those of the *Amicable*, which takes the same premium for all ages.

When the Amicable Society was formed, and continuing into Whiston's time, as seen in Table 7.1, new subscribers were admitted between the ages of 12 and 55.[21] Probably because of their financial problems in the 1720s and early 1730s, the upper limit on the age of admittance was reduced to 45 in 1737.[22] When Dodson made his application to the Amicable Society, possibly late in 1755, he was over the age of 45.[23]

Though Whiston and Dodson were both accomplished mathematicians and both fellows of the Royal Society, they were quite different in their professional interests and in their economic statuses. At his death, Whiston had property in Cambridgeshire and bequeathed several hundred pounds to each of his four children or their heirs; Dodson had nothing but expectations.[24] Whiston was a professor at Cambridge who was ejected from his professorship for holding Arian beliefs. Subsequently, he taught courses in natural philosophy in London and took a keen interest in theology. Dodson struggled to find a teaching position, eventually holding one at the Royal Mathematical School. When he died, he was nearly penniless and in debt. Dodson emerged from a group of mathematicians carrying out consultations on life annuity valuations; he was the first to try to break into the life insurance industry.

When the account of Dodson was written, the Equitable Society was divided into two warring camps squabbling over money claimed as due to them by some of the original founders, who are often called the charter fund proprietors or charter fund subscribers. The account of Dodson and the Amicable Society was written by those opposing the charter fund proprietors, whom they saw as avaricious, operating illegally, and threatening to bring the Society to financial ruin. Both sides were united in their negative feelings toward the Amicable Society, which had opposed attempts by the Equitable Society to secure a charter from the Crown. Literature from the 1760s put out by the Equitable Society (several editions of *A Short Account of the Society for Equitable Assurances on Lives and Survivorships*, none of which contain any reference to Dodson) contains several criticisms of their competitor, the Amicable Society.[25] Seen in this light, the quotation about Dodson is a snub to the Amicable Society and an elevation of Dodson to the status of "freedom fighter" for the public, who should get fairly, or equitably, priced life insurance. Those who eventually took charge of the Equitable Society wanted a good creation story to counteract the negative publicity associated with their very public spat.

Dodson may indeed have been refused membership to the Amicable Society. At the same time, he did have a keen pecuniary interest in getting the Equitable Society established. It came in the form of translating his considerable skills in the mathematics of life-contingent contracts into a consulting fee with respect to the calculation of premiums that the Equitable Society would eventually charge. This is apparent in Dodson's will, written February 9, 1757, 9½ months prior to his death. In 1735, Dodson had married Elizabeth Goodwin, ward of the very wealthy Sir John Chesshyre. The day before the wedding Dodson received a loan of £300 from Chesshyre, a loan that was still outstanding at Dodson's death, which was well after Chesshyre's death in 1738. Dodson's will does not mention any assets other than the expectation of payments from the yet-to-be-established Equitable Society. A key sentence in the will is:[26]

> Whereas it is intended to petition his Most Gracious Majesty, shortly, to grant His Royal Charter to establish a corporation for ensuring lives on more equitable terms than have hitherto been offered (which if his Majesty be graciously pleased to grant) then it hath been stipulated by and between the intended petitioners, of whom I am one (in consideration of my making certain calculations concerning the premiums to be taken for such insurances and other services by me done or to be done for the said intended corporation) that I and some other person or persons to be nominated by me within three months of the granting of said Charter shall during our natural lives and the lives of the survivors or survivor of us be intitled to and receive five shillings upon every one hundred pounds that will be insured by the said intended corporation during the continuance of such life or lives.

By 1766 the Equitable Society had written nearly £120,000 in insurance which would have brought Dodson £300, enough to pay his debt to Chesshyre.[27] In the will Dodson stipulated that the first £150 to be earned from the Equitable Society be applied to repaying half the loan from Chesshyre and the second £150 also be applied to repaying the loan. In both cases he asked the executors of Chesshyre's estate to postpone calling in the loan so that the first £150 could be paid to Dodson's wife and the second £150 to his children.

There was another way, mentioned in the will, in which Dodson was to earn money from the establishment of the Equitable Society. Obtaining the charter would cost money. Dodson subscribed £15 to a fund, eventually called the charter fund, that would pay these expenses. The charter fund subscribers would be compensated once the Equitable Society was established. It was intended that each person taking out a policy would pay an additional 10 shillings per £100 of insurance, which would be divided among the subscribers to the charter fund. Dodson's share was to be paid during the lifetimes of the last survivor of Dodson himself and his eldest surviving child. There was a twist to it that shows Dodson's economic straits. At the time that he wrote his will he had paid only £1 10s toward his subscription. He directed his executors to pay any unpaid balance on his death from a death benefit of £20 that would come to his estate from the Society of School Masters or from any other means available to his executors. The unpaid balance was to go to John Sylvester, Edward Wade, and Edward Rowe Mores.[28] These were the individuals who started and administered the charter fund.

Dodson named his wife Elizabeth and William Mountaine as his executors. When probate was granted for the will on December 8, 1757, Mountaine was mentioned as the surviving executor and so Dodson's children were left orphans. The governors of the Royal Mathematical School initially helped with some support. They paid Mountaine, as Dodson's executor, £50 (half a year's salary) for the benefit of the children.[29] Mountaine must also have paid the outstanding balance to the charter fund, either from death benefit from the Society of School Masters or from elsewhere. Dodson appears on a 1762 list as having subscribed the full £15 to the charter fund.[30] Without the establishment of the Equitable Society, Dodson's children were essentially left destitute. They were probably supported by Mountaine until they came of age or until they eventually received a settlement from the charter fund as well as a gift of £300 from the Equitable Society in recognition of their father's contributions.[31]

Dodson's impecuniousness is evident in his inability to pay the full £15 to the charter fund in 1756. He had earned extra money with the publication of his *Mathematical Repository*. After the publication of the third volume in 1755 he should have received the balance of 14 guineas owed by his publisher John Nourse for the purchase of the copyright.[32] By the time the third volume appeared he was making a reasonable and regular salary of £100 per year in his position at the Royal Mathematical School.[33] And yet in 1756 there was apparently not enough money left from Nourse's payment to make a full contribution to the charter fund. Subsequently, Dodson decided to put into his will that the balance owing to the charter fund would be paid from the death benefit of £20, money that should probably have gone to support his family. Dodson's financial situation at the time of his death may explain Augustus De Morgan's anecdote about enquiring of an aunt about Dodson, his great-grandfather. The aunt told De Morgan only, "We never cry stinking fish."[34]

The charter fund subscribers agreed with their opponents on Dodson's role in the formation of the Equitable Society. They also provided a date for when work commenced on forming the Society:

> And that he [Dodson] caused to be inserted in the publick papers an advertisement, bearing the date the 28th of February 1756, giving notice of a meeting intended to be holden the 2d of March then next following; and deciding that meeting the company of such gentlemen as might be disposed to engage in such an undertaking.

There may have been such an advertisement on February 28, 1756, but I cannot find it in the Burney Collection of Newspapers, held by the British Library. I did find an advertisement inserted in the *Gazetteer and London Daily Advertiser* for March 1, 1756 which indicates activity prior to February 28. There had been a meeting on February 26 at the Queen's Head Tavern. The advertisement states:

> At a meeting of several gentlemen, in consequence of a proposal advertised in the Daily Advertiser, concerning a more easy, general, equitable and advantageous method of insuring lives, than hitherto practised, it was resolved to meet at the same place on Tuesday next the 2d of March at six in the evening, in order to make farther progress in the consideration thereof, and to concert measures for carrying the same into execution; at which meeting the company of such other gentlemen as are disposed to engage in an undertaking of this kind is desired.

Now the *Gazetteer and London Daily Advertiser* and the *Daily Advertiser* are different newspapers. Unfortunately, no issue of the *Daily Advertiser* for 1756 survives, and only one issue from 1755, so that what Dodson did in early 1756 or late 1755 is lost in the mists of time. Edward Rowe Mores, one of the leading men behind the charter fund and its subscribers, became involved in establishing the Equitable Society on May 5, 1756.[35] Since it was the charter fund subscribers who mentioned the February 28, 1756 advertisement, it is likely that they, like Mores, date their involvement from March 2, 1756 or later.

Meetings continued throughout 1756. As mentioned in his will, written in early February 1757, Dodson calculated the premiums for the policies to be offered by the Equitable Society. His tables of premiums survive in manuscript form.[36] Perusal of the tables suggests that it was a lengthy and onerous task. There are tables for a_x, $100A_x$, $100A^{1}_{x:\overline{n}|}$, $100P_x$, and $100P^{1}_{x:\overline{n}|}$ for ages x ranging from 8 to 67 years and terms n

in the insurance such that $x + n$ is about 70 or less. There are three tables for the valuation of a_x (survivorships) reflecting Dodson's care and insight into the proper operation of the Society. Here are the titles affixed to the tables in the order that they appear in the manuscript:

1. Page 2 of the manuscript: "A Table of the present values of Annuities of 1£ each for single Lives computed at 3£ pCent compound Interest from the beforegoing Table of Decrements wherein the hazard of Life is esteemed to be the greatest."
2. Page 52: "A Table of the Present Values of Annuities for single lives computed at 3 pCent Compound Interest, upon which (as a mean Calculation) such annuities may be granted by the Corporation to persons living in London and other Great Towns."
3. Page 53: "A Table of the Present Values for single lives computed at 3 pCent Compound Interest supposing the Decrements of Life to be equal upon which (being the highest Calculation) Annuities may be granted to those whose abode & mode of Living is the most Healthy."

The gap between pages 2 and 52 of the manuscript is filled with tabular values for A_x, $A^1_{x:\overline{n}|}$, P_x and $P^1_{x:\overline{n}|}$. After page 53 there is a single table used as an aid in the calculation of annuities on two lives which explains the use of "survivorships" in the Society's full name: The Society for Equitable Assurances and Survivorships.

The table on page 2 is calculated, more or less, from the life table given on page 1 of the manuscript. This life table is based on the Bills of Mortality in London for the years 1728 through 1750. In constructing this table, Dodson took into account the variability in mortality over the 23 years in each age group and tried to capture the maximum mortality experience over the whole period. The table on page 52 loosely follows the life table of John Smart as amended by Thomas Simpson; and the table on page 53 is calculated, more or less, using De Moivre's approximation.

Valuations of contracts for life annuities and life insurance are related through the mathematical formula

$$(1+i)A_x + ia_x = 1$$

where i is the rate of interest. The formula has a very nice verbal interpretation. The right-hand side of the equation represents an investment of £1. The investment pays interest i for every year that a person is alive, valued at ia_x, and then pays the principal and interest $(1 + i)$ at the end of the year in which the person dies, valued at $(1 + i)A_x$. This is the left-hand side of the equation. This relationship between life annuities

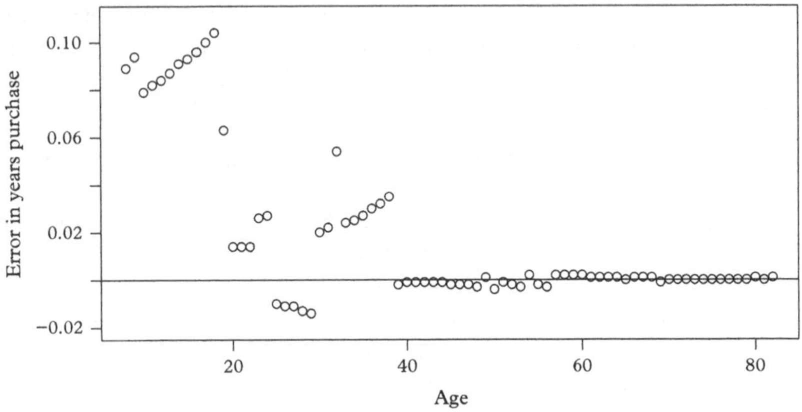

Figure 7.2. Errors in Dodson's determination of a_x from his life table

and life insurance is important when pricing the products. When mortality in one area, such as London, is higher than that in another area, such as the countryside, owing to sanitary issues and crowding in London, those at a given age in London will receive on average fewer life annuity payments than their country counterparts of the same age. By the same token insurance policyholders living in London will die sooner than those of the same age living in the countryside. At a fixed price, selling life annuities to Londoners would be more profitable than selling them to those in the country, while the opposite is true for life insurance. The formula shows that if a_x is given a low value to reflect high mortality, then A_x must have a high value and likewise if a_x is given a high value to reflect low mortality, then A_x must have a low value. Dodson recognized this. His first set of tables takes into account what he considered to be the worst-case scenario for high mortality. He took a conservative approach to life insurance by pricing the insurance at the upper level of what he thought would be the mortality experience of the policyholders. The other two tables were meant for pricing products on the life annuity side of the business, one for London and the other for the countryside.

Dodson was aware of the mathematical relationship between a_x and A_x. I recalculated the values of a_x on page 2 of Dodson's manuscript using the life table on page 1 of the manuscript; Dodson's life table is reproduced in Appendix 2. Then I calculated the differences between my determinations of a_x by computer and Dodson's determinations by hand. Figure 7.2 shows Dodson's values minus the values that I calculated. At the higher ages Dodson's calculations are quite accurate; but his arithmetical abilities seem to fall apart at lower ages. I interpret some of the distinct trends at the lower ages to Dodson's probably using a recursive formula which would accumulate any arithmetical or round-off errors. Dodson did not recalculate A_x from first principles. I checked all of his values from his table for A_x along with his values for a_x and found that $(1 + i)A_x + ia_x$ always turned out to be 1.

Before he died, Dodson wrote one more manuscript to support the establishment of the Equitable Society.[37] This manuscript has the title "First Lecture on Insurances." It is expository in nature and was meant to support the application to obtain a charter for the Society. There are references in this manuscript to the application; and arguments that were made by others against the application are refuted. Dodson writes:

> It has been supposed that James Dodsons Scheme for Establishing a Corperation for Insuring Lives is Defective because no Fund is supposed to be provided to answer Claims more than what arises from the Premiums of Insurance to be received but the fallacy of this kind of reasoning may be evident in two ways.

After arguing that such a fund is an unnecessary expense to the policyholders that may be a barrier to those seeking insurance, Dodson writes:

> Me thinks I hear the Counsel on the other side begin to open up on this.

From the first quotation, it is apparent that one of the objections to Dodson's scheme was that there was no safety net in case the premium income was insufficient to cover the death benefits in any year. This net could be funded by a flat charge made when a policy goes into effect; or there could be a provision, as there were in other companies, for the policyholders to be liable for any shortfalls. Using his mortality table, which assumes the worst-case scenario for high mortality, Dodson shows that without any such fund the Society would be in a profit position in 1750 for policies issued in 1730, given the actual mortality over those years.

Dodson applied his expertise as an accountant (he described himself as an "accomptant" on the title pages of some of his books) to demonstrate the viability of his proposed insurance scheme. He did this through an accounting of projected premium income with earned interest less death benefits over an extended period of time. In an eighteenth-century way he introduced the modern actuarial concepts of reserves (money earned from premiums invested to fund future death benefits) and asset shares (the accumulation of cash flow and investment income per policyholder).[38]

Table 7.2. *Example of reserves and asset share calculations*

(1) Age	(2) l_x	(3) d_x	(4) Income, beginning of the year	(5) Income, end of the year	(6) Death benefit	(7) Reserve	(8) Asset share
Calculations under Dodson's table of high mortality with the experience of high mortality							
55	178	8	812.4958	836.8706	800	36.8707	0.217
56	170	8	812.8498	837.2352	800	37.2353	0.230
57	162	8	776.6977	799.9986	800	0	0
58	154						
Calculations when Halley's table reflects actual mortality and Dodson's table is assumed							
55	292	10	1 332.858	1 372.844	1 000	372.844	1.322
56	282	10	1 660.056	1 709.858	1 000	709.858	2.610
57	272	10	1 951.425	2 009.967	1 000	1 009.967	3.855
58	262						

In Table 7.2 I provide a simplified numerical example in the spirit of Dodson. Suppose in a group of people aged 55 each person takes out 3-year term insurance. The policy pays £100 at the end of the year of death provided that death occurs within 3 years of the issue of the policy; if the policyholder lives until at least age 58, then nothing is paid. In the currency of Dodson's day, using a 3% annual rate of interest, as Dodson did, and his life table describing the worst-case scenario of high mortality, I calculated that the annual premium payable by each individual at the beginning of each year for 3 years is £4 11s 3½d, or £4.564583 to six decimal places. This is less than the Amicable Society's premium (£5 or more) for a policy they would not issue (the insured had to be under 45 at the time of issue). In the ideal, the insurance fund is balanced when the mortality table assumed matches the experience. Assume now that the group is comprised of 178 people, the number living at age 55 in Dodson's life table. Each of them takes out the 3-year term insurance. According to the life table, eight people die each year for the next 3 years, so that total death benefits of £800 (columns 3 and 6 in Table 7.2) are paid each year. The income at the beginning of each year (column 4) is the number of premiums paid plus the accumulated surplus from the previous year. The income at the end of the year (column 5) is the principal from the beginning of the year accumulated at 3% interest. The difference between the income and death benefits at the end of the year is called the reserve (column 7). For each individual alive at the end of the year, the asset share (column 8) is the reserve divided by the number living. From the top of Table 7.2, if the mortality experience matches the mortality assumption the reserve in each year is small but positive and becomes zero when the policy matures. The bottom of Table 7.2 shows what happens when Dodson's excess mortality assumption is made and the actual experience follows Halley's mortality table, with 292 policies issued at age 55 (l_{55} in Halley's table is 292). They all pay the annual premium of £4 11s 3½d. On making the same type of calculations as those used to produce the figures at the top of the table, there is an approximate surplus of £1,010 when the policy matures. The reserve is never negative and fairly sizable for the duration of the policy. Hence there is no need for the safety net; it is built into the mortality assumption when calculating the premium. Ignoring for the moment any expenses that the company might have and the variability in actual mortality experience, the company could refund about £3 17s 1d to each of the survivors that reach age 58. The Society would also be in surplus if its return on investments was more than 3% and the premiums were computed using a 3% rate of interest.

The petition requesting a charter for the Equitable Society was presented to the Privy Council on April 20, 1757 and very soon hit a roadblock. It was opposed by members of the Amicable Society who sought legal counsel to assist their opposition. The Amicable Society already had a royal charter to operate a life insurance scheme. Essentially, the Equitable Society was proposing to do what the Amicable was already doing, except that they were going to charge different premiums. The process stalled and Dodson died on November 23, 1757, before any progress was made in obtaining a charter.

From the beginning Edward Rowe Mores had taken the lead for the Equitable Society in the application for a charter. Mores took this role probably because of his experience. He was a member of the Society of Antiquaries, which had obtained a royal charter in 1751. Mores's efforts to obtain a charter dragged on for a few years and the Amicable Society was soon joined in opposition to the charter application by the London Assurance Corporation and the Royal Exchange Assurance Corporation, both in operation as life insurers since 1721. The full story of the Equitable's beginnings and subsequent development is described in detail in Maurice Ogborn's history of the Equitable Society.[39] It took some time, but the Equitable Society's application for a charter was turned down in a report to the Privy Council dated July 14, 1761 and signed by the Attorney General, Charles Pratt and the Solicitor General, Charles Yorke, both politicians working in William Pitt's administration. As a result of this setback, Mores changed gears and opted to go after a deed of settlement. This would establish the

Equitable as an unincorporated partnership; the holy grail of the royal charter would have provided the proprietors with the protection of limited liability. The deed of settlement was executed September 7, 1762 and the Equitable Society began operation as an insurer shortly thereafter.

All the efforts to obtain a charter and subsequently a deed of settlement had monetary costs attached, which mounted as the process bogged down in the pursuit of the charter. This resulted in an increase in the number who subscribed to the charter fund. There was a promise that those subscribers would be compensated after obtaining the charter and Mores would be a prime beneficiary in view of his work and monetary contributions. Within a few years this would become a major source of friction within the Equitable Society, eventually leading to the ouster of Mores from his positions in the Society.

The premiums charged in 1762, when the Society began operation, for £100 of whole-life insurance and of 1-year term insurance correspond to the premiums suggested in Dodson's *First Lecture on Insurances*.[40] What I find intriguing is that there are slight differences between these premiums and what appears in Dodson's premium tables. The values in *First Lecture on Insurances* are given in pounds, shillings, and pence, and the values in the premium tables are given in pounds to three decimal places. I converted the pounds, shillings, and pence into decimals, rounding the results to three decimal places. For the annual premiums for whole-life insurance, the differences in the two values for $100P_x$, for x between 15 and 67 are in the range –£0.075 to £0.053. This seems larger than a round-off error. For 1-year term insurance, the situation is slightly worse. The differences in the values of $100P^{1}_{x:\overline{1}|}$ are in the range –£0.051 to £0.213. This is definitely not round-off error. These comparisons lead me to believe that the premium tables were done first, during the planning stages for the insurance scheme. After opposition to the application for a charter became evident, *First Lecture on Insurances* was written (and premiums recalculated) to defend the proposed scheme.

What is even more intriguing is that Dodson specifically states that his values for $100P^{1}_{x:\overline{1}|}$ in his premium tables are determined from the life table that he had described on page 2 of his manuscript as the "Table of Decrements wherein the hazard of Life is esteemed to be the greatest." This is a very simple calculation (as shown in Appendix 1), probably the simplest he would need to make in life insurance or life annuity valuations. And yet in many cases what he calculates is not very close to the value that should be obtained from his life table. With the exception of a few ages Dodson's values are greater, and sometimes

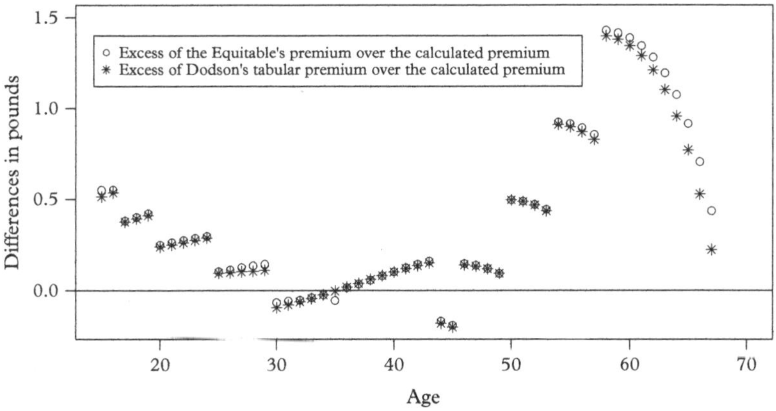

Figure 7.3. One-year limited term insurance differences between Dodson's premiums and those calculated from his life table

much greater, than what they should be. This is shown in Figure 7.3. From Dodson's premium values (taken from his *First Lecture on Insurances*, the premiums used by the Equitable Society, and from his premium tables) I have subtracted the value of $100P^{1}_{x:\overline{1}|}$ that I calculated from his table. Dodson must have used a different life table, or have been dreaming when he made his calculations. This situation is reminiscent of his very odd valuation of a_x using Brakenridge's life table published in 1755 and described in Chapter 6.

It is at the establishment of the Equitable Society in 1762 that the word "actuary" first enters the life insurance lexicon; it appears in print in *A Short Account of the Society for Equitable Assurances on Lives and Survivorships*.[41] Previously an actuary was a clerk who recorded the proceedings of a court, usually an ecclesiastical court.[42] The term was probably appropriated by Mores. The earliest actuaries of the Equitable Society were clerks. According to the Society's deed of settlement they were responsible for receiving and recording the applications for insurance, recording the fees and premiums collected, keeping the Society's books in order, and keeping the minutes of meetings of the directors and the general meetings of the Society.[43] Meetings of the directors and general meetings were called "courts" and so "actuary" in its original sense applies to the Equitable's early actuaries. The move to actuarial work in the modern sense, as it relates to the assessment and evaluation of risk for a company offering insurance products, probably first occurs with the appointment of William Morgan as the Equitable's actuary in 1775, following one year as assistant actuary.

The early actuaries at the Equitable Society were not strong mathematicians, and perhaps some were not even mathematicians at all. The Society's first actuary was William Mosdell. In 1764 Mosdell was succeeded by Dodson's son, James junior. Holding the position for less than two years, Dodson junior resigned to take a position in the Customs Office. His replacement at the Equitable was John Edwards, who became the actuary in April 1767. Neither Mosdell nor Edwards appear to have been mathematicians; the only one with mathematical ability may have been Dodson junior.

With the death of Dodson, Edward Rowe Mores apparently took it upon himself to value nonstandard life annuity contracts when tables were not directly available. For standard insurance contracts, the actuaries Mosdell, Dodson junior, or Edwards could use Dodson senior's tables or other tables the Society might have had in its possession. At the request of the customer, the Society did offer specialized contracts whose valuation went beyond standard table look-ups. In 1764 Mores issued a list of the policies that the Society had issued with the numbers of each type of policy updated by hand up to 1767.[44] The first few pages of the list show various types of life annuities and life insurances, both for a fixed term and for the whole of life. The last four pages of the list contain descriptions of the specialized policies. Here is one example from this part of the list:

> A policy indented whereby the Society assure to *F.* an annuity to be paid to his wife for the remainder of her life in the case she shall survive him. but as *F.* is entitled only to an annuity for his own life barely sufficient for the present maintenance of them both, so that he cannot conveniently spare any part of his income for payment of the premium; he grants in lieu thereof and in consideration of the assurance, an annuity to be paid to the Society during the remainder of his own life in case he shall survive her.

This quotation was confusing to me on first read. It did not seem to make any sense, since the premiums would begin only on the death of *F*'s wife, provided that *F* survives her. Who would write such a policy? Very few, if any, insurers would today. The Equitable did. This is two reversionary annuities put into one package, with reversions in different directions. The Society agrees to a reversionary life annuity payable to *F*'s wife on his death; *F* agrees to a reversionary annuity payable to the Society on his wife's death. In the event that *F* dies before his wife the Society gets nothing, which is why very few insurers would touch such a one-off policy. If *F* and his wife are of the same age, then the chance that the Society gets nothing is ½, assuming that males and females have the same mortality experience. Here is another example from the list that is a little more in the mainstream:

A policy for the following purpose. – *H.* had borrowed £500 of a friend to purchase promotion, and a further sum to pay the premium of this assurance, which was a single premium paid in hand at the time of assuring. and it was agreed between them that *H.* should repay the money borrowed by such monthly payments that at *5 per cent.* compound interest the whole of the debt would be discharged in 60 months if *H.* should so long live. – the Society therefore assure to *H.* that in case of his decease within that time they will take up the monthly payments where he shall leave them, and continue them in the same manner till the debt is paid.

The equivalent today to this type of debt insurance is mortgage insurance, the difference today being that the entire debt is paid at the time of the decease of the mortgagee.

For a mathematician such as Dodson, the valuation of these two policies is straightforward. Mosdell and Edwards probably did not have these skills. On the other hand, there is strong evidence that Mores did possess the requisite skills.[45] At his death, Mores's library contained all the standard books on the valuation of life annuities up to 1772: Abraham De Moivre's 1725 *Annuities upon Lives*, Thomas Simpson's 1742 *Doctrine of Annuities and Reversions* and his 1752 *Select Exercises for Young Proficients in the Mathematicks*, and James Dodson's 1755 *Mathematical Repository, Volume III*, which is devoted to annuities and life insurance. Mores also owned the standard works on probability: De Moivre's 1718 *Doctrine of Chances* and Simpson's 1740 *Nature and Laws of Chance*. After severing his connection with the Equitable Society, he continued to acquire books on life annuities, in particular Richard Price's 1772 *Observation on Reversionary Payments*. The strongest evidence for his abilities seems not to have survived.[46] In the sale catalog of his library dispersed after his death in 1778 there is an entry, "Calculations, Tables, &c. for the *Society for equitable Insurances on Lives and Survivorships*, by Mr. Mores, and Materials for his several Publications respecting that Society." After Mores's departure from the Equitable Society, special actuarial calculations had to be handled by a mathematician and it was not the resident actuary, John Edwards.

8 The Annuity Bubble of the 1760s and 1770s

In the decade from 1761 to 1771 several annuity societies were formed in London alone. As a result of the actions of these societies, this decade marks a turning point in the relationship between mathematicians and the life insurance and life annuity industries. Some mathematicians, whose "actuarial training" had probably been through property-based life-contingent contracts, reacted publicly to the activities of these annuity societies. Their actions led the general public to become more aware of the issues surrounding the pricing of life insurance and life annuities. The mathematicians' impact was greatest when one of them, Richard Price, made his mathematical arguments very accessible to the general public. The mathematicians were also helped by the size of the gap between the prices the societies set for the products and the prices that should have been set to break even. It was easy for them to demonstrate that in the long term the price of the product could not support the benefits on offer. There are some similarities in this situation to the financial crisis of 2008. The financial products that were on offer in 2008 were grossly overpriced (whereas they were underpriced in the eighteenth century) and the general public did not understand the pricing system behind these complex products. There are, of course, many differences between the two situations.

Very few of the annuity societies in the 1760s, perhaps none, had mathematicians involved in the design of their annuity benefits and premiums. As these new societies proliferated, they came to the attention of a small group of mathematicians, initially through one of the more responsible societies. This small group includes William Dale, James Horsfall, Richard Price, John Rowe, and Benjamin Webb. With the exception of Webb and perhaps Rowe, they were not professional mathematicians like Abraham De Moivre, who made his living as a mathematical tutor, consultant, and writer. Near the end of his career Dale was a collector of sewerage rates;[1] Horsfall was a librarian and then a treasurer of the Middle Temple, one of the four Inns of Court;[2] Price was a Nonconformist minister; Rowe's occupation is unknown; and

Webb was a writing master and accountant at a grammar school.[3] They were all very able mathematicians, and to paraphrase contemporary accounts, they were well versed in calculation. Price was the person who edited and brought Thomas Bayes's now famous essay on probability to the Royal Society and subsequently published articles on annuities and demography in the *Philosophical Transactions*.[4] Webb published some books related to the financial market, including *The Complete Annuitant: Consisting of Tables of Interest, Simple and Compound*, published in 1762.[5] Rowe published a relatively popular book on calculus that went through four editions between 1751 and 1767.[6] Although he published little, Horsfall's election certificate for fellowship in the Royal Society says that he was "well versed in Mathematical Knowledge."[7] Dale's only publications are related to bursting the annuity bubble of the 1760s and 1770s, and they show a deep knowledge of the mathematics behind life contingencies.

Of the five, only Price has gained lasting actuarial fame. Price also had the greatest impact on what happened to these annuity societies during the 1770s. There are a few reasons for his impact. They boil down to name recognition and making his work accessible. Prior to the annuity bubble, Price was known for his writing in moral philosophy and theology. He corresponded widely with many people. After the annuity bubble burst, Price gained fame as a political philosopher; he strongly supported the American colonists in their revolution to achieve independence from Britain. He continued to correspond with many people about population statistics, including several fellow clergymen interested in the subject.[8] Price also had a particular way of writing; he took what is essentially a description of a collection of numbers and calculations and made them accessible to an audience wider than the mathematically inclined. Price's situation might be compared favorably to the obscurity and writing styles of the other players. Webb's publications were mainly numerical tables that could be used by investors. Rowe left London just before the start of the growing controversy around the new annuity societies. Horsfall wrote nothing and appears to have acted quietly as a consultant to two annuity societies in the 1770s and 1780s. Dale wrote insightfully, but in a fairly technical way that might make his output difficult for the general public to digest. He also had no public presence beyond his two books related to the annuity bubble.[9]

The first in this group of annuity societies to be established was the Laudable Society for the Benefit of Widows.[10] It is difficult to say who was behind this scheme. The constant in terms of the officers of the Society is Michael Fisher, who served as secretary from the Society's

Table 8.1. *The Laudable Society reversionary payments*

Number of years the husband has been a member	>1	>2	>3	>4	>7	>10	>13
Annual payment in £	10	15	20	25	30	35	40

inception until his death in 1782.[11] If Fisher was the original promoter of the Society, either his memory was short or his knowledge of this particular market was limited (Fisher's main occupation was as a lapidary). The design of the Laudable Society's reversionary annuity scheme did not reflect any lessons that could be learned from the past. The Laudable scheme is a minor variation of the scheme of Assheton's that had been run by the Mercers' Company. Only a decade and a half before, that scheme had failed. Operating under essentially the same principles, the current scheme was doomed to fail in the long run.

Advertisements for subscriptions to the Laudable Society, along with a schedule of the proposed annuity payments, began to appear in June 1760.[12] The terms under which the Society operated were not officially enrolled in the High Court of Chancery until March 1761. In the articles of agreement are further details of interest about the scheme. Protestant married men between the ages of 21 and 45, who were neither soldiers nor seamen, were eligible to join the Society. There was no restriction on the age differential between husbands and wives. There were some fees to initiate the policy and a payment of five guineas (£5 5s, £5.25) for the capital stock of the Society as a membership fee. The annual premium payable in advance was five guineas. The benefits are outlined in Table 8.1, which can be read in the following way. Consider a man who has survived a year and a day (greater than 1 year) but dies within the next year. He makes two payments of five guineas (one at the beginning of each year), plus the five guineas for the capital stock, and his widow receives an annuity of £10 per annum. If the same man survives 4 years and a day (greater than 4 years), and then dies in that year, his widow receives an annuity of £25 per annum.

According to Price in his 1771 *Observations on Reversionary Payments*, the calculations supporting the premium and benefit structure of the Laudable Society are in a pamphlet entitled *The Possibility and Probability of a Scheme Intended for the Support of Widows Being Able to Support Itself*; the pamphlet is no longer extant.[13] The unknown method behind the calculations is highly suspect. A quick glance at Halley's table of the present values of life annuities at various ages (Table 3.3), and any thought about the experience of the Mercers'

Company, should have set off alarm bells among the proprietors of the Laudable Society. At age 25 the present value of an annuity of £1 per annum paid at the end of each year at 6% interest is 12.17, from Table 3.3. Paid at the beginning of each year, the value is 13.17. The present value of the five guineas paid in while the husband is alive, plus the initial five guineas towards the capital stock, is £74 in round numbers. The same simple arithmetic for a husband at age 45, the upper end of the age scale, is £63, again in round numbers. A lower rate than what Halley used yields higher annuity values, but will not change the overall tone of the argument. The annual payment from the Mercers' Company annuity was 30% of the amount invested. This translates to slightly more than £21 for the husband who joins the Society at age 21 and to almost £19 for one who is 45 on joining the Society. At these annual payment levels the Mercers' Company fund went broke. It took some time, but the fund still went broke. Should a husband survive 4 years after joining the Laudable Society, the annuity of £25 per annum is unsustainable no matter what age the husband is on joining the Society. What perhaps warmed the hearts and blinded the vision of the proprietors of the Laudable Society was that after about 9 years in operation the Laudable Society's net income for the year was £3,473 after annuity benefits had been paid to 20 widows.[14] The Society had not been around long enough for substantial future liabilities to take effect.

In order to better see the shortfalls of the Laudable Society's scheme, I calculated the expected profit, or loss, for a policy issued at each of the ages 21 through 45 for the husband. For ease of illustration, I assumed that husbands and wives were of the same age and used Halley's life table. As seen earlier in Figure 4.1 for the Mercers' Company, the profitability of the scheme decreases as older men marry younger women. Figure 8.1 shows, for each age at issue, the change in profitability of the scheme as the £5 increments to the annuity are added.[15] The top set of points shows the expected profits when a life annuity of £10 is given to the widow. The next set of points below this shows the profitability when the life annuity of £10 is increased to £15 if the husband survives for at least 2 years of membership in the Laudable Society. This continues in £5 increments to the bottom set of points which shows the expected profits (in this case losses) for the actual scheme as given in Table 8.1. The expected profits or losses are the differences between the expected income of five guineas per year over the husband's lifetime plus the initial capital contribution of five guineas and the expected expenses in the various reversionary annuities considered. A quick look at the solid dots in Figure 8.1 indicates that the

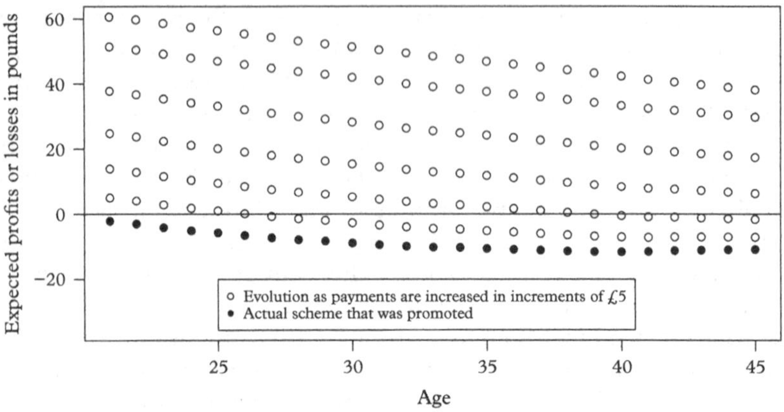

Figure 8.1. Expected profits or losses in the Laudable Society's scheme at each of the £5 increments in the annuity benefit

scheme is not viable, confirming the insights of the simple arithmetical calculations that the Laudable Society should have done in view of the Mercers' Company experience.

In my inferences from Figure 8.1, I have assumed that Halley's table accurately reflects mortality experience in eighteenth-century England. In the seventeenth century, when Halley's table was constructed, and for the next century or two, female mortality was probably higher than male mortality because of death in childbirth. On the other hand, the husband was typically older than the wife, and so that situation would increase the expense side of the equation. Simpson's 1742 table from his *Doctrine of Annuities and Reversions* and Smart's 1738 table show greater mortality at younger ages than does Halley's table. Using a different table will provide different annuity valuations. Figure 8.2 shows that losses are even greater when Simpson's 1742 mortality table is used. The additional losses are explained by the life table. As more men die at younger ages (under Simpson's mortality assumption) the amount of time for which their wives receive annuity payments increases. This harks back to the words of Jeremy Bentham that "the stock of data they [the mathematicians] have to work upon is imperfect or erroneous." James Dodson tried to address this issue by using a life table appropriate to the population purchasing an insurance policy or an annuity. Simpson's table applies to London and other large towns that may be congested and unhealthy; Halley's table applies to small towns and perhaps rural areas.

Table 8.2. *The London Annuity Society reversionary payments*

Number of years the husband has been a member	>1	>7	>15
Annual payment in £	20	30	40

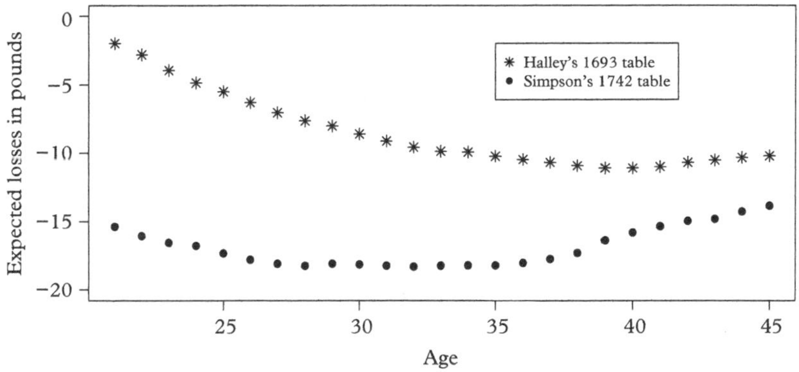

Figure 8.2. A comparison of the losses in the Laudable Society's scheme using Halley's and Simpson's mortality tables

Operating under essentially the same principles as the Laudable Society, the London Annuity Society began operation in 1765. The London Annuity Society's entrance requirements for men were the same as the Laudable's, as were the fees.[16] The new Society did admit men between the ages of 45 and 55, provided that they paid an additional one-time premium that amounted to their age next birthday minus 45, all times 5, with the final result reckoned in guineas. The benefits offered by the London Annuity Society, shown in Table 8.2, are similar, but different to those offered by the Laudable Society. The simple and approximate analysis that I used to examine the profitability of the Laudable Society also applies here. In the long run the scheme is not sustainable and will eventually run out of money.

There is a suggestion that the London Annuity Society's scheme had a mathematical foundation. John Field, an apothecary, was the principal founder of the Society. It is stated in his 1796 obituary that he "collected a great many papers from different quarters upon the probability of life in order to enable him to form the rules of his society."[17] Since this claim was made more than 30 years after the founding of the Society, it is possible that the claim is conflated with a reform of the rules of the Society in the early 1770s that put it on a firmer financial footing. Field was the treasurer of the Society from its inception until his death.[18] On the other hand, the claim in Field's obituary may be correct. There is a second approach to pricing these reversionary annuities. So far I have evaluated funds by looking at individual risks. This is done by comparing expected payments from an individual (the premiums) to the expected payments to the individual's widow (the benefits). The fund is sustainable when the expected income side for each individual equals the expected expense side. The problem can also be examined from the point of view of aggregate risk. Here the total fund is modeled in terms of its growth and diminution over time. The fund is sustainable if the risk that the fund falls into the red is very small. This was the approach taken in setting up the Scottish Ministers' Widows' Fund in the 1740s. Thirty years earlier, Daniel Cholmondeley had taken this approach when trying to justify his short-lived annuity scheme. Field may have seen the literature describing these funds.

The Scottish Ministers' Widows' Fund operated successfully initially because the assumptions that the fund's designers made in assessing aggregate risk were reasonable. Cholmondeley's assumptions were not. The Scottish Ministers' Widows' Fund looks very much like a variation on the Mercers' Company annuity and on the schemes run by the Laudable Society for the Benefit of Widows and the London Annuity Society. For an annual premium of five guineas taken from a minister's stipend, whatever his age, on the minister's death his widow would receive an annual payment of £20 for her lifetime. There were options of £10, £15, and £25 annuities with the premiums appropriately prorated.[19] The Mercers' Company scheme failed just as the Scots were starting their fund. Later the Laudable Society and London Annuity Society ran into financial difficulty and had to revise their schemes. The Scottish Ministers' Widows' Fund operated until 1993, while the Laudable Society's and London Annuity Society's funds lasted into the nineteenth century. In an aggregate risk approach to the Scottish Ministers' Widows' Fund, the total amount of funds available in any year is the balance from the previous year plus interest earned, plus the five guineas from each minister paying into the fund minus the payments of £20 made to each of the surviving widows. If it is assumed that any pulpit vacancies are replaced immediately and the annual premiums are all due on the same day, then yearly income is constant (five guineas times the number of pulpits). On the expense side the number of widows to be paid is the pool of widows from the previous year plus the women who become widows during the year minus the widows who die during the year. Modeling the expense side requires finding a way to estimate the number of ministers and widows who would die in any year.

There were mathematicians involved in the design of the Scottish Ministers' Widows' Fund: Colin Maclaurin, an eminent mathematician, and Robert Wallace, a Church of Scotland minister who had studied mathematics at Edinburgh in his student days and who had subsequently become interested in issues related to the growth of populations. It is impossible to say if either or both were part of the initial group calling for the establishment of the fund. The founding of the fund is usually credited to Alexander Webster, another Church of Scotland minister; Wallace was certainly involved at some point. What is evident from the extant sources is that early on, perhaps in 1741 or 1742, Wallace made some quick calculations on survival probabilities using Halley's life table to justify an annuity of £30 to a widow based on annual premiums of £10 paid by the minister during his lifetime. At that time Wallace was suggesting an annuity scheme for "gentlemen as have not lands, estates nor great sums of money but live by their business or yearly income which depends on their lives," a group described more vaguely than Church of Scotland ministers. For his part, Maclaurin evaluated some proposals about the scheme and suggested alterations to make them financially viable.

Maclaurin's approach was to look at aggregate risk. All ministers were required to pay into the fund on their ordination to the ministry and continue paying annually until their deaths. If ordained ministers who exited the fund were replaced by newly ordained ministers entering the fund, then the income for the fund would be approximately stable over time. To encourage timely replacement there was a tax on pulpit vacancies. Maclaurin recognized the benefit of this situation by expressing in a letter to Robert Wallace a form of the law of large numbers, combined with some ideas from risk theory that apply to this situation:[20]

> It must be advantageous, because a a [sic] greater improvement can be made of large Sums, and with less danger from the hazards to which all things are subjected, by faithfull Trustees than of small annual Sums by single Ministers; as it is a certain rule that no single man, unless he be extremely rich, ought to deal in Insurance, but rich men or companies of men only; but loss to a poor man is more sensible than an equal gain.

This was the income side. On the expense side, Maclaurin took a statistical approach. From registers that had been kept he estimated the total number of widows to be paid from the fund and the fraction of those widows that would die each year. All fees were set so that the total income and total expense in any year of the operation of the fund balanced. After Maclaurin, this idea of aggregate risk and its valuation seems almost to have gone dormant for a time and remained in

Scotland. It was Richard Price in the 1770s who introduced aggregate risk arguments into England, probably taking his cue from the Scottish experience. The concept of individual risk remained the dominant approach, widely applied in England.

Using an individual risk approach, the same approach I took to value the fund for the Laudable Society for the Benefit of Widows when husbands and wives are of the same age, I calculated the expected gain or loss per individual in the Scottish Ministers' Widows Fund. This was done assuming a 4% annual rate of interest (the current rate in the 1740s) and either Halley's or Simpson's mortality table. Under Halley's table the fund would be in surplus provided that the ministers joined the fund before age 40 and under Simpson's table the fund would only be in surplus up to age 25. Again, Jeremy Bentham comes to mind. Since the fund survived, it is likely that Halley's table, based on a town in Europe, more accurately reflects the Scottish ministers' mortality than Simpson's table, based on experience in London.

The Church of England lagged behind its Scottish counterpart. It was not until 1765 that the Fund for the Better Maintenance of the Widows and Children of the Clergy was established; and it was for London clergy only.[21] There had not been a complete absence of help for widows; distressed clergymen's widows were handled through charities in various English dioceses, but the help was often meager. The new fund, designed by the Church of England clergyman Fernando Warner, was a variation on a mortuary tontine. Clergy annually paid two guineas into the fund, or one guinea annually and a one-time two-guinea fine. Donations to the fund were also accepted. Each year the directors of the fund would declare a dividend based on the annual fees collected and income from investments, and this would be divided among all surviving widows.[22]

The legal profession in London soon tried to follow the London clergy. An attempt to establish the Law Society for the Benefit of Widows was made in 1766. The person who proposed the formation of this society, and appears to have designed the premium and benefit structure, remained in the background during the Law Society's brief existence. This was Josiah Brown. He was admitted to the Inner Temple, one of the four Inns of Court, on April 24, 1765.[23] Just before the year was out Brown put together his proposal for an annuity society.[24] A formal meeting to form the Society took place in February 1766 and a printed *Proposed Deed of Settlement* containing the rules of the Society appeared shortly thereafter.

The annual premiums charged by this society for an annuity of £50 per annum paid to the widow from the death of the husband are

Table 8.3. *The Law Society's premium structure (given in pounds decimalized rather than pounds and shillings)*

Age of the husband	25	30	35	40	45	50	55
Annual premium	3.15	3.45	3.95	5.00	6.50	8.45	10.50

outlined in Table 8.3.[25] The premium levels are based on the assumption that the husband and wife are of the same age. If that is not the case and the age difference between the member of the Society and his wife is significantly large, then it is suggested in the *Proposed Deed of Settlement* that "the annual premium paid by such a member shall be augmented or diminished, in proportion of the chance of survivorship in the opinion of the said directors ..." My first reaction to the fact that the premiums increase at a rate that is increasing with age, as well as the mention of "the chance of survivorship," is that the age-related premiums probably had a sound mathematical basis. Such was apparently not the case. Because of the premium structure, the Society was short-lived, ceasing operation possibly by the end of 1766.[26]

After advertising their premium structure, the Law Society decided to call in expert opinion on the soundness of what they had just advertised. The situation was described by Richard Price in 1771:[27]

> A plan was agreed upon and printed; but some doubts happening to arise with respect to it, the directors resolved to ask the opinion and advice of three gentlemen, well known for their skill in calculation. This occasioned a further reference to me; and the issue was, that the plan being found to be insufficient, the whole design was laid aside.

In a biography of Price, his nephew William Morgan made a stronger statement:[28]

> Mr. Price has been referred to, by some gentlemen in the profession of the law, for his opinion of a plan by which they proposed to form themselves into a Society for providing Annuities for their widows. This he found on examination to be so defective, and he represented its insufficiency so strongly to them, that they determined to lay it wholly aside.

There are truths to these statements, but the situation in more complicated than it initially appears to be. A deeper examination of the situation involves John Rowe. This examination also shows the growing persuasive power of the mathematicians.

The three gentlemen mentioned by Price whose advice was sought are Robert Montague, Joseph Waugh, and John Rowe. These names are mentioned by Rowe in marginalia that he wrote in his 1776 book *Letters Relative to Societies for the Benefit of Widows and of Age*, now held in the British Library. Rowe also states that it was the directors of the Society who approached the three and that it was Josiah Brown who approached Price privately. The Society contacted Rowe for his advice on May 7, 1766.[29] The evidence for the timing of Price's contact is much less precise. Morgan puts it in 1767 or 1768 but that cannot be if the Society abandoned its annuity scheme late in 1766.

A little further investigation provides a glimpse into the minds of the directors. Price alludes to the directors' wanting people "known for their skill in calculation." All the top choices were dead: Halley in 1742, Jones in 1749, De Moivre in 1754, Dodson in 1757, and Simpson in 1761. The last four were all known to be active in consultations related to life annuities. In view of Rowe's calculus book, he was a good choice. Since Rowe provides no further information on Waugh and Montague, their identities are subject to some speculation. There is a Richard Montague who was an accountant for the South Sea Company. There is also a Joseph Waugh who was prominent in the Mercers' Company. Both of these individuals would make sense from the point of view of the directors of the Law Society – Montague for his numerical skills as an accountant and his knowledge of annuities offered by the South Sea Company, and Waugh for his connection to the company that had offered reversionary life annuities over a period of several years.

Rowe's report to the directors of the Law Society is dated October 11, 1766.[30] Rowe says that Ward and Montague saw his report but were too busy to verify all the calculations. In general they agreed with the main thrust of the report. Rowe provides a table of premiums for an annuity of £50 calculated using a 3% annual rate of interest. The premiums are given for every age at issue, beginning at age 25, rather than at the 5-year intervals given in Table 8.3. Like the Law Society, Rowe assumes that the husband and wife are of the same age. He then adds an additional set of premiums for each of the situations in which the husband is one to 5 years older than his wife. The premiums that Rowe calculates are two to five times larger than the premiums suggested by the Law Society. To calculate his premiums Rowe used Simpson's 1752 mortality table, published in *Select Exercises for Young Proficients in the Mathematics*. What is very likely is that he used the published annuity tables and approximations given by Simpson rather than obtaining his premiums by brute force calculation using the life table. A complicating factor in using the life table directly is that, like the printed version of Halley's table, the table is incomplete. The last entry in the table is for age 79, with $l_{79} = 25$ and deaths running at two or three per year. Figure 8.3 shows the premiums suggested by the Law Society (from

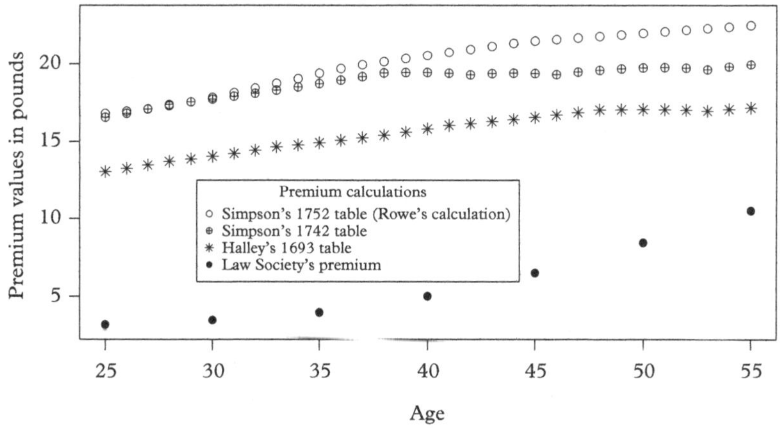

Figure 8.3. John Rowe's and related premium calculations for the Law Society benefits

Table 8.3) and the premiums under three different mortality assumptions: Halley's 1693 table, Simpson's 1742 table, and Simpson's 1752 table, but as calculated by Rowe. At any age all three premiums are well above the premium suggested by the Law Society. All calculations point to the collapse of the Law Society should their planned premium structure be adopted.

As the likely calculator of the premiums that appear in the *Proposed Deed of Settlement*, Josiah Brown was probably shocked at the large discrepancy between these premiums and the ones obtained by Rowe. And so it would be for this reason that he contacted Price. The only known surviving evidence of what Price may have calculated for Brown is in a letter from Price to his friend John Canton dated April 1768, a year or more after the demise of the annuity scheme.[31] Price's calculations were in regard to an annuity scheme that perhaps Canton was considering and in which Rowe was also involved. The annuity benefit was set at £20 per annum. Price made his premium calculation based on a 4% annual rate of interest. He compromised on which mortality table to use. First, he used De Moivre's approximation to annuity valuations, essentially Halley's mortality table. Then he also calculated the premiums based on "Mr Simpson's Valuation of Lives," which probably means he used Simpson's 1742 *Doctrine of Annuities and Reversions* and the annuity tables and approximations therein rather using the life table itself and many cumbersome calculations. The compromise was to report to Canton the average of the two premium calculations that he made.

Price's letter to Canton "contains the earliest known written discussion by Price on matters concerned with insurance."[32] It also shows that Price had a thorough knowledge of life annuity valuations at the time. The date when Price was first introduced to the topic can only be a matter of speculation. One possibility is that the introduction occurred sometime in the years 1740–44, when he was a student under John Eames at Moorfields, a dissenting academy in London. Eames, a fellow of the Royal Society, taught mathematics, Newtonian natural philosophy, and theology at the academy.[33] His brush with life annuities occurred in 1739. Edmond Halley had received a 1738 publication by Willem Kersseboom which contains a population table for Holland presented in the same spirit as Halley's Breslau table. Like Halley, Kersseboom also gives a table of values of life annuities at various ages derived from his population table. Halley sent the publication to the Royal Society. The publication was received at a meeting of the Society on May 31, 1739, and presumably since it was in Dutch, Eames was asked "to inform the Society of the Substance of it." Eames presented a short account of Kersseboom's work at a meeting of the Royal Society on June 28, 1739 and subsequently published his account in the *Philosophical Transactions*.[34] Later he corresponded briefly with Kersseboom.[35] Eames may have included life annuities in his teaching at Moorfields. Although there are surviving notes for Eames's courses in mechanics and algebra, nothing survives concerning life annuities.

The letter to Canton and other supporting material reveal some overlapping networks of friends and scientists. In the letter Price refers to meeting Canton, John Rowe, and an unidentified Mr. Lincoln at the White Hart Inn regarding an annuity scheme for widows that appears similar to the one designed for the Law Society. By the time the letter was written both Canton and Price were fellows of the Royal Society. Canton's circle of friends also included Thomas Simpson.[36] Simpson was also a fellow of the Royal Society but died before Price had any connection to it. Canton and Price often met at the Club of Honest Whigs, which met weekly and whose membership consisted predominantly of Nonconformist ministers and schoolmasters.[37] Canton was a schoolmaster by profession and at the same time a prominent experimental scientist. Thomas Simpson mentions Rowe in his correspondence and Rowe considered Simpson a friend.[38] It was a small circle that worked on the pricing of annuities in the 1760s and 1770s, as it was a small circle in the 1730–50s, at that time centered on De Moivre, who carried out annuity valuations for clients and friends.

Soon the floodgates opened and at least a dozen annuity societies opened for business over the years 1766–71, with increasing annual

Table 8.4. *Annuity societies in London 1766–71*

Society name	Date founded	Date dissolved or date last mentioned in the press
Laudable Society of Annuitants	December 25, 1766	Nineteenth century
Amicable Society of Annuitants	December 25, 1769	May 2, 1785
Provident Society	February 21, 1770	August 10, 1773
Society of London Annuitants	March 1, 1770	October 28, 1772
Equitable Society of Annuitants	April 19, 1770	April 27, 1772
London Union Society	1770	May 11, 1773
Westminster Union Society	September 29, 1770	November 21, 1774
Consolidated Society	January 1, 1771	June 6, 1771
Public Annuitant Society	January 21, 1771	July 6, 1772
Rational Society	ca January 1771	August 28, 1771
Friendly Society of Annuitants	April 12, 1771	October 26, 1771

frequency as the years progressed. These annuity societies all took a different approach. Rather than a reversionary annuity, these societies paid a deferred life annuity. As the name suggests, the first payment in this kind of annuity is deferred for a certain period of years, rather than beginning immediately. Essentially these societies were offering a form of pension income. The societies that offered deferred annuities often had "for the benefit of age" in their names or descriptions (the buyer purchased an annuity that would start in his or her old age) and the ones that offered reversionary annuities were "for the benefit of widows" (the buyer bought protection for his wife in the event that she became a widow). Whatever the age of the purchaser, and whatever the premiums that were paid in, the annuity payments made by the annuity societies offering deferred annuities typically started at age 50. If the purchaser happened to be older than 40, then the annuity payments started 10 years later. The newspaper advertisements for these schemes usually only mention the value of the annuity payable at age 50 and that premiums for a person aged 40 would continue for 10 years. William Dale collected information on many of these societies in the early 1770s, information that goes well beyond what appears in the newspapers.[39] Each society had age-based premiums and a fee, or entry fine, to join the society. A list of several of the societies in London, shown in the order in which they were founded, is given in Table 8.4. The year in which each society was established is taken from advertisements in London newspapers.[40]

There were some variations to the payment structures, probably made in an attempt to be competitive with other societies. With the appropriate doubling, trebling, and quadrupling of the premium, some societies offered annuity payments of two, three, and four times the basic amount. The London Annuity Society set their premiums and payments in guineas instead of pounds sterling. Two annuity societies allowed annuity payments to begin at age 47 instead of 50, but at a reduced amount. The Consolidated Annuity Society allowed annuity payments to commence 10 years after admission to the Society, and admission could occur at a young age. The Consolidated also had an entry fine that increased with the date of entrance, probably to try to encourage people to enter early.

The flowering of these annuity societies during the 1760s might be explained by the economic climate of the time. There had been an economic boom during the Seven Years' War (1756–63) followed by stagnation for the remainder of the decade. There was also concern about the colonial markets and growing unrest in the American colonies as the decade wore on. At the same time it was the beginning of the Industrial Revolution and the rise of "men of movable property."[41] This was a growing group of men without real property who might want some kind of pension income later in life and protection for their families that could not be derived from rents. The rate of interest over the decade was stable and relatively low.[42] All of this, combined with the apparently low price of the annuities that were offered compared to the advertised benefits, made these annuity societies attractive investment vehicles.

Despite their attractiveness to the consumer, the Laudable Society for the Benefit of Widows, the London Annuity Society, and every annuity society listed in Table 8.3 had financial difficulties. Some societies fixed their problems and continued in business; many were dissolved within 3 years of their foundation. Earlier in the century many insurance schemes had come and gone with little apparent fanfare or even comment. Likewise, when the reversionary annuity scheme run by the Mercers' Company ran into trouble in the 1740s, there was no apparent commentary in the press from mathematicians or any other members of the public about the soundness of the scheme. The press articles did mention the plight of the widows who were going to be left without any income, but again no mathematician came forward. This changed in the 1760s. Several letters began to appear in the press commenting on the shortcomings of the life annuities offered by the growing number of annuity societies.

The initial letters from the late 1760s appear in the *Gazetteer and New Daily Advertiser* printed by Charles Say. At the time, this newspaper had the highest circulation among London newspapers. Advertisements and correspondence, sometimes solicited and often political in nature, were its mainstay. What little is known of Say is that he sometimes published material in his newspaper that was controversial enough politically to get him into hot water. For example, in 1764 he was fined £100 for reprinting an article from another newspaper that was considered libellous against the Earl of Hertford. The next year he was fined another £100 for printing a false account of the proceedings of the House of Lords. When letters were published, under the pseudonym "Junius," that lampooned the government, Say reprinted some of them and in 1770 was brought before the House of Lords for interrogation to try to determine the identity of "Junius."[43] Say must have found the letters on the annuity societies sufficiently controversial and interesting to his readers that he was willing to publish lengthy and sometimes technical letters that were highly critical of these societies.

The letters in the *Gazetteer and New Daily Advertiser* made a first step in changing the practice of how life annuities were marketed and sold. Say's willingness to publish them is not the only explanation for the change. The reading public had to be receptive to the contents of these letters. By the 1760s this reading public was more knowledgeable about, or at least more aware of, pricing issues surrounding life annuities.

On the highly technical side, between 1725 and his death in 1754, De Moivre's *Annuities upon Lives* went through four English editions as well as a pirated Irish one. His work on life annuities also appears in the second and third editions of his *Doctrine of Chances.*[44] During his lifetime notice of De Moivre's work had filtered down to the less mathematically inclined. A reference to De Moivre appears in Tobias Smollett's popular 1751 novel *The Adventures of Peregrine Pickle*, in a chapter entitled "Peregrine and his friend Cadwaller proceed in the exercise of the mystery of fortune-telling, in the course of which they atchieve various adventures." The novel is a savagely satirical portrayal of eighteenth-century society. In the chapter Cadwaller poses as a fortune-teller providing advice to a number of clients on chance events. Related to leases and the chances of survival, here is some advice that Cadwaller gives through Smollett:[45]

> This client was succeeded by an old man about the age of seventy-five, who, being resolved to purchase a lease, desired to be determined in the term of years by the necromancer's advice, observing that, as he had no children of his own body, and had no regard for his heirs-in-law, the purchase would be made with a view to his own convenience only; and therefore, considering his age, he himself hesitated in the period of the lease, between thirty and threescore years.
>
> The conjurer [Cadwaller], upon due deliberation, advised him to double the last specified term, because he distinguished in his features something portending extreme old age and second childhood, and he ought to provide for that state of incapacity, which otherwise would be attended with infinite misery and affliction.

After describing a string of Cadwaller's clients, Smollett concludes with a peroration that includes reference to dubious insurance, lending, and investment practices and ending with "in short, all matters of uncertain issues were appealed to this tribunal; and, in point of calculation, De Moivre was utterly neglected."

Simpson also published his work on life annuities in 1742 and 1752. Several less technical, and hence more accessible, books were published on life annuities between 1740 and 1765. Richard Hayes's 1727 book on annuities was reprinted in 1746 and Weyman Lee's flawed 1737 book found new life in an equally flawed *A Valuation of Annuities and Leases Certain, for a Single Life*, published in 1751, with a second edition in 1754. While avoiding the mathematical theory behind annuity valuations, some professional mathematicians tried to appeal to a wider audience. Their books published between the 1740s and 1760s usually contain a life table, typically calculated from the London Bills of Mortality, accompanied by a table of the present values of life annuities, usually for one life, but sometimes for more. There are detailed descriptions of how to use the tables accompanied by worked exercises that require only facility in arithmetic.[46] At the most popular level, Edmond Hoyle expanded his horizon from books on games of chance to an explanation of the chance behind the games.[47] The final chapter of his book *An Essay Towards Making the Doctrine of Chances Easy to Those who Understand Vulgar Arithmetick Only* contains tables showing the value of an annuity on a single life at various ages evaluated at 3% and 4% interest annually, using two different mortality tables. The book went through three editions, the first in 1754 and the last 10 years later.

General references to this literature on life annuities appear in popular literature. In Henry Fielding's 1749 novel *Tom Jones* there is a description of Captain Blifil's plan to marry Squire Allworthy's sister Bridget in expectation of inheriting Allworthy's estate.[48]

> Nothing was wanting to enable him to enter upon the immediate execution of this plan, but the death of Mr. Allworthy; in calculating which he had employed much of his own algebra besides purchasing every book extant that treats of the value of lives, reversions, &c. From which he satisfied himself, that as he had every day a chance of this happening, so he had more than an even chance of its happening within a few years.

The penetration of the mathematics of annuity calculations into the consciousness of the general public may have been far from complete; but there was at least a veneer of awareness.

The first set of comments on the newly launched annuity schemes that appears in the *Gazetteer and New Daily Advertiser* is in a series of letters in 1765 supporting Fernando Warner's Fund for the Better Maintenance of the Widows and Children of the Clergy, with responses criticizing the fund.[49] The first letter writer signed himself "L.J. Brutus," probably a reference to Lucius Junius Brutus, who overthrew the last Roman king and established the Republic. The eighteenth-century Brutus supported the establishment of the fund. His concern was the inequitable way in which clergy were appointed to various livings or benefices. Beneficed clergy could hold more than one living; those that did so hired curates at much lower salaries to cover their duties. The fund was highly desirable and equitable, he said, but fixing the current state of the relation between beneficed clergy and curates (moving toward a Roman Republic of clergymen), would also fix the financial position of some of the clergy. Others pointed out specific problems with the fund as it was established. Only the beneficed clergy were responsible for the fund from which the curates might benefit. Curates could only afford to subscribe to the fund at the minimum subscription level. A final counterargument against the fund spoke to the consequences of the inequitableness of clergy appointments using some general insights from the workings of life annuities. Curates tended to come to London at a relatively young age and they were required by the rules of the fund to begin their subscriptions within 2 years of their arrival. Clergy appointed to benefices in London tended to come from dioceses outside London. Their ages at arrival in London tended to be much greater than the ages of the curates. For the same benefit curates would tend to pay more into the fund than their more wealthy beneficed colleagues.

All was quiet for a couple of years. Then John Rowe stirred things up by sharing the experience he had gained from his work for the Law Society for the Benefit of Widows. Writing a letter to the printer of *Gazetteer and New Daily Advertiser* under the pseudonym "Pro Bono Publico" (for the public good), Rowe reproduced the report that he had written for the Law Society more than a year before, demonstrating mathematically the inadequacies of the Law Society's annuity scheme. His letter is dated 1 December 1767 but it did not appear in print until the end of the month. True to his pseudonym Rowe writes:[50]

> The publication of the extract from the Deed of Settlement [of the Law Society], with the Report will probably be a great interest to the public in general; as it may be a means of preventing future Societies from falling into the like mistake with those of the late intended law Society.

It seems odd that Rowe would publish his letter at this time. The Laudable Society for the Benefit of Widows and the London Annuity

Society, which offered reversionary annuities like the Law Society, had been in operation since 1761 and 1765, respectively. The Laudable Society of Annuitants, which offered deferred annuities, had been in operation for a year. There must have been something else that moved him to write.

I think that Rowe's motivation was probably twofold. He saw some proposals for annuity societies in the newspapers. At the same time, he may have been working on setting up an annuity society, in conjunction with John Canton. The letter from Richard Price to John Canton dated April 1768 alludes to this possibility. As for other annuity societies, there were two very short-lived ones, started by an obscure individual named Thomas Paul Phillips.[51] The first was the Amicable Society for the Benefit of Widows and Children, which began operation November 21, 1766, offering reversionary annuities.[52] The benefit and premium structures for this society appear to mimic those of the Laudable Society for the Benefit of Widows, which may have prompted Rowe to reproduce his table constructed for the Law Society. The second, offering deferred life annuities, is the Guardian Society for the Benefit of Old Age which began operation on June 13, 1767.[53] Phillips' two societies may have been questionable operations, like the one started by Daniel Cholmondeley more than 50 years before. Within about 7 months of the founding of his Amicable Society, the directors decided to replace Phillips as secretary.[54] He continued to be secretary to the Guardian Society, but that society appears to have ceased operating within a year of its founding.[55] These two societies do not appear among those mentioned by William Dale in 1772; if the societies had not been dissolved in 1769 they were definitely gone by late 1771.

Between January and April 1768, Rowe's letter generated a series of more than a dozen letters in the *Gazetteer and New Daily Advertiser* concerning annuities and annuity societies.[56] Some questioned the facts about Rowe's calculations for the Law Society. Another writer, identified by Rowe as the Secretary to the Laudable Society for the Benefit of Widows, defended the Laudable Society claiming (incorrectly) that it was on a firm financial foundation. John Edwards, actuary to the Society for Equitable Assurances used the situation to promote the Equitable as one that was based on sound principles. The remaining letters by Rowe and Benjamin Webb contain calculations and discussions addressing the long-term viability of some annuity societies.[57] There is a brief hiatus in the exchange during March and April, while the London part of the 1768 general Parliamentary election took place. As the election drew closer all the letters to the printer were about the candidates. On March 25, the printer Charles Say inserted into his newspaper the notice, "The City Election now finished, this paper is open again for all kinds of instructive and entertaining subjects." Then other issues intervened which attracted the printer's attention. The paper devoted a great deal of space to a property dispute between Sir James Lowther, later Earl of Lonsdale, and the Duke of Portland, and to issues over the politician John Wilkes's failure to get a London seat in the House of Commons and his attempt to get one just outside of London. It was not until April 18, that the annuity society controversy was taken up again in the newspaper, at which time a letter written by Benjamin Webb and dated March 6, was printed. The issue had lost traction, at least with the printer, and there was only one more letter printed on annuity societies. On May 13, Rowe left London to live in Exeter.

Initially in this exchange of correspondence, Webb checked one of Rowe's premiums using his own tables from the *Complete Annuitant* and found that Rowe's value agreed with his. He concluded his letter by recommending that the annuity societies should "consult such gentlemen who are versed in computations of this nature." While Rowe responded to some critics of his calculations, Webb focused on various shortfalls of some individual annuity societies. He singled out one society that he said had a five-guinea premium with a £50 benefit to surviving widows. Here he was conflating the Laudable Society for the Benefit of Widows (five-guinea premium) with the Laudable Society of Annuitants (£50 paid every year beginning at age 50). Making a reasonable assumption about the age distribution of the society members, Webb demonstrated that the fund "will be exhausted before the younger widows claim." Rowe followed with a letter showing that the premiums for the Laudable Society of Annuitants were too low. He justified the writing of his letter with two concluding sentences:

> If you saw a blind man walking towards a well, ought you not to caution him of his danger? Whether this be a similar case, you, Sir, can easily determine.

Both Rowe and Webb continued with premium calculation examples showing the inadequacy of the funds, at times disagreeing on the values of the premiums. At the end of this sequence of correspondence, Webb reports that some members of the Laudable Society of Annuitants had come to him for advice on the viability of this annuity society. He responded that the premiums were not sufficient to meet the promised benefits. Despite this, the premium and benefit structures did not change in any substantial way. More generally, there was no move at this time by any of the annuity societies to reform their premium and benefit structures. The letters in the *Gazetteer and New Daily Advertiser* had little or no impact on the societies.

The complete disregard of these annuity society critics continued into 1770. A letter to the printer of the *Gazetteer and New Daily Advertiser* in July of that year and signed J.J. again demonstrated the quicksand on which these annuity societies stood.[58] Using Halley's life table as well as some London tables, the writer calculated what the premiums for the Laudable Society of Annuitants should be. As a member of that society he was concerned that the amounts he calculated were much less than the amounts the Laudable Society charged, fearing that the society would not be able to meet its obligations.

From Christmas 1769 to the end of September 1770 at least six annuity societies were formed (Table 8.3). It was an advertisement for the founding of one of these societies that led to the bubble finally bursting. In his *Observations on Reversionary Payments* Richard Price writes:

> At the beginning of last winter a letter was published to the *Provident Society*, containing a clear proof of the insufficiency of the plans of all these societies.

It was probably this letter that motivated Price to look carefully into the annuity societies then operating in London and to write *Observations on Reversionary Payments*. In September 1770 a lengthy advertisement for the Provident Society appeared in both *London Magazine* and *Gentleman's Magazine*.[59] The advertisement contains all the rules of the society, a list of the officers, and a table of premiums for ages 1 through 70. This advertisement for the annuities offered by this society is much more detailed than what appears in the London newspapers for the Provident Society or any other annuity society. The letter to which Price refers is signed W. and appears in the November issue of *Gentleman's Magazine*.[60] With a little algebra that is absent from all earlier letters to the newspapers on the topic of annuity societies, with references to Halley and De Moivre, and with a reasonable assumption about the cash flow of the Provident Society, W. concludes, "That the annual contributions to be paid, are by no means equal to the support of the annuities to be expected."

In a letter dated March 22, 1771 to Elizabeth Montagu, Price says that *Observations on Reversionary Payments* would soon be published and that it "has taken up all my time and attention this winter." He also expressed to her the expectation that the work would be ignored. Unlike his assessments of the annuity societies, this expectation was very wrong.

Soon after his 1768 letter to John Canton, Price demonstrated that he was well versed in the finer points of the mathematics of life annuity calculations as well as in issues surrounding the measurement of mortality and population. In a 1769 letter to Benjamin Franklin published in *Philosophical Transactions* Price took up the issue of estimating the size of populations, an issue first treated statistically by John Graunt in the 1660s.[61] It is obvious from the letter that Price had read most or all of the literature on the subject that had been published. In modern parlance, Price had good data sense; he was able to discern what was good and bad about the data collected and how to tease information from the data. His major "technical" contribution in the paper is that he found a method to obtain population estimates based on the concept of expected future lifetime calculated from a mortality table combined with the yearly number of births in the population. With some more or less reasonable assumptions, he was able to take into account migration, to London in particular, by considering the differences between numbers of yearly births and burials in London. The next year Price published another paper in *Philosophical Transactions*, addressing an error that he had found in De Moivre's *Annuities upon Lives*. It is a fairly complex calculation involving a valuation related to the order in which people die.[62] Price's nephew, William Morgan, reports that Price believed initially that the error was his and puzzled over it so much that some of his hair turned white.[63]

Price's *Observations on Reversionary Payments* contains many pages of well-reasoned sage advice ranging through the annuity societies to insurance companies to the national debt, all connected through life-contingent calculations and arguments. The first 120 pages of *Observations on Reversionary Payments* deal with the annuity societies – how they currently operate, how they are failing their annuitants in the long run, and how they should operate so as not to go bankrupt. Price opens his arguments by showing through numerical examples and the use of life annuity tables how to find the values of reversionary annuities and deferred annuities, as well as how these are paid for through annual premiums. All his arguments can be understood through the use of simple arithmetic. He leaves the mathematical formulae and demonstrations to an appendix, saying:[64]

> These demonstrations I have chosen to keep out of sight in the body of the work, in order to avoid discouraging such readers as may be unacquainted with mathematics.

This decision makes his arguments readable and easy to follow. Price then takes his initial numerical examples and applies them to the analysis of several annuity societies. In his analyses he uses very effectively both individual risk arguments, as Rowe had done, and aggregate risk arguments, as Maclaurin had done. Numerical results on reversionary annuities are applied to the Laudable Society for the Benefit of Widows and to the London Annuity Society. Similar results on deferred annuities are applied to the Laudable Society of Annuitants, the Amicable Society of Annuitants, the Provident Society, the London Union Society, and the Equitable Society of Annuitants, all of which appear in Table 8.4. Price finds all these societies wanting and concludes:

> They are all impositions on the public, proceeding from ignorance, and encouraged by credulity and folly.

Price does not concern himself solely with the secular. He is also critical of the Church of England scheme for London clergy designed by Fernando Warner. His insightful comments on this scheme go beyond the problems and inequities of curates and beneficed clergy that were voiced at the scheme's inception. Since the annuity provided depends on the number of surviving widows in any year, the yearly payment to a widow will decrease over time as more widows come into the system, until a steady state is achieved. On the positive side, Price praises the design of the Scottish Ministers' Widows' Fund, with one caveat: the calculations used to design and maintain the scheme may have included an underestimate of the number of widows that may soon come into the system.

Life annuity calculations, when done directly from life tables accompanied by interest tables, are time-consuming and onerous. For his valuations Price relies on Thomas Simpson's tables of life annuity values and on Abraham De Moivre's time-saving assumption that for a given group of people of the same age, the number of survivors decreases linearly as the people in the group age. Based on his own mortality investigations for the towns of Northampton and Norwich, as well as Halley's life table, Price embraced De Moivre's assumption. Figure 8.4 shows the number of survivors from ages 10 to 93 in each of Northampton and Norwich, along with a fitted straight line; the linear approximation is reasonable for both towns.

The problem with De Moivre's overall approach is that for valuing joint life annuities he had made two contradictory assumptions about mortality, the linear and exponential assumptions for survival. Price shows that the valuation of joint life annuities employing De Moivre's two assumptions together results in the annuity's being undervalued. Consequently, Price took a result from Simpson's 1742 *Doctrine of Annuities and Reversions* which values joint life annuities based on the linear assumption only and still provides a shortcut to calculations directly from a life table.

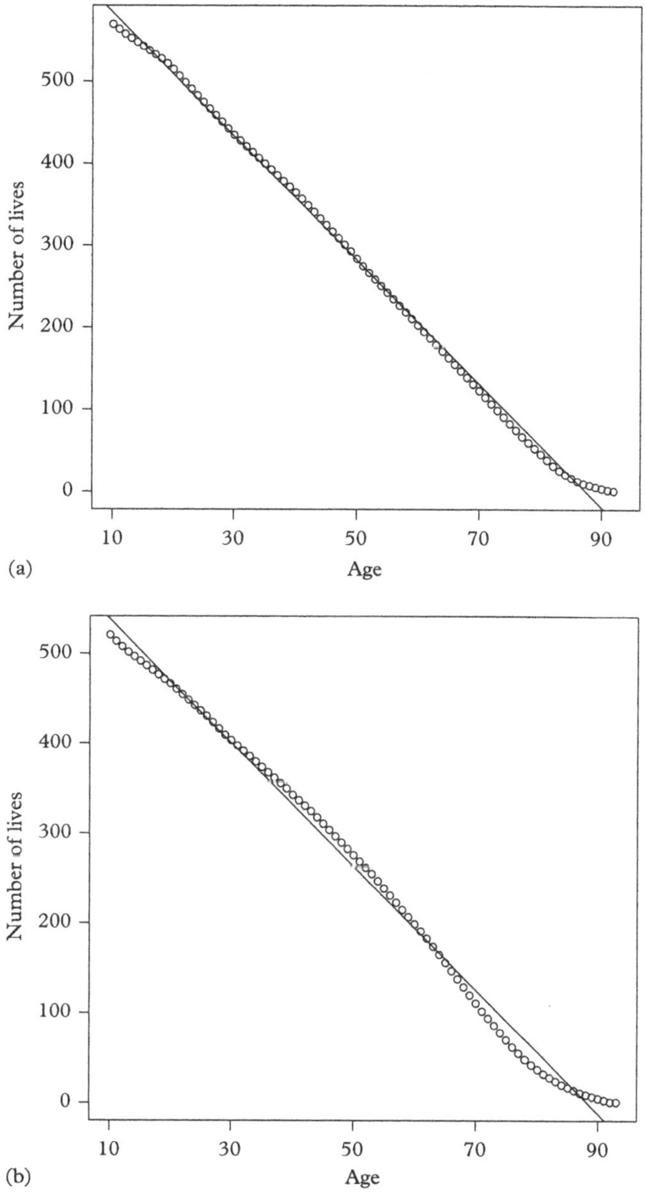

Figure 8.4. The survivor functions for Northampton and Norwich approximated by a straight line

Table 8.5. *Income and benefits of seven annuity societies in London*

Society name	Age at membership	Initial payment (£)	Annual premium (£)	Annuity payment (£)	Income to benefits (%)
Laudable Society of Annuitants	20	11.55	2.20	44	57.6
	40	105	6.70		64.7
	60	0	6.70		36.7
Amicable Society of Annuitants	20	1	1.35	26	46.0
	40	31	6.00		52.7
	60	1.05	3.60		34.8
Provident Society	20	1.05	1.80	25	63.7
	40	31.5	8.40		68.1
	60	0	5.25		51.0
London Society of Annuitants	20	2.125	2.80	50	56.5
	40	35.125	14.70		59.0
	60	0.125	6.70		36.8
Equitable Society of Annuitants	20	1.525	2.50	50	49.9
	40	32.125	13.00		52.6
	60	0.125	6.70		36.8
London Union Society	20	9	3.075	54.6	28.6
	40	63.25	16.133		30.3
	60	10.25	8.40		22.1
Rational Society	20	0	2.35	30	66.0
	40	8.4	8.80		43.9
	60	0.525	6.10		49.7

To understand the severity of the shortfall in funds for the annuity societies in London, I examined some of the societies that offered deferred annuities as shown in Table 8.4. Slightly narrowing down the list, I focused on those societies whose annuity benefit payments typically began at age 50. Information on the societies' premiums and annuity payments are taken from William Dale's 1772 *Calculations Deduced from First Principles.* As Dale did, I used Simpson's 1742 life table for London and a 3½% annual rate of interest compounded semi-annually. Simpson's table was used in order to reflect the potential mortality experience of the annuity societies in London and the interest rate was the approximate current rate at the time. To find the shortfall in each society, I calculated the ratio of the present value of the premiums charged by a society to the present value of the benefits paid by the same society. The results are shown in Table 8.5. In all cases, the premiums cover less than 70% of the value of the benefits to be paid.

Each society is eventually headed for bankruptcy. The "best" society of them all is the Provident Society, with premium to benefit ratios coming close (but not very) to 70%, while the worst is the London Union Society, which barely covers 30% of its expected costs. Bankruptcy will happen later rather than sooner in these operations, since the first annuity benefit to be paid is 10 years in the future. Further, as Price noted, the annuitants who will be hurt the most are those joining these societies when they are younger than 40; their benefits will be deferred more than 10 years and may begin only when a society is starting to feel financial stress.

I have made reference to William Dale and his 1772 work *Calculations Deduced from First Principles*. Just prior to Price's publication of *Observations on Reversionary Payments* Dale became interested in life annuity societies. From 1766 to 1770 he had been the household steward for Henry Somerset, 5th Duke of Beaufort, where his duties included paying the servants their wages, and the tradesmen who were hired to carry out work at the Duke's country residence, Badminton House, as well as paying taxes and buying provisions for the household.[65] As he expressed it in his book, while he was in the Duke's employ 100 miles from London, he saw a manuscript copy of the terms of admission to one of the London annuity societies (most likely the Laudable Society, based on the value of the entry fine and the premiums that Dale describes). He wrote to the society in June 1768 expressing his desire to become a member, and at the same time his concern that the capital of the society would not be sufficient to pay the annuities that would be drawn on the society, beginning in 1776. He became a member and thought no more about his financial concern until he left the Duke's employ and went to London, where he attended his first general meeting of the society in 1770. At the meeting he learned that the managers of the society had never properly ascertained whether, in Dale's words, "the foundation was a rock or sand." The experience led him to challenge the management of the Laudable Society and to investigate the viability of several annuity societies. *Calculations Deduced from First Principles* contains the results of his investigation.[66] Along the way, in September 1771 he noticed an advertisement for the position of Secretary to the Provident Society, that was open.[67] In his letter of application, Dale outlined in detail the financial shortcomings of the Provident Society, a précis of which is given in the Provident Society's entry in Table 8.5. Dale also let the proprietors know that he was making similar calculations for all the other societies and that these should appear in print early in the next year. He did not get the job.[68]

Table 8.6. *An extract of Dale's calculations to compute the present value of a life annuity*

Age 50	Living 224	Reversion	Pres. value of pay. To survivors	Total of the products
50½	219½	× 0.982801	= 215.7248195	
51	215	× 0.965898	= 207.66807	
51½	210½	× 0.949285	= 199.8244925	
52	206	× 0.932959	= 192.189554	
52½	202	× 0.916912	= 185.216224	
53	198	× 0.901143	= 178.426314	£1 000.62316
53½	194	× 0.885644	= 171.814936	
54	190	× 0.870412	= 165.37828	
54½	186½	× 0.855441	= 159.5397465	
55	183	× 0.840728	= 153.853224	
55½	179½	× 0.826269	= 148.3152855	£829.0125005
56	176	× 0.812058	= 142.922208	

The full title of William Dale's 1772 book is *Calculations Deduced from First Principles, in the Most Familiar Manner, by Plain Arithmetic; for the Use of the Societies Instituted for the Benefit of Old Age: Intended as an Introduction to the Study of the Doctrine of Annuities*. It is apparent from the latter part of the title that there was a pedagogical aspect to the book. Certainly everything, theory and calculation, is explained in great detail. After about 275 pages of explanation of the working and pricing of annuities, along with examples, there is finally an application showing the inadequacies of the pricing of the products that were being promoted by the annuity societies. Instead of the premium to benefit ratios I have given in Table 8.5, Dale calculated the present value of the premiums and the length of time it would take a society to run out of money paying its advertised benefits. Dale did not take Price's route of leaving the mathematics to an appendix and it detracts from the readability of his central argument that the annuity societies were headed for trouble.

In the first 275 pages, one of the explanations, which is unique among all of these annuity books, is of how to carry out the onerous calculations that were involved in finding the present value of a life annuity. It was an explanation by example. How Dale did his calculations is probably close to what Edmond Halley, Richard Hayes, and perhaps a few others did. The entries in Table 8.6 are the first dozen entries out of a total of 85 from a table in *Calculations Deduced from First Principles* used to compute the present value of a life annuity for a person currently aged 50 who pays £1 every 6 months where interest is 1¾% compounded semiannually. The life table that Dale used for Table 8.6 was calculated by Richard Price based on the Bills of Mortality of London from 1759 to 1768. This life table shows lives and deaths at integral ages. Dale obtains the midyear number of lives by taking the average number of lives at the two surrounding integral ages. This is the same as assuming a uniform distribution of deaths between the two ages, an assumption that actuaries today commonly make. The first column in Dale's table is age, followed by the number living at each age in the second column, taken from Price's life table. The third column shows the present value of £1 to be paid one, two, three, etc. time periods in the future, calculated at 1¾% interest. The numbers were probably taken from some published tables of compound interest. The fourth column, the present values of the payments made to the surviving lives, is the product of the second and third columns. Since paper was expensive, the multiplication was probably carried out longhand on a slate. To reduce addition error, five numbers at a time are summed from column four to obtain column five. Dale's table extends to age 92½. The final tally in the fifth column is the present value of £1 paid every 6 months for life to a person currently aged 50. The fifth column can also be used to find the present values of term life annuities and deferred life annuities. For an annuity for a person aged 50 who pays until age 60 or death (a term life annuity), whichever comes first, the value is the sum of the numbers in the fifth column up to age 60. For an annuity that begins after the 60th birthday (a deferred annuity) the value is the sum of the numbers in the fifth column after age 60 to the end of the table. To find the present value at another age requires another table of calculations.

Price's *Observations on Reversionary Payments* had a nearly immediate impact. In a June 1771 issue of *Bingley's Journal or Universal Gazette* a reader wrote to the printer quoting extensively from a section of Price's book which condemned several of the annuity societies on their lack of long-term viability.[69] In the same month *London Magazine* reproduced the introduction to Price's book in its book review section and concluded with:[70]

This work seems to be the result of much study, and is at this time, when annuity societies are hourly multiplying, particularly necessary for the perusal of the public.

By August the *Gazetteer and New Daily Advertiser* prefaced a news report with:[71]

> The Observations of Dr. Price on the many Societies for the Benefit of Age, having caused great difficulty in the minds of the public, respecting the probability of their permanence.

The writer went on to say that the Provident Society met to adopt a plan that they thought would fix future financial shortfalls, but that no other society had made any reforms. The Provident Society carried on until August 10, 1773, at which time, at a general meeting of the society, it was dissolved.[72] Price himself recognized his impact, as evidenced in a letter dated August 3, 1771 which he wrote to his friend George Walker, another Nonconformist minister and mathematician, like Price, whom Price had recently successfully nominated to fellowship in the Royal Society. Price writes:[73]

> The Treatise I have lately published has gone off better than I expected. The London Societies are in general alarmed. I wish I may prove the means of breaking them, or engaging them to reform. They have in their present state a very pernicious tendency.

Price went on to say that his comments on the national debt were of more importance and that he wanted Walker's comments on that part of his work.

What was probably the first of these societies to fall, fell quickly. The Friendly Society of Annuitants did not last long enough to undergo Dale's analysis, published in 1772. Within months of the publication of *Observations on Reversionary Payments*, a member of the Friendly Society wrote to Price with a printed description of the premiums and benefits of the society. As Price describes it, some of the members wanted to dissolve the society, while several older members and a few younger ones wanted to carry on. Price wrote to the directors of the Friendly Society with an analysis of their scheme, tearing it apart. Subsequently, the directors called a meeting of the society, published Price's letter in the *Public Advertiser*, and in the same issue of this newspaper published the following advertisement:[74]

> At a General Meeting of the Members by Adjournment, on Friday last the 26th ult. [26 Oct 1771] the Plan of the Society was taken into Consideration, and proved insufficient to answer the Purposes set forth therein; the Members then present were fully convinced that the younger Members would never receive the Annuity promised, and that the older Members could not enjoy it many Years: A Motion was therefore made to dissolve the Society, and to return each Member a just Proportion of the Admission Fines and Quarterly Payments; the numbers for the Dissolution were forty-nine, against it eleven.

Most of the remaining societies collapsed within the next 2 years.

Throughout this entire episode no new mathematical theory was developed for the valuation of annuities. All the groundwork had been laid by Halley in 1693, by De Moivre in 1725, and to a lesser extent by Simpson in 1742. And this groundwork was inspired mainly by property-based life annuity questions. The work done by the mathematicians in the 1760s and early 1770s was for the most part calculation combined with practical perspicacity. Mathematicians like Price used time-saving approximations and tables. Others, like Dale, abandoned the approximations and spent many hours making longhand calculations when they determined that the published tables, also calculated by longhand, were not available.

9 The Aftershocks of the Bubble, Their Impact on Life Annuities

Did the annuity bubble of the 1760s end in complete victory for the mathematicians and lead to the new establishment of an industry whose product design and valuation would be dominated by mathematicians as protoactuaries? The answer is a definitive no. Even in the nineteenth century there was a proliferation of life insurance companies that ran into financial difficulty. What did happen from the 1770s to the end of the century was a slow but growing appreciation in the general public of mathematics and mathematicians in the insurance and annuity industries, and in other areas that dealt in life-contingent contracts. This is seen almost exclusively in life annuities. With the exception of the Equitable Society, life insurance companies continued for the most part to ignore the mathematicians.

Three annuity societies survived the annuity bubble: the Laudable Society for the Benefit of Widows, the Laudable Society of Annuitants, and the London Annuity Society. These were also the three that had been longest on the scene. Their desire to carry on might be related to the amount of investment that had accumulated in these societies by the time Price called the viability of each of their operations into question. What turned out to be a stumbling block for many, especially rank and file members of the societies, is that they saw large positive balances on their society's books. There was no appreciation of the need to maintain a reserve of funds to cover the large expected future liabilities of the society. What eventually allowed these societies to survive is a reformation of their premiums and benefits. Reform, when it came, was sometimes slow to happen and sometimes insufficient.

The London Annuity Society was the first to reform. Price's *Observations on Reversionary Payments*, which was critical of the London Annuity Society, was in the booksellers' stalls by early June 1771.[1] The society's reform was made by early February 1772.[2] No society records survive, so that it is difficult to pinpoint exactly what reform was made; and other surviving sources are not in total agreement. For a five-guinea entrance fine and a five-guinea annual premium payable in advance, the original annuity benefits were £20, £30, and £40 per annum, provided that the husband had been a member of the society for at least 1, 7, and 15 years, respectively. In 1773 Price reports that the annuity of £40 was removed and the membership time required to obtain the annuity of £30 was increased to 15 years or more.[3] This reform, Price says, would still not be enough to keep the society from running out of funds. A comment about the society's annuities that appears a year earlier in the press claims, in agreement with Price, that the benefits had changed to an annuity of £20 per annum. At slight variance with Price, it is claimed in the letter that after 15 years as a member the annuity benefit would increase above £20 to an amount that the society could afford. After 25 years an additional increase might be made.[4]

An argument against this reform using the society's own deed of settlement was made by a lawyer, Thomas Warren of the Inner Temple. It hinged on the wording of Article 10 in the deed of settlement from 1765, which states:[5]

> In Case it shall happen by Reason of great Mortality, or any other unforeseen Cause, that the Interest of the Capital and annual Payments should not be sufficient to pay the said Annuities, it shall be lawful for the Directors to make a Call, upon each of the Members equally of such a Sum, as shall in the whole be sufficient, to make good such Annuities, provided only that the said Call, shall not raise the annual Payments of each Member above six Pounds; but should it so happen that the payment of fifteen Shillings extraordinary from each Member, in any Year shall prove insufficient, the highest Annuities at that Time existing shall be reduced, so far and so long only, as shall be necessary to make and keep the Income and Expense of the Society equal.

On the surface it looks as if the directors of the society, after reading Price's criticisms of their society, were correct in taking some action. There was evidence that the funds would "not be sufficient to pay the said Annuities." The action they took was that "the highest Annuities at that Time existing shall be reduced." Warren focused on the concluding part of that phrase, "so far and so long only, as shall be necessary to make and keep the Income and Expense of the Society equal." He argued that the society's fund was currently in surplus, so that the actions taken by the society violated the deed of settlement; no changes could be made until the fund was reduced to zero. Warren was an early antagonist, who ignored expected future liabilities in the balance sheet and the necessity to maintain a reserve of funds to meet these liabilities.

The reforms, though insufficient, were made and the issue was not revisited until 1780, when again the directors saw that the financial situation of the society called for action.[6] Both the directors and the membership liked the concept that the size of the annuity payment to the widow should be tied to the husband's length of membership in the society. They thought that more contributions over time deserved more benefits. They considered three different benefit plans, each of which had an increasing benefit amount as the length of membership increased. The simplest of the three under consideration was a base payment of £20 per annum payable on the death of the husband. Should the husband reach the milestone of 16 years as a member of the Society the annual payment would be £25 and at a milestone of 26 the annual payment would be £30. The directors consulted with William Dale, by that time known for his publications relating to annuity societies, and James Horsfall from the Middle Temple, known for his mathematical abilities. The two evaluated each plan and made comments on them. In his fourth edition of *Observations on Reversionary Payments*, published in 1783, Price reports on the end result only.[7] Saying that "some able judges were consulted," he thought that, if he had been correctly informed, the benefit structure had been set at an annuity of £20 per annum, which would increase to £24 if the member survived in the plan for 15 years. Price thought the plan was feasible provided that the five-guinea entrance fine and the five-guinea annual premium, payable in advance, went toward financing the benefits only and did not include any administrative expenses. Price died in 1791. Near the end of his life the London Annuity Society was taken over by the Society for Equitable Assurances on Lives and Survivorships. Price was probably involved in the valuation of the London Annuity Society's policies.[8]

The oldest of the three societies, the Laudable Society for the Benefit of Widows, has the most surviving information, allowing a more detailed look into the role of mathematicians after the annuity bubble burst. It took about 3 years from the time that Price's *Observations on Reversionary Payments* was published in 1771 (there was a second edition in 1772 and a third in 1773) until the Laudable Society carried out some reform of its premiums and benefits at a meeting of the Society on June 23, 1774. Three major changes were made at this meeting:[9]

1. For new members, the original admission fine of five guineas was augmented by another fine, depending on how many years older the husband was than his wife. The amount was two guineas times the age difference if the husband was more than 2 years older than his wife and three guineas times the age difference if the age difference was more than 5 years.
2. The original plan, which had no restriction on the age differential between husbands and wives, was changed to a maximum of 10 years for new members.

Table 9.1. *Changes to the Laudable Society's benefit structure*

	Number of years the husband has been a member						
Original	>1	>2	>3	>4	>7	>10	>13
Reformed	>2	>3	>6	>8	>11	>13	>15
Annuity payment	10	15	20	25	30	35	40

3. The annuity amounts to be paid remained as given in Table 8.1, but the length of time that the husband had to be a member before the payments came into effect was increased as shown in Table 9.1.

The road to reform in the Laudable Society for the Benefit of Widows was not an easy one, and the reforms that were carried out do not appear to be the reforms that the mathematicians consulted may have recommended. Benjamin Webb also resurfaces as a kind of rogue mathematician. Earlier in 1768, in his exchange with John Rowe in the *Gazetteer and New Daily Advertiser*, he had been inconsistent regarding some calculations. When pressed he agreed with Rowe. This time he was again inconsistent, and this inconsistency was used by the forces lining up against reform of the Laudable Society.

At first glance, the three reforms instituted in 1774 appear to have been a late response to the mathematicians' criticisms concerning the long-term viability of the society. The mathematicians, Price in particular, had predicted that the annuity societies would run into trouble in the long term as more wives became widows. Rather, the reform that happened was the result of a long struggle between the directors of the society, who wanted reform using the help of mathematicians, and many members who did not.

No reform had occurred by early 1772. A strongly worded letter to the printer of the *Morning Chronicle and London Advertiser* appeared on February 8, 1772. The writer, who called himself "Benevolus," called for the Laudable Society for the Benefit of Widows to follow in the footsteps of the London Annuity Society and reform their scheme. Benevolus used calculations from Price's recently published *Supplement to the Second Edition of the Treatise on Reversionary Payments* to demonstrate the insufficiency of the society's scheme. He concludes his letter with:

> What is it, or who is it, that so perniciously misleads you? Ought you not to consider, that, by carrying on a scheme so insufficient, you are providing relief for present annuitants by plundering future annuitants, and subjecting yourselves to their execrations?

Whether it was this letter or their own reading of Price's work, the chairman and directors of the Laudable Society decided to take action. Their first step along the road to reform was to call in some mathematicians to provide advice about what the premiums and benefits should be. They aimed for the top and consulted Richard Price, Daniel Harris (James Dodson's successor as Master of the Royal Mathematical School at Christ's Hospital), and James Horsfall. All three were recognized mathematicians and fellows of the Royal Society. Presumably Harris and Horsfall were approached additionally because Price, in view of his book, was not exactly an unbiased observer. Their report, now no longer extant, ran to at least 60 pages.[10] In the end the three mathematicians recommended increases in fees. For husbands and wives of the same age, the entry fine should be increased from five guineas to 10 guineas and the annual premium should be raised from five guineas per annum to eight. During September 1772 a letter was sent from Michael Fisher, the secretary of the society, to the membership, supporting the mathematicians' recommendations. He made an additional offer. Those who were not in agreement with the reform could opt to be paid 15 shillings in the pound for their investment; it was determined that if the society had been wound up in 1771, then all members would get about 13 or 14 shillings in the pound. The proposal was to be considered at a meeting of the society on October 8, 1772.

The proposal did not sit well with the membership. There were at least three letters of complaint in the newspapers. On receiving his letter from Michael Fisher, one member, who signed himself "Meanwell," argued on the basis of the society's current surplus. There was enough money to make a settlement of more than 15 shillings in the pound. An alternative was that current members should remain under the current plan and new members would pay the higher fees. Echoing the suggestion made by Thomas Warren, Meanwell argued that if the society ever ran out of money and could not fulfill its annuity obligations, then the clause in the deed of settlement (clause 27) could be invoked that would allow the society to collect fees from the members to cover any shortfall.[11] A little more than a week after this letter appeared, a woman wrote in with another argument. The letter begins:[12]

> Hearing you have it under the consideration of the members of your society whether they should spend a little more annually, or whether you should diminish our yearly slender allowance, at a time when we can least admit of it, viz. when we become widows, we, your petitioners, most humbly pray that you will take some pains (before you positively determine this measure) to consider of our husbands abilities to augment their expenses, and our readiness to submit to a diminution of our undoubted right and property.

The writer went on to say that if the reforms were carried through the members would "unite and combine against you to take the direction of affairs into our own hands." The last letter appeared on October 8, the day on which the general meeting was scheduled to take place.[13] Here the writer introduced the complicating factor of Benjamin Webb. The writer, who signed himself "Minos" (presumably after the King of Crete in Greek mythology who became a judge of the dead in the underworld), opened his letter with:

> The following observations on Messrs. Price, Harris, and Horsfall's Calculations, on a supposition that they are in the right, and Mr. Webb are in the wrong, are offered to your consideration.

In November 1771 Webb had written that the society would have no trouble in meeting its obligations. When confronted with Harris's calculations Webb wrote (after Minos had written his letter) that, based on his own calculations, the society's premiums should be about eight guineas (Webb says £8 9s 1½d), now agreeing with Harris, and essentially Price and Horsfall, who were all in agreement.[14] Putting Webb's submission aside, Minos took Harris's calculations and redid them under his own "traditional" assumption. Citing the common selling price in the marketplace of a life annuity of 7 years' purchase and remembering a case in the Court of Chancery from 1751, in which a widow aged 36 had the jointure in her marriage settlement valued at 7 years' purchase, Minos valued all the widows' annuities currently being paid by the society at the standard 7 years' purchase. Using this value and paying all the current members the full 20 shillings in the pound on their investments instead of 15, there would be about £228 left over from the society's current capital of £28,319. Consequently, there was no reason, Minos contended, to make any reformation of the society.

Just prior to the general meeting of October 8, a group of society members met twice, a week before and then 2 days before, to fight the proposed reforms.[15] Their agitation was probably effective. At the meeting on October 8, a majority of the members rejected the proposal. The chairman and directors of the society printed the decision in the newspapers and responded with a declaration:[16]

> The Chairman and Directors with several other Members present have signed a protest against the above resolution looking upon it to be inconsistent with the real interests and welfare of the Society which (according to the opinions of the most able Mathematicians and Calculators) stands in need of an immediate reformation.

What followed was more than a year of unrest within the society. Many members wanted to maintain the status quo. A smaller number saw the future financial problems that the society would face and wanted to take corrective action.

Since those in favor of reform had Price, Horsfall, and Harris on their side, the opponents of reform recruited Benjamin Webb (or he volunteered his services; it is impossible to say which). In mid-January 1773, there was some jockeying in the background over the credibility of Webb's opinion. Word had been circulated that Webb had written to Price and had agreed with Price's conclusions about the viability of the Laudable Society. Webb wrote to the newspapers stating that this was not true.[17] What is odd is that apparently Webb agreed with Price, Horsfall, and Harris that the annual premium should be eight guineas, but still thought that the society was in good financial shape. He seems to have been of the opinion that the financial problems facing the society were too far in the future to worry about now. In a letter to the *Public Ledger* he advised the Laudable Society:[18]

> A future and far distant Period, which I believe none of the present Members will ever live to see, may perhaps require such an Alteration [in the premiums]; but till that happens would advise you to remain as you are.

In other words, instead of planning to avoid a crisis, wait until the crisis occurs and then fix the problem.

Webb shows his incompetence in the interpretation of mortality data in a letter to the Laudable Society published in the newspapers.[19] He had been to the Laudable Society's office and had collected some data. He found that over a 10-year period, 18 members had died without leaving widows, 20 members had died leaving widows, 38 wives had died before their husbands and the husbands had quit the Society, and 16 members had been expelled. He gave a table of the numbers in each year from 1761 to 1770. He argued that if these 92 members leaving the Society were replaced by new members, then over the 10-year period the premiums collected would be over £4,000, enough to pay each of the 20 widows a reasonable annuity for their lifetimes (£18 10s, he calculated). He concluded that this argument is "plain Proof that your Society is not on a rotten and sandy Foundation." Webb's aggregate risk argument that supports the viability of the Laudable Society is fallacious. What Maclaurin, Wallace, and Webster had done for the Scottish Ministers' Widows' Fund was to take into account how the pool of participants and beneficiaries would grow and change over time until there was a maturity in the fund in terms of a steady state (income in a year matches annuity payments in a year). Webb immediately assumed the steady state situation and looked at the wrong group. He focused only on those leaving and being replaced, and the number of widows that these replacements could support. He grossly underestimated the number of widows that would receive annuities in the future. Of his 20 widows from the past 10 years of experience, there were none in the first 4 years that the Society was in operation, and then two per year for the next 3 years. In the final 3 years there were three, five, and six, respectively. Clearly the number of widows was increasing, so that past averages would not be good predictors of future ones.

Late in January 1773 the directors and a "considerable body of respectable members" were able to convince the membership at a general meeting to adopt a set of reforms, which would reduce the annuity payments by a factor that could be sustainable with the current premiums. The plan was approved by Price, Horsfall, and Harris. The only stipulation that the members put to the directors was that money should be raised to maintain the current widows at the annuity levels they were already receiving. Of the 300 or so members at the meeting the reforms were approved by a "prodigious majority."[20] Less than a week after the decision had been made, the opposition met and decided to hold meetings rallying those opposing the changes.[21] They invited Webb to present his case against Price, Horsfall, and Harris. For some months the press seems to have gone silent on the issue. The opposition must have won; beginning as early as the end of April, advertisements began appearing in the newspapers advertising Laudable Society's annuities at their original levels in 1761 and at their original premiums. The advertisements continued into February 1774.

What had been simmering for a year came to a boil in 1774. In January a petition was being organized to ask Parliament to dissolve the Laudable Society. The opposition mustered their forces. On January 20, 1774, a letter to the printer of the *Morning Chronicle and London Advertiser* made the basic arguments of the opposition. The society was flush with money, properly put into safe investments (3% consols). It had no problem paying the current set of 50 widows their annuities. There were 700 members in the society; they were satisfied with the status quo and not convinced by the argument that the society was not viable in the long term. What the writer missed in his analysis, as had Webb, is that the number of widows funded by the society was growing. There were 4 widows receiving annuities in 1766, 18 in 1770 and 50 in 1774. The opposition met during February and put forward a counter-petition. The petition to dissolve the society reached Parliament on February 25, 1774.[22] It was referred to a committee for consideration, chaired by the MP William Dowdeswell, who was recognized for his financial expertise. Dowdeswell had some prior experience with annuity schemes and their proper funding. Fourteen months earlier he had presented a bill to Parliament with the title "Bill for the better support of poor persons, in certain circumstances, by enabling parishes to grant annuities for life, upon purchase, and under certain restrictions."[23] Three days after the submission of the petition to dissolve the Laudable Society there was a general meeting of the society and a majority opposed the petition for dissolution. The petition to dissolve was signed by 46 members. By the end of the meeting the counter petition had been signed by 150 members and by the middle of March the number had risen to 248. Soon after the original petition was presented to Parliament, Dowdeswell was ready to consider writing a bill to dissolve the society but the House, possibly hearing of the opposition, decided to refer the matter to committee for further study. The counter petition was presented to Parliament on March 14. The whole matter was referred to committee to hear the arguments for and against dissolution.

The committee did its due diligence. It viewed the books of the society and questioned the secretary and other directors of the society. The committee also interviewed Price and Horsfall about the viability of the Laudable Society. The committee may have interviewed the opposition but to my knowledge no records have survived. What do survive are printed arguments from each side, three in favor of dissolution and one against.[24] From contents of the documents I would arrange them in sequence with the following interpretation.

1. In January 1774, when making a petition to dissolve the society was first considered, representatives of those favoring dissolution put together a three-page printed document outlining the poor state of the society and citing the plight of the Mercers' Company, which had to petition Parliament for money when its funds to support widows' annuities were depleted. They sought legal advice and found that the petition to dissolve would not be recognized in a court of law. Further, submitting the case to the Court of Chancery would be very time-consuming, since there would be many interested parties in the case. In the end they decided that the speediest solution was to petition Parliament.
2. When opposition to the proposed petition grew and Benjamin Webb was employed to demonstrate the viability of the society, the petitioners in favor of dissolution had another three-page document printed. This document contains, verbatim, what is in document (1). Added to it is a rebuttal of the arguments of the opposition and a list of quotations from letters by Benjamin Webb showing the inconsistencies in his opinions over a period of time from November

1771 to October 1772. This document was probably submitted to Parliament along with the petition to dissolve the society.

3. In response to document (2), the opposition printed a document that supported the continuance of the Laudable Society. They put forward two counter arguments. Firstly, they quoted several rules of the society from the deed of settlement including one stating that any amendments to the rules should be brought to general meetings of the Society. These rules had always been followed. The motions to dissolve the society (essentially an amendment to the deed of settlement) were denied by substantial majorities. The decisions of the membership should therefore be respected. Secondly, they argued, with the support of Webb, that the actual number of widows supported by the Laudable Society was much smaller than what Price, Horsfall, and Harris had predicted. They also brought in the experience of the Stationers' Company, which had a pension scheme for members and widows; this experience was also of a smaller number of payees than what the mathematical trio had predicted. What they glossed over was that the experience that they were using in support of their argument was in the short term (15 years or less) and Price, Horsfall, and Harris were arguing that problems would occur in the longer term. This document was probably submitted to Parliament at or near the time of the submission of the counter petition.
4. The document that was probably last in its composition is written by Richard Price and is dated March 22, 1774. Price testified before the House of Commons committee near the end of March, and so Price may have submitted this document to the committee during his testimony. Based on data from the Laudable Society and assuming that the society did not take in any new members, Price argued that the Society would be in a deficit position in about 20 years. The consequence of adding new members would be to postpone the time to bankruptcy by a few years. He used an aggregate risk argument estimating the yearly revenue and expenses of the society each year until the deficit occurred. Price published a similar but less detailed argument the year before in the supplement to the third edition of his *Observations on Reversionary Payments*.[25]

What the committee initially decided was to seek the opinion of another mathematician, hopefully with impeccable credentials. They chose Edward Waring, Lucasian Professor of Mathematics at Cambridge. Waring made his recommendation, which was reported to Parliament on May 17, 1774. Waring's recommendation was to make four changes to the premiums and benefits. Three of these changes were the ones

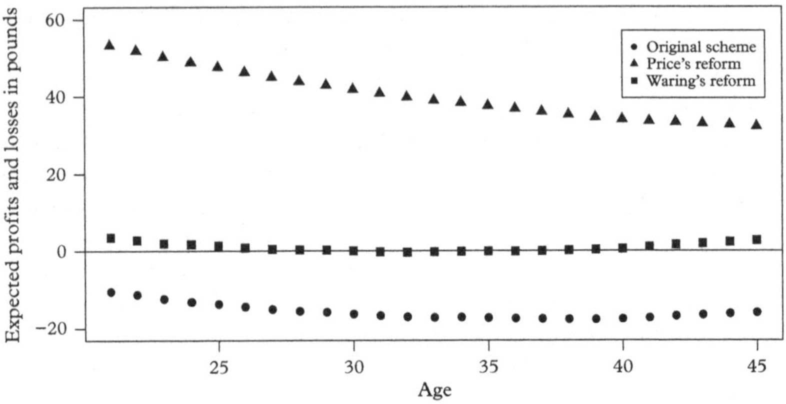

Figure 9.1. Reformed schemes for the Laudable Society: Expected profits and losses

that were adopted at a general meeting of the Laudable Society on June 23, 1774 and appear in Table 9.1. His fourth recommendation was to increase the annual premium of current members to six guineas. No changes were made to the annuities that were already being paid to widows and it appears that Waring's fourth recommendation was not implemented.

The simple reforms of a 10-guinea entrance fine and premiums of eight guineas suggested by Price (as well as Horsfall and Harris) applied only to the premium structure for the reversionary annuity offered by the Laudable Society; their proposed benefit structure remained unchanged. As before, the premiums are constant no matter what the age of the member or the difference in the age between the member and his wife. Consequently, if the reform is to cover the average couple, it will be conservative for couples who are of the same age. Waring's reform takes into account some age differences between the husband and the wife. Using Halley's life table (recommended by Price as appropriate to this society) and 3½% annual interest (also recommended by Price), I calculated the expected differences between the income and expenses under both reforms and compared them to those of the unreformed society. The results are shown in Figure 9.1. The unreformed society will lose money in the long run, Waring's reform brings the society very close to balance, but positive, and Price's reform is very conservative, as expected. On the surface it appears that Price was wrong; his premiums are far larger than necessary. That conclusion is too simple. Price's reform, based on an aggregate risk argument, was meant to correct for the 13 years of inadequate funding from the time of the Laudable Society's inception in 1761 to the early 1770s. Waring's reform, as implemented, ignored this.

Once the dust had settled on this reform the editor of *Gentleman's Magazine*, Edward Cave, writing under the pseudonym Sylvanus Urban, decided to ask the question generally about the financial situation of annuity societies. He set his question in the context of MPs in the House of Commons forming an annuity society. In the November issue of the magazine for 1774, Cave provided a list of MPs who had died each year between May 11, 1768, when the first session of Parliament was held after the 1768 general election, and October 1774, when a general election for the next Parliament began.[26] Then he imagined a scenario similar to that of the Laudable Society for the Benefit of Widows. Each member deposits five guineas at the commencement of Parliament and five guineas annually. Those members who die are replaced in by-elections. Their widows receive annual payments of £30, beginning a year after the death of the member. Assume a rate of interest of 3½% annually, the mean rate in the "public funds." Cave wanted to know what would be the capital of this imagined society in 6 years and 6 months, the total length of this particular Parliament. It was William Dale who responded to this query. His response was to provide a very clear and easy-to-follow aggregate risk analysis, clearer than the one presented by Price to the Parliamentary committee on the Laudable Society. Dale's clarity comes from the description of his assumptions and his explanation of them. Dale assumed that everything was computed semiannually, as was done in the Laudable Society. He assumed semiannual premiums of 2½ guineas, and benefits of £15 payable to surviving widows semiannually. He had deaths by calendar year and needed to have his results expressed on a May to April basis because of the beginning of the Parliamentary session. To do this he assumed that the deaths were evenly spread over the year, or in other words a uniform distribution of deaths. Based on this assumption he calculated the number of deaths in a year with the year beginning on the first of May. This gave him the number of widows each year that would begin receiving their annuities. For female mortality, he first calculated the average number of deaths per year among the 558 members and hence the estimated chance of death in any year among the members. This chance turning out to be about 1 in 46, he assumed the same rate of mortality for women. The pool of widows in any year then is the number from the previous year plus the new widows for the year (the known number of deaths of MPs given by Cave) minus the expected number of deaths (using the 1 in 46 model) in the pool of widows.

Dale further assumed that this imagined society was not a group of MPs but a "regular" annuity society, so that those men who became widowers during any year would quit the society and lose their contributions, but would be replaced immediately by other men. Using the 1 in 46 mortality rate among women, Dale estimated the number of widowers created each year that would drop out with each being replaced by another member paying the 2½-guinea fee on entrance. Dale then set out what in modern terms is a spreadsheet showing at every 6 months the value of the capital of the society. The capital is the income received from the members (558 plus the replacements during the 6 months, all times 2½ guineas) plus the interest earned on the accumulated capital at 1¾% semiannually minus £15 times the number of surviving widows.[27]

Waring's reform for the Laudable Society lasted 7 years. The most likely reason is the shortfall in income during the first 13 years of operation of the society that was never recouped. In April 1781 substantial changes were made to the scheme. The oldest age at admission was reduced from 45 to 35 and the annuity payments currently made to the widows were reduced by amounts that ranged from 15% to 35%. About 6 months later the annuity payment structure was changed. The payment classes were reduced from seven to four – £10, £20, £30, and £40 per annum, with associated membership lengths of 3+, 7+, 13+, and 20+ years. The author of the 1781 reforms is unknown. Waring's 1774 reform is his only known practical contribution to the valuation of life annuities. As a mathematician, he is much better known for his work on algebraic equations and number theory. Waring did make one foray into probability and annuities with a very difficult-to-read book published in 1792 and entitled *On the Principles of Translating Algebraic Quantities in Probable Relations and Annuities*. The nineteenth-century historian of probability, Isaac Todhunter, comments that Waring and his printer "have combined their efforts in order to render the work as obscure and repulsive as possible."[28]

The struggle to reform the other Laudable Society, the Laudable Society of Annuitants for the Benefit of Age, was just as intense but less visible. There are very few reports in the surviving London newspapers about the need for reform; and the directors of this Laudable Society were less inclined to reform than those of the older Laudable Society. The main driving force behind reform was William Dale, who had been a member of the Laudable Society of Annuitants from about 1768 or 1770. In his 1772 book, *Calculations Deduced from First Principles*, Dale shows the inadequacies of most of the existing annuity societies that offered deferred annuities rather than reversionary annuities. Dale's later book, *A Supplement to Calculations of the Value of Annuities*, published in 1777, is devoted mainly to addressing the problems and shortcomings of the Laudable Society of Annuitants, the only annuity society left from the group listed in Table 8.3 that offered deferred annuities. Like his 1772 book, the one from 1777 is not an easy read; but it is an accurate assessment of the situation. As one reviewer wrote in 1777, "Mr. D's manner of composition is rather unpleasant; he is however right in the main point, his calculations being just, and sufficiently accurate."[29]

One of the issues in the reform of the Laudable Society of Annuitants is which life table to use in making annuity valuations. With respect to the Laudable Society for the Benefit of Widows, Price recommended using Halley's life table and 3½% interest annually. Dale makes the same recommendation for the Laudable Society of Annuitants and goes into some depth concerning his reasons.[30] There were only two generally available choices of life tables to use in the annuity valuations: tables based on the London Bills of Mortality, including Simpson's 1742 life table, and Halley's 1693 table. When comparing these tables, more die before the age of 70 in tables based on the London Bills of Mortality than in Halley's table. When translating this to the valuation of a life annuity issued at age 50, the valuation based on London tables will be lower than for Halley's table. In particular, the value of a life annuity issued at age 50 is 10.68 under Simpson's 1742 life table and 11.45 under Halley's table. If there is a fixed pool of money to buy the annuity, then the annual payments would be lower under Halley's table than under Simpson's table. For the financial health of the annuity society it would be better to be conservative and offer the lower annuity payment. A wrinkle in the decision to pick a life table is that Dale found among the members of the Laudable Society of Annuitants that even fewer members died before the age of 70 than was predicted by Halley's table. The opposition would not trust any life table and quoted from the first edition of William Maitland's *History of London* to make their point.[31] The opening sentence of the quotation is, "The Bill of Mortality of the City of London is certainly one of the most defective of its kind." The defect lay in the incompleteness of the data collected. Only the numbers of burials in parish churches in London were recorded; there were many other burial grounds in London for which no data were collected.

One of the stumbling blocks to reform in the Laudable Society of Annuitants was the admission fine system. For a person aged 40 joining the Laudable Society the fine as given in Table 8.4 is 100 guineas, or £105. Using Simpson's 1742 life table, at this level of the fine the income accounts for only 64.7% of the benefits to be paid. The fine had not always been set at 100 guineas. When the society first started in 1766 there was no fine. As the number of members in the society grew, it was decided to institute, and then to increase, the fine. The fine grew in seven increments until the level of 100 guineas was reached in 1770. The graph at the top of Figure 9.2 shows the number of members who joined at each admission fine level. The number of new members generally increased as the fine increased. The one large deviation from the trend is at 30 guineas, at which level 273 members joined the society. The trend in this graph seems counterintuitive; one would expect that as the fine increases the annuity scheme would become financially less attractive and so the number of additional members would decrease. The graph at the bottom of Figure 9.2 perhaps explains the increasing popularity of the scheme and also the resistance to reform. For this graph I used Halley's life table and a 3½% annual rate of interest, as recommended by both Price and Dale. From this graph it can be seen that those who bought in at the inception of the society had the expectation of enjoying benefits that were worth more than five times what they paid on average. Even at a fine of 30 guineas the benefits were worth in expectation about 3½ times what would be paid in. At the highest level of 100 guineas the member would still expect more from the scheme than what was paid in. The members may not have been capable of calculating exact numbers as I have done (or as Price and Dale could have done), but some quick arithmetic might make the scheme attractive to many. For a person aged 40, take the 100 guineas (£105) and add the premiums of £6.70 that would be paid for 10 years. This yields £172. Ignoring interest and mortality, the annuity of £44 would need to last only 4 years ($44 \times 4 = 176$) until the member made a profit from his payments. Without further examination this seems like a good risk to take, and the lower the fine the better the risk. It is no surprise that the main opposition to reform came from the group that had paid lower fines.

After publishing his *Calculations Deduced from First Principles* in 1772, Dale continued to agitate for reform of the Laudable Society of Annuitants. A committee of managers and members was formed to examine the state of the society's finances. They worked for a year and a half, and consulted both Richard Price and Benjamin Webb. What came back from the consultations, mainly from Price it appears, is a recommendation to follow one of four options:

1. For each member in the society, change the life annuity benefit so that the present value of the benefit is equal to the present value of the amount that the member has contributed.

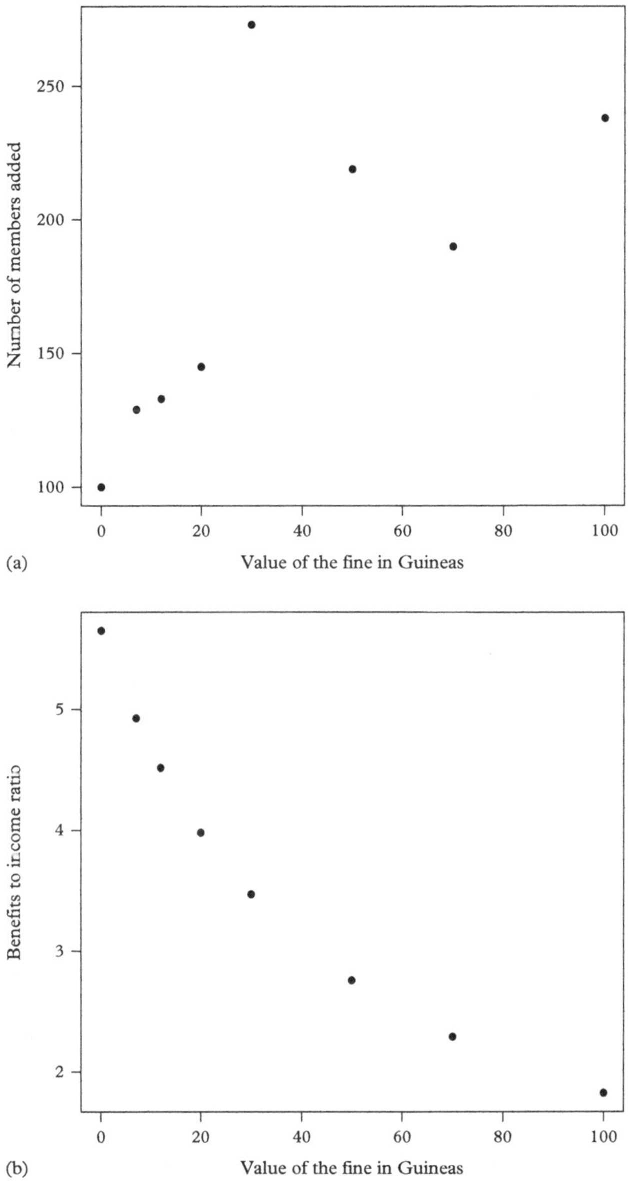

Figure 9.2. Effect of admission fine values in the Laudable Society of Annuitants

2. Keep the original life annuity benefit at the original level of £44 per annum. Find the present value of this annuity and compare it to the present value of the amount that the member has contributed. The member is required to make up the difference.
3. Change the starting age of the life annuity of £44 per annum from 50 to a greater age, so that the present value of the value of this annuity is equal to the present value of the amount that the member has contributed.
4. Return all the money that the member has contributed with simple interest at 3% per annum.

All the present value calculations for the benefits would be done using Halley's life table.

The decision that the Laudable Society of Annuitants took was to ignore all the recommendations and reduce the original annuity payment of £44 per annum to £24 per annum. This decision was made at a meeting of the society on October 26, 1775.[32] Price thought that the amount should be at most £15 and perhaps as low as £12. Price reported in 1783 that the annuity had been reduced by that time to £20 per annum.[33] Whatever decisions were made subsequently, the Laudable Society of Annuitants was still in operation in 1823.[34]

The methods for valuation of deferred and reversionary annuities all originate with De Moivre's 1725 *Annuities upon Lives*. The use of aggregate risk to value schemes, used extensively by Price, originates with the Scottish Ministers' Widows' Fund in the early 1740s. The one new concept that Dale introduces in *A Supplement to Calculations of the Value of Annuities* is the standardized mortality ratio (the ratio of the actual number of deaths to the expected number of deaths), although he does not call it that, calculating only the numerator and denominator, without making the final division. It is motivated by the discussion around the use of Halley's life table for these annuity societies.[35] If Halley's table accurately reflects the mortality of the members of the Laudable Society, then setting premiums based on this table would be a way to balance with the expenses that would be paid as annuity benefits. Dale then considers the pool of annuitants in the Laudable Society who would receive annuity payments beginning at age 50 or later if the member joins the society after age 40. He reasons that if mortality for this group is greater than what would be predicted by Halley's table, then the society would be in a surplus position. On the other hand, if the reverse is true and the annuitants tend to live longer than expected, then the society would be in a deficit position. In his actual study, Dale goes beyond this by finding the actual and expected number of deaths in six age groups: under 21, 21 to 30, 31 to 40, 41 to 50, 51 to 60, and over 60 years of age. From the records of the society, Dale was able to have before him the number of society members living and the number dying at each age in steps of 1 year for each of the years 1767–74.[36] He could find the expected number of deaths at each age by multiplying the number living at any age by the probability of death of an individual over a 1-year period, using Halley's table to obtain the expected number of deaths. The summation of the actual and expected numbers for the entire study period in each of the six age groups provides an assessment of the mortality experience. Dale found that the actual number of deaths was greater than expected in the under 21 and 21–30 age groups, while the reverse was true in the higher age groups. Overall, summing over all age groups, the actual number of deaths was about 57% of the expected number of deaths.

During the turmoil over the financial viability of the annuity societies, the sun seemed to be rising on a properly funded annuity scheme; this was the scheme that William Dowdeswell submitted as a bill to Parliament late in 1772. The insight to be found in the events surrounding the bill seems more theological and political than actuarial. The bill had its origins the year before in a proposal made by Francis Maseres, a lawyer of the Inner Temple. The proposal was in a lengthy letter that Maseres wrote to the *Public Advertiser*; it appeared on July 22, 1771. The letter has the title "A Proposal for the Establishment of Life Annuities in the several Parishes of England, for the Benefit of the Infirm and Aged Poor." Through acts called Poor Laws, dating from late in the reign of Elizabeth I, there existed a system in England for the support of the poor. It was administered in every parish in the country and financed by property taxes in each parish, known as the Poor Law Rate. Maseres's proposal was meant to lessen the number that needed to be supported under the Poor Law system. Participants in Maseres's scheme would invest some of their savings with the parish authorities (the churchwardens and overseers of the poor), who in turn, would invest all the funds received in 3% bank annuities. Maseres recommended this investment since it was trading at below par. Using the life tables in Simpson's *Doctrine of Annuities and Reversions*, the annuities would be valued and paid at 3% per annum while the investment in the public funds bought below par would pay more than 3%, thus providing room to cover some administration costs. The whole idea behind the scheme was to get some of the people to save and invest, so that when they became aged and infirm, and unable to support themselves through their daily work, they would not need to draw on the Poor Law system. This would save the ratepayers money in the long run. The red flag to those opposed to the proposal was that Maseres also suggested that the Poor Law Rate would back these annuities. With the annuity bubble bursting and many annuity societies dissolving, property owners could envisage their Poor Law Rates rising rather than declining.

Maseres used the pseudonym "Eumenes" when he signed the letter in the *Public Advertiser*. It was an interesting choice, as Maseres probably saw parallels between himself and the original Eumenes. The original was secretary to Philip of Macedon and then to Alexander the Great, following in Alexander's train during his conquests in Asia Minor and India; Maseres served as attorney general in Quebec from 1766 to 1769 under the governor Sir Guy Carleton (later 1st Baron Dorchester) after the British conquest of French Canada. Eumenes was the only ethnic Greek who rose to power among the leading Macedonians after the death of Alexander; Maseres was a third generation Huguenot who had risen through the system in England. Eumenes was betrayed by his Macedonian soldiers and executed; Maseres had a serious disagreement with Carleton over how the newly conquered French Catholic population should be assimilated into the Protestant British colonies and was sent back to England. Eumenes is seen as a tragic figure, and 2 years after leaving Quebec Maseres probably also saw himself as one.[37]

Richard Price probably saw Maseres's proposal as printed in the *Public Advertiser* and commented on it favorably in a letter to an unknown correspondent.[38] One of Price's suggestions to his correspondent is that the annuities should be valued using Halley's life table, or the Norwich or Northampton tables that appear in the first edition of his *Observations on Reversionary Payments*. Simpson's tables applied only to mortality in London and were not applicable to the whole country. Using arguments similar to those Price used in examining the Laudable Society for the Benefit of Widows, Price contended that Simpson's table would tend to overvalue the price of a life annuity for areas outside London, so that income from the contributions would not support the scheme. Maseres followed Price's advice to the letter in a later version of the proposal that he published in October 1771 in the *Sussex Weekly Advertiser, or Lewes Journal*.[39] The revised proposal begins in exactly the same way as the letter to the *Public Advertiser*. Maseres then added some tables of annuity values using Simpson's life table, followed by a discussion of the appropriateness of Halley's life table or Price's Northampton table for country parishes. The proposal was now long enough (about 4¼ columns of print) for the printer to have to publish it in two parts over two issues of the paper.

Price also praised Maseres's proposal in the supplement to the second edition of his *Observations on Reversionary Payments*, which appeared in his publisher's bookshop early in January 1772.[40] As in the letter to the unknown recipient, the praise came with some suggestions. One suggestion, which appears in both the letter and the supplement, reflects some of the theological thinking of the time on poverty. Price did not want to discourage work while a person was capable of work and so he suggested that the annuity payments should not begin until age 55 or 60.[41] Maseres was of the same mind-set. In his original proposal in the *Public Advertiser*, although the title has the phrase "for the Benefit of the Infirm and Aged Poor," the proposal was meant for what Maseres called the "industrious poor." These were journeymen working in handicraft trades and household servants. According to Maseres, this group tended to spend their surplus wages on "idleness and pleasure," rather than planning for old age so as not to be a burden on the parish. When Maseres published his revised proposal as a pamphlet in 1772, his theology was the same as Price's but his conclusion was different.[42] He would not be strict on the annuity payments beginning at age 55 or 60 because the participants, by buying into the scheme, had already shown that they were "well disposed to an industrious course of living." Maseres sent his proposal to Benjamin Franklin, then living in London. Franklin wrote back praising the proposal and adding some of his own comments. Among Franklin's papers is a commentary (probably not Franklin's) on the proposal that reflects the same theology, but with different conclusions. The major issue was around making a single payment to buy this annuity early in one's career. The commentator thought that this might discourage marriage as the purchaser, because of saving for the single payment, may not be able to afford to get married. Perhaps more importantly from the point of view of the work ethic, the single premium followed years later by the annuity payment would lead the purchaser to think that the parish must maintain the purchaser in old age. To dispel this idea, the commentator suggested that the purchaser should make weekly contributions to the fund until the annuity commenced.[43] The theology of labor, with its Calvinist overtones, that is expressed in Maseres's proposal, and the comments on it, originate in the work of the seventeenth-century Puritan theologian, Richard Baxter.[44]

A few MPs led by William Dowdeswell took an interest in Maseres's proposal. Probably early in 1772, Dowdeswell met with Maseres and two other MPs, Edmund Burke and Sir George Saville, at Saville's house.[45] There the MPs suggested some changes to the proposal.

Subsequently, Maseres rewrote the proposal, published it in pamphlet form by mid-1772, and had printed enough copies "for use of such members of both houses of Parliament as shall be inclined to support it."[46] The three MPs met on several occasions, along with other interested MPs, at Saville's house to put the bill in a form to submit to Parliament.[47] It took until December 23, 1772 before the bill was given a first reading in the House of Commons. Prior to the first reading, Dowdeswell spoke to the intended bill in the Commons on December 11, 1772. In the speech, Baxter's theology peeks through as Dowdeswell outlines some of the advantages of the bill. In particular, Dowdeswell says:[48]

> In the first place, the poor will be the gainers, not only because the plan will make some provision for their old age, but because the prospect of future comfort, by means of sobriety and industry, will actually render them sober and industrious, and thus beget a habit, which will make their bodies more healthy, their lives longer, and their happiness greater.

There were several objections to the bill that Maseres lists and then refutes.[49] Baxter's theology again peeks through some of the objections. The bill would encourage idleness among men who could work and would also discourage ambition. Despite the many objections, the bill passed a third reading on March 5, 1773, and was sent to the House of Lords. Attached to the bill were two sets of annuity tables drawn up by Richard Price: one, meant for country parishes, was based on the Northampton life table in Price's third edition of *Observations on Reversionary Payments* and the other was based on the London table in Simpson's *Select Exercises*.[50] To deal with the practicalities of the proposed bill (not giving the poor too much money at once to fritter away), rather than annual payments, which appear in most tables of annuity valuations, Price makes his valuations based on quarterly payments. The bill passed its first reading in the Lords and then stalled at the second reading. A motion was passed on March 25, 1773 to postpone the second reading for 6 months. It was a motion meant to kill the bill. Since Parliament was normally prorogued for the summer – this time on July 1, 1773 – the bill died on the order papers.[51]

Ten years later Maseres was still interested in seeing this bill come back to life. His book *Principles of the Doctrine of Life-Annuities* contains a copy of the bill, a discussion of the benefits of passing the bill, and an expression of hope that the bill will be again brought before Parliament. Beyond the bill, the book was meant to be an introduction to life annuity valuations for people who did not know probability theory. In addition to copious calculations and lengthy numerical examples, it contains reviews and discussions of many previous books on life annuities and, in concert with Price's *Observations on Reversionary Payments*, a lengthy discussion of the British national debt. The most important contribution in the book is a review and comparison of several different life tables. In view of the overly meticulous attention to detail, the book is not a particularly easy read.

Through the efforts of Church of England clergyman John Acland, Price was involved in one more ill-fated attempt in Parliament to provide support in the form of annuities to the "industrious poor." Acland was motivated by what he considered the wrong-headed approach of MP Thomas Gilbert to reform the Poor Laws; Gilbert advocated increasing the size of workhouses, as well as other measures to tighten administrative and financial control over the application of the Poor Laws.[52] By contrast, Acland proposed the establishment of a nationwide friendly society financed by regular contributions from the working poor. His idea came from examining some friendly societies that had been established in Devon, where he had his parish. These friendly societies were small; they were not necessarily well run or properly financed; and their funds were not necessarily put into interest-bearing investments. Acland suggested a nationwide society with compulsory contributions from anyone ("anyone" is restricted to those earning about 4 or 5 shillings a week, i.e. the industrious or working poor) aged 21 or over. The contributions were set at 1½ pence a week for women and 2 pence a week for men, about 4% of wages earned. The benefits provided by this national society would be similar to those of the existing friendly societies: financial support in times of sickness or infirmity, financial support in old age, and a lump sum payment to cover burial costs. Price supported Acland's proposal and provided some calculations regarding the proper funding of the scheme.[53]

Acland's proposal was published late in 1786.[54] Very quickly there was interest in it, not only in Devon, but countrywide. Within a month of its publication Acland received letters of support signed by about 2,000 people.[55] Early in February a meeting was held in Exeter, during which a committee was struck to write a bill for Parliament that would put Acland's proposal into effect. Counterbalanced by this positive support, there were others who favored Gilbert's approach of expanding the workhouses.[56] While the two sides debated what each considered the appropriate approach for supporting the poor, the House of Commons gave permission to consider the bill on April 30, 1787.[57] Subsequently, the bill was brought before the House of Commons in May for the first two readings, was sent to committee, and then amended. It did not make it to the third reading before Parliament was prorogued. When the bill was first mentioned in the House of Commons on April 30, one of the MPs for Devon, John Rolle, rose to speak to it. Here is a key element from the report of the speech:[58]

> It was so extensive in its object, and of such serious importance in its consequences, that he should not have presumed to have taken the lead in such a very delicate and difficult business, had it not been at the express desire of his constituents, whose plan for the better regulation and provision of the poor, his worthy friend and himself were directed to submit to the consideration of the Legislature.

The quotation shows the influence of the February meeting at Exeter and points to the role that Rolle played over subsequent Parliamentary sessions. Rolle presented the bill again, or an amended version of it, twice before the Commons. The first revision, in 1788, suffered the same fate as had the original the previous year, and the second successfully passed the Commons on June 10, 1789. As with Maseres's proposal in 1773, the Lords used the same tactic to kill the bill – let the bill pass at least one reading and postpone the later reading until after Parliament is prorogued.

On the third and successful attempt in the Commons, the bill was accompanied by a set of tables. Price again enters the scene; he constructed the tables which show the costs for both pension and disability benefits. Attached to the original bill there are four tables showing:[59]

1. weekly contributions intended to cover the disability benefits associated with sickness and infirmity, where the contributions vary with the age of entry into the proposed national friendly society;
2. weekly contributions in the same form as (1) but directed to the pension benefit;
3. total weekly contributions for both disability and pension benefits; and
4. the lump sum fee or fine that a member would pay on entry to the society after age 21 if the member opted to make weekly contributions at the level of a 21-year-old.

The basic scheme and benefits can be deduced from these tables. It was intended that an individual would join this national friendly society at age 21 in one of 11 classes. The class corresponded to the amount the member was willing to pay each week; the base amount was 2 pence per week, covering pension and disability benefits, and rose by 1 pence in each of the remaining ten classes until the highest payment, 1 shilling per week. At age 65 the member was to receive a weekly payment or pension in shillings corresponding to what the member had paid weekly in pence (payments into the fund of 2 pence per week, for example, would result in weekly payments to the member of 2 shillings per week). At age 70 the benefit payments doubled. There were two kinds of disabilities, described as bedridden and infirm but walking, with associated benefits. Those who were considered bedridden would receive amounts equal to the pension benefits of a person aged 70 and those who were infirm but walking would receive the same benefits as those aged 65. After the bill was amended Price calculated additional extensive sets of tables. These are tables that determined "surrender values," or the amounts paid to a member on withdrawing from the society categorized by one who joined the society at a certain age, quit at another age, and did or did not pay a fine on entrance. There were tables for various ages at entry and exit, and for whether or not the member paid an entry fine.

Price's tables for sickness and infirmity benefits were probably the first actuarial tables of this kind.[60] There is no explanation with the tables attached to the bill before Parliament concerning how Price made his calculations. The explanation is given by Price's nephew, William Morgan, in a posthumous edition of *Observations on Reversionary Payments*.[61] Price had been working on revising *Observations on Reversionary Payments* but died in 1791 before it was complete. Morgan finished the revision and, based on Price's manuscripts, added in material on the national friendly society. He reproduced the four tables calculated for the first version of the bill and left out the extensive tables done for the amended bill. Following the table for sickness and infirmity, Morgan gave Price's two assumptions behind the calculation of it. First, Price assumed that for those under 32 years of age, about 1 in 48 of this group "will always be in a state of incapacitation by illness and accidents." This assumption for the most part was statistically based on the experience of various friendly societies already in existence; the 1 in 48 was a reasonable upper bound on the probability of finding a person under the age of 32 disabled. Second, Price assumed that this disability probability increases with age, and is related to increases in mortality with age. At higher ages the disability probability was a multiple of 1/48. The multipliers that Prices assumed are: 1.25 for ages 32 to 42, 1.5 for ages 43 to 51, 1.75 for ages 52 to 58 and 2 for ages 59 to 64. The only comment he gives for this sequence of multipliers is:

> The reason for assuming this rate of increase is, that the probability of duration of human life decreases after age 30 nearly in this manner, or so that a person of age 60 has but half the probability of living any given time that a person at 32 has, and consequently must be then doubly subject to the causes that produce sickness and mortality.

Taken literally, Price's obscure reasoning is false. Using Price's Northampton mortality table published in the first edition of *Observations on Reversionary Payments*, the survival probability of a person aged 32 to age 33 is 0.983, while the same probability for someone aged 60 surviving to 61 is 0.961. What Price probably meant was the median age at death for someone aged 32 was about age 60 (l_{32}/l_{60} is approximately 2 or half the people aged 32 would be alive at 60). Price's Northampton table gives age 59 and his Norwich table gives age 60 or 61.[62] The other multipliers are obtained approximately when examining l_{32}/l_x in the two tables when $x = 42$, 51, and 56 (rather than 58). However questionably he obtained his probabilities, the weekly contribution by the member was set at the maximum weekly benefit (given for those who are bedridden) times the probability of becoming disabled during the year.

10 Developments in the Life Insurance Industry in the Later Eighteenth Century

The turmoil in the Equitable Society over the charter subscriptions with Edward Rowe Mores at the center of the controversy eventually brought Richard Price into a 15-year relationship with the Society. The problem for the Society was that Mores seems to have done valuations for the special or unusual contracts and John Edwards, who became the actuary in 1767, was not a strong mathematician capable of easily making these valuations. Also, many of the directors who were opposed to Mores thought that he had set the premiums at too low a level. It is in this atmosphere that John Edwards began corresponding with Price; what survive are Price's replies to Edwards's queries written between August 1768 and March 1771. It is impossible to say why Price was chosen to be contacted or who in the Society recommended him. My guess is that it was Dr. John Silvester, one of the charter subscribers. During the controversy that erupted, Silvester chaired the meetings of the court of directors. He had at least some passing interest in pricing the insurances offered by the Society; he thought they were too low. And in the latter part of 1768 he was the only fellow of the Royal Society who was working actively in the Equitable Society's business dealings; Price had been elected a fellow in 1765. It was only in October 1768, after the correspondence with Edwards had been initiated, that William Mountaine, a charter subscriber as well as Dodson's friend and executor, commented very positively on Price. At the same time Mountaine said that he knew Price only by reputation. It seems that Price had been previously selected and Mountaine was called on to provide a character reference, probably because of the distrust that some of the new directors had in Silvester. If Silvester was the one to select Price it may have been through another Royal Society fellow, Price's friend John Canton. A few months prior to Price's initial involvement with the Equitable Society, Price was corresponding with Canton about calculations he had made concerning an annuity society.

The first set of questions that John Edwards posed to Price was concerned with annuity valuations. Here are the first two questions:

1. To find the value of a life annuity that would commence on the death of a man currently aged 60 and that is payable to two women aged 62 and 64 as long as either is alive.
2. To find the value of a life annuity payable to the same two women as long as either is alive, but which ceases on the death of the man.

Price looked through the same collection of annuity books that Mores had in his library, all the books on the topic by De Moivre, Simpson, and Dodson. He writes in his letter to Edwards that the first question could be solved using a result in Simpson's *Doctrine of Annuities and Reversions*. There was no published solution to the second question and so Price worked it out by himself. In these initial letters to Edwards, Price refers to calculations that were done "some years ago." It is apparent that Price had been working on annuity calculations long before his correspondence with Canton.

A question that Price answered in a letter of August 27, 1768 speaks directly to the issue of the charter fund subscribers, an issue that had been increasing in intensity throughout 1768. The original intention to compensate those subscribers who put up money to obtain a charter for the Equitable Society was to charge an additional 10 shillings per £100 of insurance sold, or ½% of the amount of insurance written. This amount would be divided among the charter fund subscribers. The question put to Price was how this should be reflected in single premiums and annual premiums both for insurance and annuities. Price pointed out that taken literally, this charge would be inequitable. For example, the single premium paid for £100 of insurance for a younger life is less than that for an older life, so that a younger person would have a higher portion of his or her premium go to the charter fund. These arguments carry over to annual premiums for both insurance and reversionary annuities. Price's general recommendation is that:

> The right way is to make additions to the annual payments less or greater in proportion to the greater or less value of the lives.

This is the basic idea behind the pricing of annuities and insurance.

Subsequent questions by Edwards and answers by Price cover a range of issues. There are practical issues, such as advice on table calculation; Price recommends that two people calculate tables for the Society independently and then compare the results. In a few letters Edwards appears to be learning and then practicing the fundamentals of life-contingent calculation; Price checks some of his calculations.

Some new ground is also covered on life insurance products and issues. With respect to products, Price explains how to value an insurance involving two persons, A and B, in two situations: (1) the insurer pays an amount to B on the death of A provided that B survives A for a given period of time and (2) the insurer pays an amount to B on the death of A provided that A dies within a fixed period of time and B is still alive after the fixed period. With respect to issues, Price explains how much to pay the insured if the insured is alive and wishes to sell his policy back to the Equitable Society. In more modern jargon, this is called the surrender value of the policy.

There is one question that Price could not answer. He was asked to calculate the probability that an unmarried person will marry and have a son. He could only reply, in his letter dated June 9, 1769, that "there are no rules by which the Chance can be determined." Price was confronted with this question 8 years later and, in view of the circumstances in which the question was framed, was forced to come up with an answer without data. He assumed that the probability is ½, essentially invoking the principle of insufficient reason.

In a letter to Edwards dated December 19, 1770, Price says that he has a book that he is sending soon to a printer for publication. This is his *Observations on Reversionary Payments*. He also wants to check some facts with Edwards. Was the Equitable Society founded under the direction of James Dodson? Did the Society offer single life annuities to commence immediately after purchase or after a specified age? It is interesting that in his 2 years of dealing with the Society he knew very little about what products the Society offered, even though in 1768 Edwards had sent Price a printed account of the Society. In the published book, Price says correctly that the Equitable Society was founded as a result of proposals made by Dodson and also describes generally the annuity products that the Equitable offered. Price also thought that the Equitable would be a great benefit to society if it operated properly.

Price's comments on the Equitable Society in his *Observations on Reversionary Payments* followed immediately after he had criticized the oldest existing life insurance company, the Amicable Society for a Perpetual Insurance Office, which had been in operation since 1706.[1] He acknowledges that the Amicable Society was useful but in a limited way. The policies were too restrictive. Access to membership was only for those in a certain age interval. There was no option for term insurance. There was no option for special insurances, for example a policy in which a husband could insure his life with the death benefit payable only if he predeceased his wife, a situation similar to that of a reversionary annuity or a marriage settlement. Further, the policies were inequitable: the benefits received did not depend on the value of the contribution but on the number of members who die in a year and the payments into the fund were the same regardless of age. Like a good philosopher, Price constructed a counter example which demonstrates how such an insurance scheme can be grossly inequitable. He assumes a society consisting of 1,000 members, all aged 36 on entry. At the death of a member, that person is replaced immediately by someone aged 36. Price then demonstrates that the early claimants will receive large death benefits and that these benefits will decrease over time, so that after 50 years of operation of the society the claimants will receive about half the original amount.

Just as the directors of the Amicable Society ignored William Whiston in the 1730s when he suggested that the Society move to age-based premiums, the later directors ignored Price and kept their life insurance benefits in the form of a mortuary tontine with level premiums for all ages upon joining the Society. Price's criticism did prompt a response from Charles Brand, a clerk in the Amicable Society serving as assistant to the Register.[2] The response came in the form of a 100-page book published in 1775 under the title *A Treatise of Assurances and Annuities on Lives*.[3] The trailer to the main title is *With Several Observations against Dr. Price's Observations on the Amicable Society and Others*. Only about three or four pages are devoted to the trailer. After a short introduction nearly 60 pages are devoted to reprinting the articles of association of the Amicable Society and subsequent amendments and bylaws. The last 30 pages or more of the book are devoted to interest and annuity tables, followed by a number of solved problems related to life annuities. Almost all of this material has been taken from other publications, including Simpson's *Doctrine of Annuities and Reversions*. Furthermore, some of the lifting of this material had not been done well; one contemporary, and very knowledgeable, reviewer of the book pointed out a number of errors and inconsistencies in Brand's treatment of life annuities. Further, tables from John Smart's *Tables of Interest, Discount, Annuities &c.* were copied incorrectly. Smart provides table values to eight decimal places, Brand to five. The copying was done by deleting the last three digits instead of rounding to five decimal places.

Several reviewers found the book wanting. Here are some quotations from their reviews:

The Critical Review (August 1775):[4]

We recommend the perusal of p. 133 of Mr. Dale's calculation to Mr. Brand, which may thoroughly convince him of the inequity of the plan of the Amicable Society.

The reader who knows where to find them all [the life annuity problems treated by Brand], and that there is not one Algebraical definition among the 21 problems he has borrowed, will be ready to smile on this, and will not deny that Mr. Brand is most completely qualified to write A Treatise on *Assurances*.

The Monthly Review (March 1775):[5]

We have been favoured with some pertinent and just remarks on this publication by an anonymous Correspondent; but it is hardly necessary to trouble our Readers with them: more especially as Mr. B. does not seem to be capable of misleading those who are at all conversant with subjects of this nature.

London Magazine (September 1775):[6]

Our author would have been much better employed in sitting at Dr. Price's feet to learn of, than in cobling together this treatise against him. He hath borrowed the tables and problems from Simpson and Smart Very little is his own, and from what is, he appears unequal to the subject of assurances and annuities on lives.

At eight pages, the review from *The Critical Review* is the longest and most profound and insightful of the three. Brand thought that perhaps Price wrote this review.[7] The above review in *London Magazine* is quoted in its entirety and may be just a very short précis on the editor's part of what had appeared a month before in *The Critical Review*. These magazines for the most part were literary magazines. What these reviews (at least two and possibly three independent ones) show are further examples of a growing appreciation among segments of the population of the mathematical issues behind life insurance and annuities on lives.

One point that Brand makes against Price's criticisms relates to the inequity of the premiums charged to members of the Society; Price wanted age-based premiums. Brand's response was that the Society admitted people in a 20-year age interval, of ages 20–40, and paid close attention to the health of the applicants. Brand thought that the risks associated with variation in health were much greater than the risks associated with the variation in age in this narrow age interval. The care the Society took in screening for health probably stemmed from its experience early in the century when the Society nearly collapsed, in part owing to insuring bad lives. The reviewer in *The Critical Review* dismissed Brand's point and pointed to page 133 of Dale's *Calculations Deduced from First Principles* where any scheme, and in particular the Amicable Society's scheme, with level premiums for all ages is described as a "glaring absurdity." Much more recently, Geoffrey Clark has argued that Brand's response was reasonable, since the risk of death in that age range over 1 year varied from about 1 in 100 to 2 in 100, according to Halley's life table.[8] Assuming that this negligible difference carried on as the policyholder aged, then other factors, such as screening for health status at admission, might outweigh these differences.

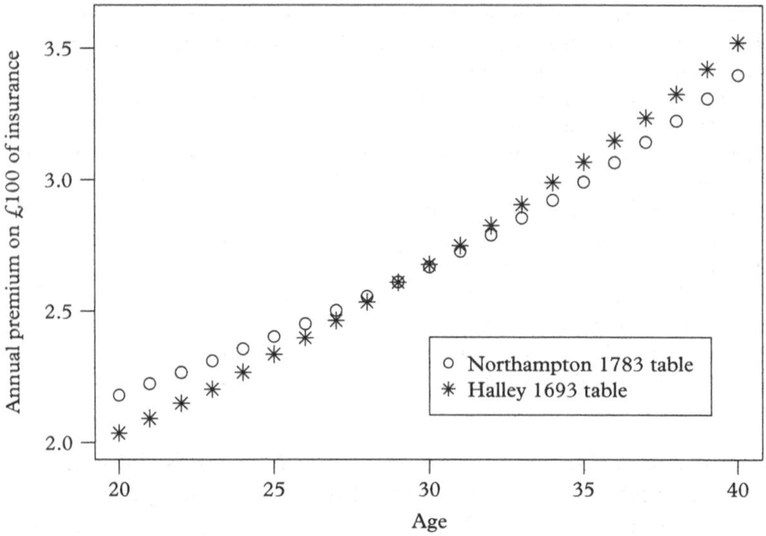

Figure 10.1. Premiums for a whole-life insurance of £100 payable at the end of the year of death

Although the risk of death is small, the age-based premium for a 1-year term insurance would double over the age interval 20 to 40, since the 1-year risk of death doubles over that age range.

The Amicable Society did not offer 1-year term insurance; rather it was insurance that extended over the life of the individual, with an annual contribution from the insured. To examine the differences in the risks of death more closely, consider the similarities between a whole-life insurance policy that Price was promoting and the mortuary tontine offered by the Amicable Society. In both cases a fixed premium is paid in and at death an amount is paid to a beneficiary. Of course, there are major differences. For the Amicable Society the annual amount paid in is constant over all ages (initially £6 4s when the Society was formed) and the death benefit is variable, depending on the number of deaths in the year. In whole-life insurance the annual amount paid in varies with age and the death benefit is constant. What kind of variability is there in the premiums for a whole-life insurance policy in the age range 20–40 years? Figure 10.1 shows the value of these premiums with a death benefit of £100, assuming either Halley's life table or the 1783 Northampton table and a 3% annual rate of interest, as suggested by Brand. Both life tables give similar premium levels at each age. In contrast to the situation pertaining to 1-year term insurance, the largest differences are less than double: under Halley's table the largest premium is 1.73 times the smallest and under the Northampton table the largest premium is only 1.56 times the smallest. Were these differences large or small in the eyes of a late eighteenth-century consumer? I will return to this question after examining some of the life insurance products of the London Assurance Corporation.

Brand responded at length in *The Critical Review* to the negative comments about his book that the magazine had published the previous year.[9] The article comes with a set of footnotes, almost certainly written by the reviewer from the previous year, which severely mock Brand's points of rebuttal of the original scathing review. The editor or editors must have been somewhat knowledgeable in the issues of annuities and insurance to allow this kind of response to Brand's response. On the positive side, Brand's response has the germs of a later publication that shows Brand in a much better light. Brand provides a table of mortality experience for the Amicable Society. From the Society's registers over the previous 11 years he tabulates the numbers who have died by each age of admittance between the ages of 20 and 45 (grouped for the early ages where there is little data), and then calculates the average number of years lived by those individuals by each age of admittance, as well as overall. The footnote writer complained about the "obscurity" of the last number. It is not stated in the article, but clearly Brand meant the average number of years lived after entry into the Society, not total lifetime. The footnote writer also knew what Brand meant and stated he had recommended the use of average future lifetime (or duration of life) in his previous review. Brand's calculated average future lifetime is about 19 years. He uses this number to argue in favor of the equitableness of the Amicable Society, saying firstly:

> I think the durations thus marked [average lifetimes at each age] will evidently shew and confirm the reason for my objecting against Dr. P. and his adherents, who suppose the plan of the Amicable Society inequitable, without their knowing anything of the matter.

Brand goes on to argue that the average future lifetime of 19 years that he has calculated exceeds what might be calculated from mortality data from the general population, and so calculations of premiums from mortality tables are deceptive. The footnote writer at this point likes Brand's calculation of average future lifetime, but gives credit to the original reviewer of Brand's book, which is the footnote writer himself, by saying that such a calculation had been suggested in the original review. With the exception of perhaps one or two more positive comments, he continues to mock Brand's rebuttal throughout the rest of the article.

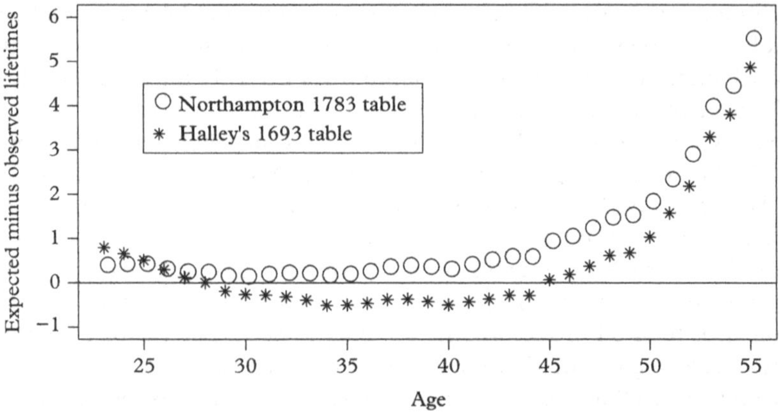

Figure 10.2. Differences between the expected lifetimes according to Halley's life table and the Northampton life table, and the observed lifetimes as calculated by Charles Brand for the Amicable Society

Brand delved further into the Amicable Society's registers going back from 1777 to the Society's inception in 1706 and extracted all the deaths. He published his results in the form of a broadside in 1778.[10] The first table in the publication has the same structure as what appears in *The Critical Review* – the average number of years lived by individuals extracted from the registers at each age of admittance. With 72 years of mortality experience he was able to provide a table for ages 12 through 75, with grouping of ages at the high and low ages, owing to the small number of lives at those ages. In his second table he essentially responds to the criticism of his table published in *The Critical Review.* Using the first table he calculates the average future lifetime for individuals at each of the ages 23 through 55, which is different from, but related to, the future lifetime from the time of admittance. To make the comparison, as Brand and his nemesis tried, to the mortality tables that were being used, I took the expected future lifetimes calculated from Halley's 1693 life table and the 1783 Northampton life table, and subtracted Brand's observed average future lifetimes. The differences are shown in Figure 10.2. A look at the x-axis begs a question. The maximum age at admittance was 45. James Dodson could not get insurance from the Amicable Society, since he was over 45. Why are the ages in Figure 10.2 given up to 55? The answer is given in the broadside. Some younger members sold their memberships to new members who were over 45. From the graph it may be seen that the Amicable's experience up to age 45, the official age of admittance, resulted in up to a year of additional lifetime when compared to the Halley's table and up to a year in lost lifetime when compared to the 1783 Northampton table. After the age of 45 the expected lifetime according to either life table is increasingly greater than Brand's observed averages. Two things may account for the differences in mortality experience at the higher ages. The first is adverse selection, which would tend to reduce the average future lifetime among Brand's policyholders. Older individuals buying their memberships from younger members may not be healthy lives. The other is that Brand only took into account those who died, and did not include any of the survivors in his analysis. This would give a downward bias to the calculation of average future lifetime.

The Amicable Society finally made the transition to age-based premiums in 1807.[11] It required a change to the charter incorporating the Society. The reason for the change may have been as a result of increased competition. In the 1790s at least two new life insurance companies began operation. The pace increased in the early nineteenth century with three new companies in each of 1806 and 1807.[12]

Another insurance company, the London Assurance Corporation, which had offered life insurance since 1721, was under Price's radar – or Price knew of it and ignored it. Premiums charged by London Assurance were not based on the probabilities of death as determined by life tables. Rather the person seeking insurance appeared before a committee to determine the applicant's health and lifestyle. Based on this information only, the committee decided whether or not to write a policy and then set the premium level.[13] Most policies were 1-year term insurance, while some were for less than a year and a very few for up to 2 years. Standard charges per £100 of insurance were £5, £5.25 (5 guineas), or £5.50 (£5 10s). The rates set were not arbitrary, but reflected the opinion of the committee on the risk to be assumed. Often insurance on soldiers was at the higher end of the scale. Sometimes the rate went to £6 or higher if the insured was over the age of 60 (the only situation in which the premium was "age-based"). Higher rates were also charged for someone doing a significant amount of traveling by sea during the period of insurance. Figure 10.3 shows the entry in London Assurance Corporation's books for a typical policy on an atypical person. In 1745 Philip Baker took out a 1-year term insurance policy of £110 on the life of Sir Alexander Cuming, best known for his single-handed efforts, in 1730, to negotiate a treaty with the Cherokee nation in America, which eventually brought the Cherokees under the sovereignty of Britain. The cost of the policy was 5 guineas per £100 of insurance. Cuming, who was in debtors' prison at the time that the policy was purchased, was also the person who had suggested a probability problem to Abraham De Moivre in 1721 that led to one of De Moivre's

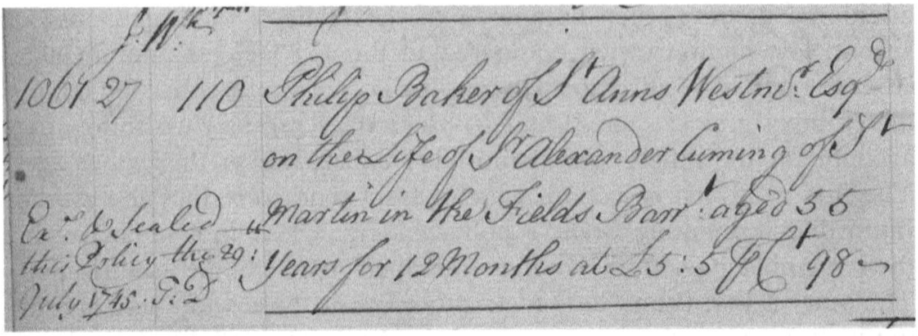
1061 27 110 Philip Baker of St Anns Westmr Esqr
on the Life of Sr Alexander Cuming of St
Martin in the Fields Bart aged 56
Years for 12 Months at £5:5 PCt 98

Figure 10.3. London Assurance Corporation policy on the life of Sir Alexander Cuming. *Source*: Photo by the London Metropolitan Archives, reproduced with permission from Royal & Sun Alliance Insurance plc

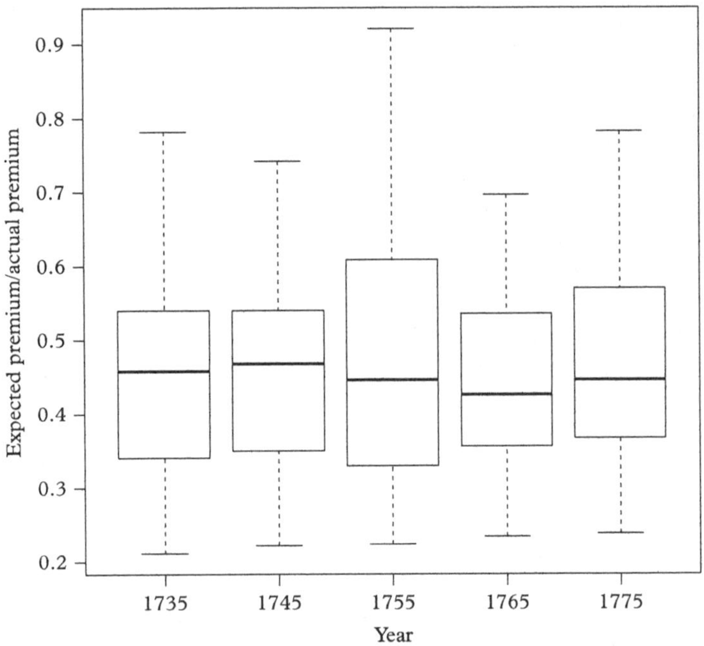

Figure 10.4. London Assurance policies by decade

greatest results in probability theory, the so-called normal approximation to the binomial. In prison during the 1740s, Cuming was still throwing out challenge problems in probability to other mathematicians.[14]

The fact that the premiums were not related to age can be seen in Figure 10.4. I have extracted the premiums from the corporation's books that show the premiums charged on all policies offered by London Assurance Corporation where the age of the insured has been given (the vast majority of cases).[15] This was done from the year 1735 in 10-year increments to the year 1775. Using the 1783 Northampton life table, I calculated the actuarially-based premium (the expected value of the benefit) for each of the policies written in the company's books and divided this amount by what London Assurance actually charged. In all cases the ratio is less than 1; the average amount required is less than what was charged. Figure 10.4 shows side-by-side boxplots of these ratios for each of the 5 years studied. A boxplot shows the distribution of the data, in this case the calculated ratios. The ends of the upper and lower lines show the maximum and minimum ratio values respectively. The upper end of a box shows the third quartile (25% of the ratios are greater than this value) and the lower end shows the first quartile (25% of the ratios are smaller than this value). The line within a box shows the median value of the ratios for that year. Not shown in the graph is that the number of life policies issued declined over the 40-year period; over 80 policies were issued in 1735, declining to 25 or less in 1775. What can be observed from Figure 10.3 is that the amount of variation in the ratios is similar for the 5 years that were considered. From the graph and from looking at the raw data, it appears that the mix of ages remained similar over time, as did the approach to premium pricing.

For some reason that I cannot uncover, there appears to have been a change in company policy regarding premiums in 1785 and/or 1787. No life insurance policies were written in the 2 years 1785 and 1786. Beginning in 1787, very few policies were issued each year (none in 1793, 1794, and 1795). One policy issued in 1787, which I have left out of the analysis, was much more complex than the others. It was a 5-year term insurance (previously the maximum had been about 2 years) in which the death benefit decreased in each of the 5 years during which the insured survived. The only thing I can connect to the changes that began in 1787 is that Edward Austen, who had held the position of secretary of the company, became the company's accountant in that year. Starting in 1787 and for the remainder of the century, the actuarial premium to actual premium ratio is higher and less variable. This is shown in Figure 10.5. It possibly indicates that some attention was paid to life tables and the proper mathematical calculation of premiums.

Near the end of Austen's term as accountant, London Assurance began charging age-based premiums. The first policy written this way was in 1808; it was a whole-life insurance policy with a death benefit of £1,000 for Stephen Lee, the company's secretary at the time.[16] The annual premium was set at £33.13 (in modern decimal currency). By 1809 the age-based premiums that were charged according to the

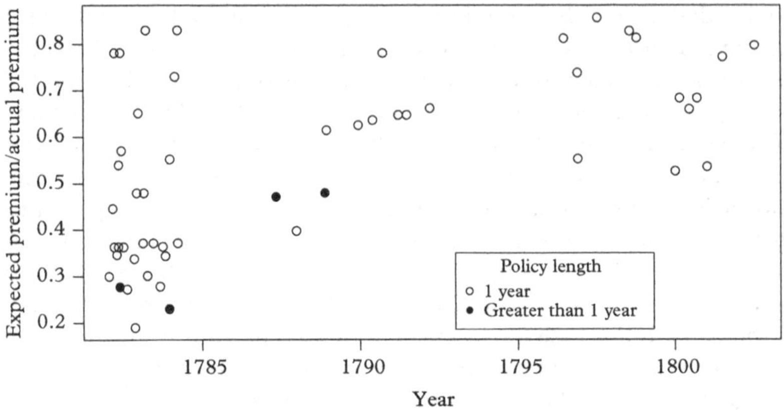

Figure 10.5. London Assurance policies 1782–1802

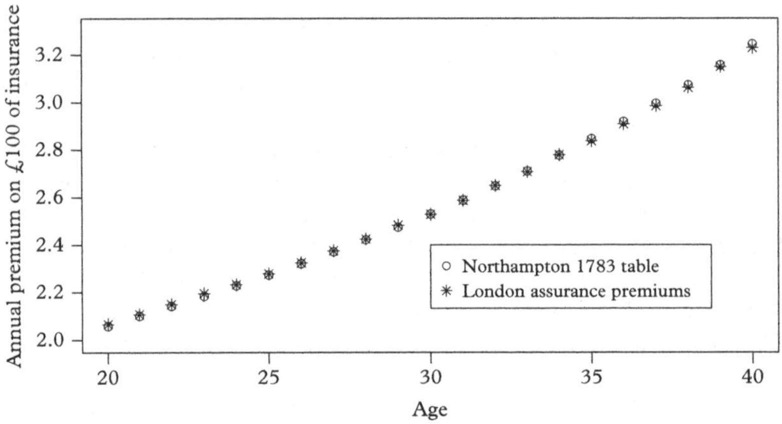

Figure 10.6. London Assurance premiums and the Northampton life table

Corporation's books conform, more or less, to an undated broadside advertising the premiums at various ages for whole-life and term policies offered by London Assurance.[17] The premiums were probably based on the 1783 Northampton life table using an annual interest rate of 3¾%. Figure 10.6 shows London Assurance Corporation's new age-based premiums for the ages of 20 through 40 and the calculated premium from the Northampton life table. London Assurance's change to age-based premiums may have been motived by the age-based premium structure instituted by the Amicable Society for a Perpetual Assurance

Office in 1807, as well as the entry of several new life insurance companies into the market in the late eighteenth and early nineteenth centuries. What is interesting about London Assurance Corporation's age-based premiums is that administrative expenses do not seem to have been taken into account in their calculation; no additional charges for applying for the insurance or for handling a policy claim appear on the broadside. These expenses must have been met either by wise investments of the premiums yielding a return of greater than 3¾% or by a careful screening of the health of the applicants.

The experience of the London Assurance Corporation can be used to address Clark's point about the small risk of death between ages 20 and 40. Figure 10.2 shows that the mortality experience of the Amicable Society is about the same (within 1 year for the average future lifetime) as indicated by figures given in the major life tables for policies issued before age 45. This gives strength to Clark's point. Brand's data cover the entire period 1706–77. In the early 1730s the Society was in financial difficulty due, in part, to its insuring bad lives. The fact that the Amicable's mortality experience is comparable to the Northampton life table, for example, means that the Amicable's later prudent approach to insuring lives provided a better than average mortality experience, which in the final statistics compensated for the early bad lives.

For me a greater question is whether the small variation in age-based premiums in the 20 to 40 age group is large or small in the eyes of a late eighteenth-century consumer. In the first half of the eighteenth century, many were willing to pay the London Assurance Corporation £5 or more for £100 of 1-year term insurance. Demand tended to fall off substantially in the last quarter of the century, and only a few policies were issued in the 1780s and 1790s. Following the bursting of the annuity bubble and the several editions of Price's book, I suspect that those in the populace who were interested in life insurance and could afford the premiums were becoming a little more savvy about issues surrounding the pricing of life insurance products. Earlier in the century consumers were interested in the product. They may also have been concerned about the viability of an insurer but were unable to assess it. Later in the century they became more aware of the issue of equitability and the connection between the mathematicians' approach to equitability and the viability of a company. The demand shifted to products that were equitable in terms of their premium structures.

Companies like the Amicable Society and the London Assurance Corporation had relatively simple business models, which included simple ways of determining the financial positions of these companies. London Assurance sold mostly 1-year term insurance, so that profitability could be roughly determined by finding the difference between premium income and death benefits in a year. The Amicable Society sold mortuary tontines. Its profitability for the year roughly would be the year's income from the subscribers less the total amount paid that year in death benefits. The situation for the Equitable Society is much less simple. There would be cash from premiums coming in during the year; but expenses to be taken into consideration would include not only the death benefits paid during the year but also the liabilities, in the form of future death benefits that the current premiums are paying for. In the very early days of the company, if it sold only whole-life insurance, there should be an accumulated surplus to cover future death benefits perhaps years away. What part of that surplus is profit or loss?

In a report to the Equitable Society in 1774, Richard Price outlined three ways to determine the financial position of the Society at any given time. The first is to look at the mortality experience of the Society and compare it to the mortality tables used to price the insurance. If the observed number of deaths is less than the expected number (fewer benefits paid than expected) then the Society is in good financial shape. If the situation is reversed, then the Society is in a loss position. This is essentially what Brand was doing in 1775 and 1778 for the Amicable Society. Price's use of this measure in 1774 gives credence to Brand's claim that Price wrote the review of Brand's 1775 book in *The Critical Review* and the footnotes to Brand's rejoinder. Price's approach is also the same as that of Dale's analysis of the Laudable Society of Annuitants in 1777.[18] The second way to assess the Society's financial position is a quick and dirty method resulting in a rough approximation of the financial position. In any year, sum the premium income from all whole-life policies and sum the total benefits paid on whole-life policies. Find the ratio of the two sums. Do the same for all term insurance policies for terms of up to 7 years and find the ratio. If the first ratio is greater than 1.5 and the second ratio is greater than 1, then the Society is in a good financial position. The third, and to Price the most useful, way is to find the present value of all future benefit payments the Society might make and the present value of all future premiums. The financial health of the Society is measured through an actuarial balance sheet: the funds on hand or invested plus the present value of future premiums minus the present value of future benefit payments. The construction of such a balance sheet can be a very time-consuming process when done by hand.

Price made at least two more major contributions to the Equitable Society. The first was that he encouraged his nephew, William Morgan, to study mathematics. Subsequently, Price recommended Morgan for the new position of Assistant Actuary at the Equitable Society when the position was created in 1774.[19] Morgan became Actuary in 1775 on the death of the incumbent actuary, John Pocock. The second contribution was the construction of a second and more extensive life table based on data from Northampton, a table that I have used earlier in the chapter for my analysis of the Amicable Society and the London Assurance Corporation.

The first Northampton life table appears in Price's 1771 *Observations on Reversionary Payments*. It was constructed from the parish registers of All Saints, Northampton. Like John Smart with his 1738 life table, Price had deaths or burials recorded for the age intervals of under 2, 2–5, 5–10, 10–20, and every 10-year group thereafter. There were 3,690 burials for the years 1735–70 in the registers, and 3,242 christenings. Since most burials were done in Church of England cemeteries and not all christenings were done by the Church of England (and not all were recorded in the parish registers), then both burials and christenings were underestimated, christenings more so than burials. Price's reasoning behind his method for life table construction ignores this issue. He considers the excess of burials over christenings (448) as the number of immigrants (he uses the words "settlers") into Northampton. To construct his life table he wants the number of christenings to be equal to the number of burials, and so the immigrants must be eliminated from the calculation. He assumes that immigration occurs at age 20 and above, and that the number of immigrants in each group is proportional to the number of deaths in that group. These numbers are subtracted from the reported deaths to get the number of deaths among those born in Northampton. Price uses 1,149 as the radix of his table ($l_0 = 1{,}149$) and so the numbers have to be further prorated to obtain 1,149 as the total number of deaths.

I have illustrated Price's method with the 1771 Northampton data in Table 10.1. The column labeled (1) in Table 10.1 is the number of deaths from 1735 to 1770 in Northampton as reported by Price.[20] The total number of deaths is 3,690. The deaths over the age of 20 appear in column (2) with the total number of deaths given as 1,898. The number of immigrants or "settlers" is the difference between the total number of deaths (3,690) and the number of births (3,242) or 448. These 448 deaths must be distributed over the age groups of 20 and over and subtracted from the deaths in these age groups to obtain the deaths among those born in Northampton. For example, in the 20 to 30 age group there are 297 deaths, of which 448 × (297/1,898), or 70, can be attributed to the immigrants, leaving 227 deaths among those born in Northampton (the entry in column (3)). Essentially column (3)

Table 10.1. *Construction of Price's 1771 Northampton life table*

Age group	(1) Reported deaths	(2) Deaths over 20	(3) Adjusted deaths	(4) Prorated deaths	(5) Deaths from the 1771 life table
0–2	1 206		1 206	427	427
2–5	276		276	98	97
5–10	155		155	55	55
10–20	155		155	55	55
20–30	297	297	227	80	80
30–40	257	257	196	69	70
40–50	297	297	227	80	81
50–60	300	300	229	81	81
60–70	293	293	224	79	80
70–80	285	285	218	77	77
80–90	155	155	118	42	42
90–100	14	14	11	4	4
Totals	3 690	1 898	3 242	1 149	1 149
Births	3 242				
Settlers	448				

is obtained by multiplying column (1) by 1 (first four entries) or by 1,450/1,898 or by 1 – 448/1,898 (last eight entries). The adjusted total number of deaths is 3,242. Since the radix of Price's 1771 table is 1,149, column (3) is multiplied by 1,149/3,242 to obtain the final table. This is shown in column (4). When the deaths in the 1771 life table (given in Appendix 2) are totaled by age group, column (5) is obtained. The slight difference between columns (4) and (5), my calculation and Price's calculation, is probably due to round-off error.[21]

Once the deaths for each age group had been found, Price had to distribute the deaths to each age within the group. In the age range 20–80 he did this by making an approximately equal number of deaths at each individual age. The age group totals conform, approximately, to De Moivre's linear survivor assumption and so the deaths at the individual ages should also conform.

The second Northampton table appears in the 1783 edition of *Observations on Reversionary Payments*. To construct this table, Price used the same parish in Northampton with an additional 10 years of data. He also reported deaths by the same age groups he had used in 1771. Price says that he used the same method of construction as he used in 1771 with one minor change. In the age groups 20–30 and 30–40, there were 373 and 329 deaths, respectively. In all other mortality data that he had examined, the younger age group always experienced fewer deaths than the older one. Consequently, Price set the deaths in

Table 10.2. *Construction of Price's 1783 Northampton life table*

Age group	(1) Reported deaths	(2) Deaths over 20	(3) Adjusted deaths	(4) Prorated deaths	(5) Deaths from the 1783 life table	(6) Adjusted deaths	(7) Prorated deaths
0–2	1 529		1 529	4 221	4 367	1 529	4 367
2–5	362		362	999	1034	362	1 034
5–10	201		201	555	574	201	574
10–20	189		189	522	543	189	540
20–30	351	351	283	780	747	262	749
30–40	351	351	283	780	750	262	749
40–50	365	365	294	812	778	272	778
50–60	384	384	309	854	819	287	819
60–70	378	378	304	840	806	282	806
70–80	358	358	288	796	763	267	763
80–90	199	199	160	442	423	149	424
90–100	22	22	18	49	46	16	47
Totals	4 689	2 408	4 220	11 650	11 650	4 078	11 650
Births	4 220						
Settlers	469						

these two age groups as the average of the two numbers, or 351.[22] As I have done with the 1771 data, I tried to reproduce Price's results for 1783. This is shown in Table 10.2, columns (1) through (5). The method is the same; the reported deaths have changed, as well as the multiplier, to get from column (2) to column (3). The 1771 multiplier is 1,450/1,898 or 1 – 448/1,898; the 1783 multiplier is 1,939/2,408 or 1 – 469/2,408. On comparing columns (4) and (5), no close agreement can be found, unlike looking at the results for 1771. Price must have done something different. In decimal form Price's multiplier 1,939/2,408 is 0.80523 to five decimal places. I tried different multipliers and found one that fit the 1783 table. The multiplier is 0.7465, resulting in columns (6) and (7). There is a much closer agreement between column (7) and the deaths from the 1783 life table shown in column (5). It is a mystery why Price changed his methodology; the 1783 *Observations on Reversionary Payments* gives no hint and based on the data, I cannot justify the multiplier that I used to get column (7).

Price was motivated to construct the second Northampton table as a result of his work with the Equitable Society. He saw the Society as a useful and valuable institution and wanted to see it prosper. One of the routes to prosperity was through the proper construction and use of annuity and insurance tables.[23] Dodson had intentionally constructed a mortality table to be very conservative in the pricing of life insurance. Price felt that now that the Society had been in operation for several years, such extreme conservativeness was no longer necessary. Rather, a life table such as Halley's life table would be appropriate, since it captured an average mortality between the high mortality in large cities like London and the much lower mortality in villages and small country parishes. Added into this mix is that further tables were needed for the operation of the Equitable Society. The Society sold annuity products, including those valued on two or more lives. Since Simpson's tables for joint life annuities were based on London data, they were not appropriate for the Society in that they priced the annuity products too low. Other joint life annuity tables or valuations, those done by Dodson for example, were based on the linear survivor curve assumption, which would approximate Halley's table. Such an assumption was not appropriate for those who were under the age of 20 and over the age of 70. As a first step to computing actuarial tables, Price decided to construct a new life table from the Northampton data. Why not stay with the first Northampton table and make all the table calculations necessary for insurance and annuity values? These would be the numbers attached to all those symbols a_x, a_{xy}, A_x, $A^1_{x:\overline{n}|}$, P_x, and $P^1_{x:\overline{n}|}$. The most probable answer is that the Equitable Society wanted its tables calculated to a higher degree of precision than what had been available. Simpson's tables, for example, were calculated to one decimal place. Price reports that the Equitable Society's tables calculated from the second Northampton table were made to four decimal places.[24] I would conjecture that by increasing the radix in the first Northampton life table by an order of magnitude ($l_0 = 1{,}149$ in the first table to $l_0 = 11{,}650$ in the second table), it was felt that the second life table with a larger radix would improve the precision in the calculations. Price does comment that when the larger radix is used it is easier to approximately equalize the number of deaths at each age within an age group.[25]

The second Northampton life table may have been published in 1783, but it was constructed in 1781.[26] In the 1783 *Observations on Reversionary Payments* Price indicates that the Equitable Society had already calculated some tables. This was actually an extensive set of tables done by Morgan and his assistant, covering several manuscript pages in notebooks, that includes annuities for single and joint lives as well as insurances for single and joint lives, calculated during 1781.[27] The final table ("Table the Ninth," in Morgan's words) covering several pages of a notebook in which Morgan and his assistant made their calculations shows the complexity of the products that were offered (compared to those offered by the Amicable Society and London Assurance Corporation) and the amount of work that went into pricing them. It is a table that shows the value of the benefit of £100 to be paid provided that one life survives another. The table includes by age the value of the single premium if the contract is paid at once, the annual premium, and the annuity payment to the beneficiary if the £100 is converted into a life annuity. The amount of work that went into constructing this table is indicated by two notes inserted by Morgan. Written on the fly-leaf of the notebook is: "Begun this Table May 31st 1781 WM." At the end of the notebook is: "Finis W Morgan Novem^{r} 3^{d} 1781."[28] In all, a 5-month labor with all arithmetical calculations done by hand.

In his role as actuary, William Morgan applied Price's methods of determining the financial position of the Equitable Society. He found Price's second method, the rough approximation to the financial position, of little use and discarded it. Price's other two suggestions have evolved into standard fare for actuarial valuations. Morgan calculated the mortality experience of the company on an annual basis. He also constructed an actuarial balance sheet showing the surplus of the Society. This he did beginning in 1776, not annually but initially irregularly, settling into about once every 10 years.

In 1790 Morgan was elected fellow of the Royal Society. Two of his sponsors were Richard Price and Francis Maseres.[29] Two years prior to his election, Price presented to the Royal Society the first of a series of five papers by Morgan, all published in the *Philosophical Transactions of the Royal Society*, on valuing some fairly complex life-contingent contracts.[30] They were in the general area where Price had pointed out an error made by De Moivre for the specific case in which the benefits paid depend on the order in which people die. Over five papers Morgan outlined a whole series of situations and provided solutions for them all. Here is one of the more complicated cases that Morgan solved. There are three people in the contract. Call them A, B, and C. The policy pays £1 if A is the first or second to die of the three and B dies before C. Morgan's solutions were obtained using a life table like the Northampton table and assuming that deaths in any year of age are evenly distributed over the year, or the "uniform distribution of deaths." I recall solving this kind of problem in an actuarial examination I wrote more than 45 years ago.

Morgan continued to work for the Equitable Society until his retirement in 1830. Until about 1800 he was the only person working in the life insurance industry with the title "actuary." It was at the turn of the century that more mathematicians became involved as actuaries in the life insurance industry. By 1848 there was a professional association of actuaries, the Institute of Actuaries, established in London.

11 A Return to Roots

Richard Price's impact was enormous, not to developments of actuarial theory but to actuarial practice. He was the leading figure who publicly promoted the idea of the proper actuarial valuation of annuities. The impact of the work of John Rowe and William Dale was important but less far-reaching than that of Price's. With the help of William Morgan, there was a spillover effect into the proper pricing of life insurance. Though old habits die hard, the bursting of the annuity bubble in the 1770s marked the time when the general application of actuarial methods in the life insurance and life annuity industries began to take hold. At the same time, the mathematicians did not lose sight of their roots. Many who were active in the 1770s and 1780s (Rowe, Price, and Morgan among them) continued to carry out work as consultants when life-contingent contracts arose involving property. As for the earlier generation of consultants that included De Moivre, Dodson, Jones, and Simpson, the information on these consulting activities is sparse: Rowe's notebook on his consulting cases between 1775 and 1790 happens to have survived in a transcription, and what little information exists about Price's and Morgan's activities was found by chance discoveries and careful combing of online catalogs of archives.

Perhaps the mathematicians' biggest client in regard to property was the Church of England. Throughout the eighteenth century, many landowners moved away from leases for lives to leases for fixed terms. The dioceses of the Church of England did not, and many continued to hold leases for lives well into the nineteenth century. The easiest (and standard) way at the time for a church official to evaluate fines for the renewal of leases was to equate a lease on three lives to a lease for 21 years and then to refer to published tables, such as Mabbut's *Tables for Renewing & Purchasing of the Leases* or later versions of them. By the end of the eighteenth century this had changed slightly. In the Exeter Cathedral Archives there is a manuscript from 1806 that shows a table comparing the renewal fines for various types of leases – leases for lives and leases for fixed terms.[1] For fixed-term leases, the table produced by Newton, the successor to Mabbut, was used. For leases on lives, standard values are mentioned in only two cases: replacing one life in a lease when the remaining two are under 50 years of age, and replacing two lives when the third and surviving life is under 50. The renewal fines in these cases are 1½ years' purchase and 6 years' purchase, respectively. These two amounts are only slightly greater than the traditional 1 year's and 5 years' purchase for church-held lands.[2] The other difference from tradition is that there is some minor recognition given to age.

As in Thomas Simpson's experience, outlined in his letter of January 21, 1756 to the Dean and Chapter of an unnamed cathedral, mathematicians were called in to consult on "difficult" cases, which might be described as complex life-contingent contracts not covered by tradition or published tables. There are a few surviving records of consultations on these issues, made by mathematicians in the 1780s and 1790s. They all come from Exeter and the mathematicians consulted were John Rowe and William Morgan.

In 1781 and 1782, the priest vicars of Exeter Cathedral consulted Rowe on two nonstandard (for them) cases in leases for lives. The cases were nonstandard because the surviving lives were over 50 years of age. In one case Rowe was asked to evaluate an estate that brought in £95 per annum in rent that was leased on three lives aged 82, 53, and 52. The valuation was requested and given in two situations: either the youngest or the oldest life was replaced by a person aged 8. The second case was a house rented on one life aged 60. In this case the valuation was requested and given for adding two lives aged 20 and 15 to the lease.[3]

William Morgan was consulted in 1786 concerning a case involving lands held by the Bishop of Exeter.[4] It appears that that there was some dispute over some leases on lives for a manor in Cornwall. The manor was let on a lease for lives and the remaining (or perhaps only) lessee was aged 64. This lessee had subleased the manor into 108 farms let on leases for one, two, and three lives. By mutual agreement, by paying a fine the lessee could renew his lease with the bishop. Also by mutual agreement, the lessee could renew his subleases with his subtenants at any time before the renewal of his own lease. Should the bishop let his tenant's lease run out (i.e. his tenant dies without renewal) then all renewal fines from the subtenants would go to the bishop. This leads to a conundrum. If the bishop decides to let the lease run out, so that he becomes the landlord for the subtenants, then it is in his tenant's interest to renew as many subleases as soon as possible, to maximize his collection of renewal fines before he dies. The bishop is also aged 64, and if he takes the option of running out the lease, the subleases may not come up for renewal until after he is dead, so that the renewal fines will go to his successor. In the dispute it became necessary to know the value of the manor. Morgan was called in to do the valuation and did so in light of two different scenarios. These were based on the information that the current nominal rent for all subleases was £1,390 per annum with renewal fines bringing in an average of £300 per annum. Morgan reasoned that if the bishop renews his tenant's lease, then the value of the estate would be the present value of a life annuity of £300 per annum on two or three lives. If on the other hand the bishop lets the lease run out, the value is instead the present value of the reversionary annuity, £1,390 per annum, paid after the deaths of all the subtenants. In the documents the outcome of the dispute is not given.

As has been mentioned, for lands held by Exeter Cathedral the fine for replacing one life in a lease on three lives was typically 1½ years' purchase. In 1791 those in charge of the finances of the Cathedral wanted an estimate of the average yearly revenue in a portfolio of forty of these leases, totaling £550 per annum in value. They consulted Morgan, who made some simplifying assumptions to do the calculations: everyone on the leases was under age 75; when someone died, the person was immediately replaced on the lease; and there were lives of all ages on the leases. Among the 120 lives in total, Morgan assumed a yearly death rate of 1 in 40. He probably got this value by calculations from a life table; using the Northampton life table, the death rate per year in a group of people between the ages of 18 and 75 is about 1 in 40. Among the 120 lives on the leases, about three per year would be expected to die. With the average lease valued at 550/40 and a fine of 1½ years purchase, the expected annual revenue would be 3 × 1½ × 550/40, or 61.875. Without giving the details of his calculation, Morgan estimated the revenue at £62 per annum.[5] Morgan continued to carry out work for the diocese into the nineteenth century.[6]

The first set of tables to deal directly with leases on lives appeared in 1802, Francis Baily's *Tables for the Purchasing and Renewing of Leases*.[7] Baily was greatly influenced by Richard Price's work on annuities. Within a decade Baily's tables were joined by another publication, *Tables for the Purchasing of Estates* by William Inwood.[8] Inwood's tables became the standard into the 1880s. By the early nineteenth century these tables had replaced fixed-term annuity tables and were used by several dioceses in valuing renewals of leases for lives. An 1839 report on property held by the Church of England attests to this and also indicates that some mathematicians, now referred to as actuaries, were brought in for consultation on difficult cases.[9]

In the earlier generation of consultants that began with De Moivre, there was usually a direct contact between a person with landed or financial interests and the mathematician. This had changed by the 1780s. The bulk of Rowe's clients were Exeter lawyers or law firms representing clients with landed interests. Rowe was often called upon by the lawyers to find the value of various estates of interest to their clients when there were special conditions attached to the estate. Some were quite simple, such as the value an estate held for the lifetime of one individual (essentially the value of a single life annuity), or the difference in the value of an estate held on three lives when two of the lives are to be replaced by two others (essentially the difference in the values of the joint life annuities based on each of the three lives). Others were reversionary annuity calculations taking into account the line of inheritance of an estate. In one case the person who held the estate wanted to buy back the reversion from the person with the reversionary interest in order to hold the estate in perpetuity. There were complicating factors in this case, such as a marriage settlement charged to the estate and the ability of the estate holder, who was married and childless, to remarry on his wife's death and have children who could inherit. Another case shows the plight of Church of England curates, as previously illustrated in Fernando Warner's attempt to establish an annuity fund for London clergy. One of the law firms was handling the purchase of an advowson. The living would bring the clergyman who was the purchaser nearly £112 per annum gross. There were no clerical duties attached; the purchase price took into account a payment of £40 per annum to the curate, who would carry out all the clerical duties in the parish. Perhaps the saddest case was the valuation of an annuity held by the wife of a bankrupt that was held jointly on her and her mother's life with an additional reversionary interest on her mother's death.

Among Rowe's clients who were not lawyers were two clergymen and a builder from Exeter, as well as two gentlemen with landed interests, Edmund Granger and John Dunning, 1st Baron Ashburton. Granger and Dunning seem to have been acting in the way clients of mathematicians had in the earlier generation. Granger, a wealthy Exeter merchant, was inquiring of Rowe the value of an estate that Lord Ashburton was considering purchasing. There was some back and forth in the consultation. Rowe presented his calculations to Granger, which resulted in a letter from Ashburton (which has not survived) which apparently questioned the valuation. Part of the query was over the annual interest rate – Rowe had used 4½% instead of 5% – bringing to mind De Moivre's request in a newspaper advertisement in 1739 that the client should tell him in advance the agreed-upon rate of interest.

Rowe redid the calculation and thought the difference inconsequential, but said that if Lord Ashburton thought otherwise he could raise the rent by £1 a year. What other issues there were is not known, but some might be hinted at from Rowe's short concluding response to Ashburton via Granger:[10]

> Sure I am, that my friend Dr. Price, were he to be consulted, would join with me in opinion; and, I believe, my Lord Ashburton, will not dispute his understanding the subject of annuities; nor, indeed, does his Lordship mine.

Rowe's other clients, the clergymen and the builder, were also in direct contact with him. It is not entirely clear from Rowe's notebook, but it is a reasonable conjecture that the consultations were about the clients' personal finances. The Rev. Richard Hole asked Rowe to value a complex reversion on an estate held by a person aged 40. In 1787, when the question was posed, Hole was about 40 years of age. Two years later, Hole asked Rowe what £1,000 might buy in a life annuity for a person aged 78. Hole's father was about 78 years of age at the time. The Rev. James Bryatt and Giles Painter, an Exeter builder, both asked specific questions about life annuities and reversions for people who may have been of their ages.

William Morgan also carried out some consulting work outside the Church of England. In the 1790s the Duke of Marlborough apparently needed to pay some back taxes on his estates and decided to raise £30,000 to pay them. It was to be done by selling life annuities.[11] The novel attraction to his scheme was that the annual payments would increase over time. There were five different options to choose from; and the annuitants had to be between 45 and 70 years of age at the time of purchase, presumably so that the Duke's debt would be amortized sooner rather than later. For each scheme, based on an investment of £100, there were initial annual payments set for each of the age groups: 45–50, 50–55, 55–60, 60–65, and 65–70. Each of the options had a different amount by which the annual payment would increase. For example, in the first option the payment increased by 5 shillings every year; and in the second by £1 at the end of every 10 years. Morgan was involved in the design of the scheme in 1792 and with some corrections to the payment levels in 1798.

There was also a budding need for actuarial consultations in cases that went before the courts, the High Court of Chancery in particular. While the case of the sale of a reversion from the 1750s (*Nichols* v. *Gould*) mentions De Moivre and his "rule," no consideration was given to the fair price of the sale since, as the Lord Chancellor determined, no fraud was committed in the actual sale. By the 1770s and into the

1780s the fair price of annuities and reversions was again material in some legal proceedings, but with the courts listening to actuarial valuations. The earliest example I can find is in John Rowe's notebook. On June 19, 1779, the Exeter solicitor Christopher Gullett wrote to Rowe with a request for a valuation of a reversion (A grants to B a life annuity on the death of C, provided both A and B are alive at C's death):[12]

> Mr. Gullett's compliments wait on Mr. Rowe, with a Case, to desire his solution of the mathematical question there stated, which is of very considerable moment to Mr. Gullett's clyent, and therefore Mr. Rowe will please to give it due attention, as at all events it will be laid before the Lord Chancellor, either with or in preference to Mr. Horsfall's.

By the early 1770s James Horsfall was already known for his ability in annuity valuations regarding the dispute in the Laudable Society for the Benefit of Widows. Presumably, to make his case stronger, Gullett needed a second opinion. The outcome of the case is unknown.

The courts came to smile favorably on the mathematicians and their methods of valuation. The case of *Heathcote* v. *Paignon*, heard in 1787, was a precedent-setting case.[13] One of the issues was the price of a life annuity. The defendant Paignon had paid the plaintiff Heathcote £200 to buy an annuity that would pay £50 per annum to Paignon during Heathcote's lifetime. The market price (in this case 4 years' purchase) for a life annuity depended on a number of factors beyond health (Heathcote occasionally suffered from gout). It could be purchased in the marketplace at one price but sold only in the same marketplace by the same individual at a lower one. The price might also depend on whether the purchaser was buying the annuity on his own life or on someone else's life, and on what kind of security there was (such as land) backing the annuity payments. William Morgan was involved in the case, but only as a witness, testifying that Paignon had also taken out an insurance policy for £200 on the life of Heathcote through the Equitable Society. It was Charles Brand of the Amicable Society who gave testimony to the "fair" price of the annuity, which he put at 11.6 years' purchase. The court ruled in favor of the "fair" price, reasoning that:[14]

> If the court should take such a ground as to rest the case on the market price, every transaction of this kind would come into a court of equity.

From that point in time the court favored actuarially-based valuations when considering disputes over life annuities that came before the courts.

At about the same time Brand, Horsfall, and Morgan all had brushes with another Chancery lawsuit, *Clayton* v. *Kenrick*. There were four plaintiffs altogether, two Claytons and two Greshams. In his version of the case, John Kenrick claimed:[15]

They all admit, in their several answers, that it appears from a book by Mr. Morgan, Actuary to the Society for equitable Assurances on Lives and Survivorships, that 10,000 l. improved by the accumulation of interest, for a term of years equal to the probability of Sir R. Clayton's life, at the time aged thirty-eight years, will amount to 32,500 l. and upwards.

Horsfall, Brand, and Morgan were all called in to verify the calculation. From Morgan's book, the expected lifetime of a life aged 38 is 23.98 years; the accumulated value of £10,000 at 5% interest for 24 years is £32,251.[16]

The most complex life annuity consultation goes to Richard Price. It arose in 1777 when John Arthur Worsop, a wealthy but financially constrained landowner, wanted to get married. He needed to settle a sufficient sum on his bride-to-be that would pay her a life annuity if he predeceased her during the marriage. No marriage settlement, no marriage. His wealth amounted to £1,200 per annum in rents from his estates. From these rents he wanted to settle £400 per annum on his wife. The constraint was in how he held the land. It had come to him as an inheritance from a cousin, Richard Worsop, who had died in 1758. Richard Worsop left his estate to his cousins, siblings John and Hester Arthur. Hester never married but was alive in 1777, aged 69. Her brother John died in 1773, with his share of the inheritance going to his son John, who took the name John Arthur Worsop, as requested in the will of Richard Worsop. The constraint was that there was an entail on the estate. On Hester's death, the entire estate would go to John Arthur Worsop or his estate. Should he die without male offspring, the estate would go to another cousin of Richard Worsop, Herbert Ferreman. Herbert had died in 1760 and his heirs were his son George and daughter Ametha. To make the marriage settlement, John Arthur Worsop needed to put aside a fund that would compensate George and Ametha for their lost expectations of the £400 per annum put aside for the life of John's bride. It required an Act of Parliament to make the marriage settlement valid and all parties agreed to have Richard Price work out the expectations of each party.[17]

The question posed to Price is in two parts. The first is to find the total value of the reversion. The second is to find the shares in the reversion to which each interested party is entitled. The second part was expressed as:[18]

An Estate is to descend after the lives of H.A. [Hester Arthur] aged 69, and J.A. [John Arthur Worsop] aged 27, to the male issue of J.A. and the male Issue of that male Issue. But if J.A. does not leave male issue, or no male issue that leaves male issue, the Estate is to descend to G.F [George Ferreman] aged 22 [who was actually 25 at the time], for life; and after the 3 lives H.A. __ J.A.__ and G.F. it is to descend to the male issue of G.F. And for want of such male Issue, it is to descend after the three lives to H.F. [Herbert Ferreman] and his Heirs and Assigns for ever [meaning his daughter Ametha and her children].

Conforming to the differences between city and country mortality (Worsop's was a country estate), Price used De Moivre's approximations for life annuities, essentially Halley's life table. It was a reversionary annuity valuation with a twist. Price needed to make some additional assumptions about whether John Arthur Worsop and George Ferreman would have male children. He had no data and consequently set the probability for each to have a male heir at ½. Price found that the total value of the reversion of the £400 per annum was £1,556. Then he valued the interests of each of the four parties: the male heirs of J.A., G.F., the male heirs of G.F., and the heirs of H.F.

It sometimes happens when a consultation is requested that the consultant is not given all the information. This happened to Price in this case. After submitting his opinion on the value of the reversion and how it should be divided among the four parties, he was given an important extra bit of information. John Arthur Worsop's wife would not be entitled to the £400 per annum until after the death of Hester Arthur. Price redid his calculations and the total valuation dropped to £1,400. Again he found the share for each of the four parties. These revised amounts appear in the Act of Parliament, and by the act the funds were to be placed in trusts in the event that any of these four parties inherited the estate. Following the passage of the act, in 1778 John married Sarah Mauleverer, from a landed family.[19] Subsequently, the couple had a son and grandson.

12 Conclusion

Before about 1760, life insurance and life annuities in the marketplace in England had very little to do with mathematics, or actuarial science as we know it today, and at the same time mathematicians as a group took little interest in the life insurance and life annuities markets. What motivated the mathematicians to evaluate life-contingent contracts was land and property. That is where the major interest lay among those who were the patrons of the mathematicians. This is best expressed in the mathematical work of Abraham De Moivre, who by 1725 had laid the mathematical foundations for the majority of life-contingent contracts offered during the eighteenth century. Although this is never explicitly stated in his book, De Moivre's *Annuities upon Lives* addresses the valuation of a wide variety of property contracts where the length of the contract depends on the lengths of the lives of those entering the contract.

The major mathematical developments in the valuation of life-contingent contracts all occurred prior to 1760. Edmond Halley set the stage for the construction of life tables based on available data that did not include a proper count of the total size of the population. Later mathematicians continued to be faced with a lack of an accurate population count. Their contribution was that they tried to account for immigration in the construction of these tables, Thomas Simpson not very successfully and Richard Price moderately successfully, after making some strong assumptions about the nature of immigration. As mentioned already De Moivre worked through many of the scenarios for life-contingent contracts. Halley had demonstrated how to calculate single life annuities from his table and had made a stab at joint life annuities. This involved an onerous set of calculations done by hand. This led to De Moivre's other contribution to the mathematical theory. By making a data-based model assumption after examining Halley's life table (the probability of survival decreases linearly over time assumed) he was able to find expressions for the value of life annuities that required much less calculation. Until Thomas Simpson's work on annuity problems in the 1740s, other, and lesser, mathematicians tried unsuccessfully to find their own time-saving approximations to the values of life annuities. Simpson devised a number of approximations that worked but were dependent on a life table based on data from London that could give quite different results from data from the rest of the country. By the mid-1750s James Dodson had developed the mathematical tools for valuing various kinds of life insurance contracts other than 1-year term insurance.

My claim that most of the mathematical work up to about 1760 was motivated by property issues is supported by manuscript evidence, scanty as it is, showing clients seeking out mathematicians to obtain annuity valuations. These annuities were mostly related to marriage settlements, reversions on estates, and leases whose terms were based on the lengths of lives of the lessees. There are only one or two instances of requests for the valuation of a life annuity without reference to property. Mathematicians continued to carry out this kind of consulting work throughout the eighteenth century. The law is notoriously conservative, but eventually the courts sided with the mathematicians. The proper mathematical valuation of life-contingent contracts related to property was given the official court blessing in 1787.

James Dodson's idea, in 1756, of establishing an insurance company offering products with mathematically based premiums, is and is not a turning point in the history of the life insurance industry. It is, in the sense that the Equitable Society was the first to operate in this way. It is not, in the sense that the Society experienced strong opposition from the established companies that delayed its establishment. Further, no other company followed in the trail blazed by Dodson for at least 30 years.

What is a turning point that brought the mathematicians and the annuity sector of the industry together is the response to a perceived imminent financial crisis after a number of annuity societies were established and underfunded in the 1760s. The demand for the products offered by these annuity societies increased over the century as the growing middle class sought financial protection for their families and for their own declining years. All but one of the annuity proprietors ignored the mathematicians and made the mistake of undervaluing, in some cases grossly undervaluing, their advertised benefits. For the first time some mathematicians took to the public press to raise the alarm about these societies and how they operated. Over a few years the public became more aware of the issues. This awareness was greatly helped by Richard Price, who was able to express the technical issues in a nontechnical way that made his arguments accessible to a wider public.

As a result of his efforts, more mathematicians became involved in the life annuity industry as consultants and commentators.

Richard Price provided no major mathematical breakthroughs related to the valuation of life-contingent contracts. Consequently, I think his work as a protoactuary has been underestimated by the mathematical community. He is known mainly for the construction of the Northampton life table that was used by the insurance industry into the nineteenth century. His contributions to the development of the practice of actuarial science were far-reaching. Early on, he was responsible for educating the public in issues related to life annuities. Later, he provided the Equitable Society with much practical advice as well as a mortality table applicable (at least for some time) to the insurance industry. Finally, he was proactive with Francis Maseres and John Acland in trying to establish pensions for working people. The trio was held back by property interests that sabotaged their efforts.

The eighteenth century did not end in a victory for the mathematicians within the life insurance industry. After 1800 the number of insurance companies founded in England exploded. Of the more than 200 companies formed, many failed and most were taken over by larger companies. Despite the establishment of a professional organization, the Institute of Actuaries, in 1848, there continued to be questionable companies and questionable practices, as satirized in the early 1840s by Charles Dickens, in his novel *Martin Chuzzlewit*, in the form of the Anglo-Bengalese Disinterested Loan and Life Assurance Company.

Appendix 1 Technical Appendix

A standard reference for the theory of annuities certain is S.G. Kellison's *The Theory of Interest*.[1] The development and discussion of the valuation of life annuity and life insurance functions can be found in C.W. Jordan's *Life Contingencies*, which was written for students taking the examinations of the Society of Actuaries.[2] It has been replaced by another textbook. The modern examination syllabus for actuarial examinations no longer stresses topics such as reversionary annuities and so Jordan's book provides better coverage of topics important in the eighteenth century.

In a fixed-term annuity, or an annuity certain, an amount 1 (the annuity payment) is paid at the end of every year for n years. At an interest rate of i, the present value of these payments is worth

$$a_{\overline{n}|} = \frac{1}{(1+i)} + \frac{1}{(1+i)^2} + \cdots + \frac{1}{(1+i)^n} = \frac{1 - \frac{1}{(1+i)^n}}{i}.$$

It is usual to denote $\frac{1}{(1+i)}$ by the letter v, so that another expression for $a_{\overline{n}|}$ is

$$a_{\overline{n}|} = v + v^2 + \cdots + v^n = \frac{1 - v^n}{i}.$$

If the amount 1 is paid at the end of every year beginning at the end of the $(m+1)^{\text{th}}$ and ending at the end of the nth year, then the present value of the annuity is

$$v^{m+1} + v^{m+2} + \cdots + v^n$$

or

$$(v + v^2 + \cdots + v^n) - (v + v^2 + \cdots + v^m) = a_{\overline{n}|} - a_{\overline{m}|}$$

In the seventeenth and eighteenth centuries this would be called a fixed-term reversionary annuity. Today the term is "deferred annuity." If the annuity is paid forever, then $n \to \infty$ and $\frac{1}{i}$ is the value of the perpetuity.

In a single life annuity issued to a person aged x, payments are made at the end of each year until death. The values of the payments are v, v^2, v^3, etc. The probability of making a payment t years in the future is the probability that the annuitant will survive at least t years into the future, which from the demographical results is l_{x+t}/l_x for a person who is currently aged x. The expected value of this payment is the value of the payment times the probability of making it or $v^t l_{x+t}/l_x$. The value of the life annuity is then

$$a_x = \sum_{t=1}^{\omega - x} v^t \frac{l_{x+t}}{l_x}$$

where ω is the highest age in the life table (at age ω there is no one left living). The upper limit of the sum could be conveniently replaced by the symbol ∞, since $l_\omega = l_{\omega+1} = l_{\omega+2} = \cdots = 0$. The life annuity could be limited to a term of n years. In this kind of life annuity payments are made to a person aged x at the end of each year until death or for n years, whichever comes first. The expected value of these payments is

$$a_{x:\overline{n}|} = \sum_{t=1}^{n} v^t \frac{l_{x+t}}{l_x}.$$

To obtain the value of a_x under a linear survivor model set

$$\frac{l_{x+t}}{l_x} = 1 - \frac{t}{\omega - x}.$$

Then

$$a_x = \sum_{t=1}^{\omega - x} v^t \left(1 - \frac{t}{\omega - x}\right) = \sum_{t=1}^{\omega - x} v^t - \frac{1}{\omega - x} \sum_{t=1}^{\omega - x} t v^t.$$

The first term on the right-hand side of the equation is the sum of a geometric progression and the second term is the sum of an arithmetic geometric progression. After some algebra this reduces to

$$a_x = \frac{1}{i}\left(1 - \frac{1+i}{\omega - x}\right) a_{\overline{\omega - x}|}.$$

There are several variations on contracts that could be offered when there are two or more lives: joint life annuities, reversion, and last survivor annuities. In a joint survivor annuity for two persons aged x and y, the value of 1 is paid at the end of the year while both persons are alive. The value of this annuity is given by

$$a_{xy} = \sum_{t=1}^{\infty} v^t \left(\frac{l_{x+t}}{l_x}\right)\left(\frac{l_{y+t}}{l_y}\right)$$

where l_{x+t}/l_x is the probability that the individual aged x survives to age $x + t$ and l_{y+t}/l_y is the probability that the individual aged y survives to age $y + t$. In a reversionary life annuity an amount of 1 is paid annually to an individual currently aged x, beginning at the end of the year in which an individual currently aged y dies. The value of this annuity may be expressed as

$$\sum_{t=1}^{\infty} v^t \left(\frac{l_{x+t}}{l_x}\right)\left(\frac{l_y - l_{y+t}}{l_y}\right) = a_x - a_{xy}$$

where l_{x+t}/l_x is the probability that the individual currently aged x survives t years and $(l_y - l_{y+t})/l_y$ is the probability that the person aged y is dead within t years. The right-hand side of the expression gives a nice interpretation of the value of a reversionary annuity; it is the value of a life annuity paid to the person aged x minus the payments made when both people (aged x and y) are alive. For a last survivor annuity an amount of 1 is paid at the end of each year until both individuals, one aged x and the other aged y, die. Since the value of the payment at time t is v^t and the probability of making the payment at time t is

$$1 - \left(1 - \frac{l_{x+t}}{l_x}\right)\left(1 - \frac{l_{y+t}}{l_y}\right),$$

which is the probability that at least one is alive at time t, then the present value of the payments is

$$\sum_{t=1}^{\infty} v^t \left[1 - \left(1 - \frac{l_{x+t}}{l_x}\right)\left(1 - \frac{l_{y+t}}{l_y}\right)\right] = a_x + a_y - a_{xy}.$$

The right-hand side may be interpreted as the present value of the payment of 1 made to each person while they are alive minus the value of the payment made while they are both alive. These concepts can be extended to three lives aged x, y, and z.

Here is De Moivre's approximation to a_{xy} under an exponential survival model. Assume that $\omega \to \infty$ and that

$$\frac{l_{x+t}}{l_x} = \left(\frac{l_{x+1}}{l_x}\right)^t = (p_x)^t.$$

Then

$$a_{xy} = \sum_{t=1}^{\infty} v^t (p_x)^t (p_y)^t,$$

which is the sum of an infinite geometric progression, is $vp_xp_y/(1 - vp_xp_y)$. Since under this model $a_x = vp_x/(1 - vp_x)$, we can solve for

$p_x = (1+i)a_x/(1+a_x)$. Substituting this and the equivalent expression for p_y into the formula for a_{xy}, De Moivre's approximation is

$$a_{xy} = \frac{(1+i)a_x a_y}{(1+a_x)(1+a_y)-(1+i)a_x a_y}.$$

Here is a justification of one of Simpson's approximations to a_{xy}. Simpson suggests that if $x = y$, one should use the tables to find a_{xx}. When $x \neq y$ and $25 \le x, y \le 50$ then let $w = (x+y)/2$ and approximate a_{xy} by a_{ww}. To justify this approximation go back to the definition

$$a_{xy} = \sum_{t=1}^{\infty} v^t \frac{l_{x+t}}{l_x}\frac{l_{y+t}}{l_y}.$$

Suppose the survivor function l_x is linear. By the properties of the linear relationship (or linear interpolation), when $w = (x+y)/2$ then $l_w = (l_x + l_y)/2$. Let $\varepsilon = (l_y - l_x)/2$. Then $l_x = l_w - \varepsilon$ and $l_y = l_w + \varepsilon$. To understand the approximation we need only look at

$$\frac{l_x l_y}{l_w l_w} = \frac{(l_w-\varepsilon)(l_w+\varepsilon)}{l_w l_w} = 1 - \left(\frac{\varepsilon}{l_w}\right)^2.$$

The "error" ε is one half the number of deaths occurring between ages x and y. If the number of deaths is small relative to the number alive, then $(\varepsilon/l_w)^2$ will be close to 0. As age increases the term $(\varepsilon/l_w)^2$ may not be negligible. However at higher ages $(l_{w+t}/l_w)^2$ is multiplied by v^t, which is decreasing exponentially as t increases, so that the contribution of the higher ages to a_{ww} will be small.

For two lives aged x and y, there is a functional relationship between the life annuities a_x and a_y where $y - x = z$. This is given by

$$a_x = \frac{1}{l_x}(vl_{x+1} + v^2 l_{x+2} + \cdots + v^z l_y + v^z l_y a_y).$$

From this relationship, an expression of the 1-year survival probability $p_x = l_{x+1}/l_x$ can be obtained. In particular

$$p_x = \frac{(1+i)a_x}{1+a_{x+1}}.$$

In an insurance contract, a payment is made on the death of an individual. In a whole life insurance issued to a person aged x, a payment of 1 is made at the end of the year of death. The net single premium for this insurance, or the cost of the insurance paid in a lump sum at the beginning of the contract, is given by

$$A_x = \sum_{t=0}^{\infty} v^{t+1}\frac{d_{x+t}}{l_x}.$$

As with annuities, the term could be limited to n years of coverage. For an n-year term insurance an amount of value 1 is paid at the end of the year if death occurs within the n years and nothing is paid if the individual survives the n years. The net single premium for this insurance is

$$A^{1}_{x:\overline{n}|} = \sum_{t=0}^{n-1} v^{t+1} \frac{d_{x+t}}{l_x}.$$

The numeral 1 over the n indicates that death must occur before the term n if a payment is to be made. A special case of the term insurance policy is 1-year term insurance which has value

$$A^{1}_{x:\overline{1}|} = v \frac{d_x}{l_x}.$$

Insurance policies are usually paid by annual premiums. The present value of the premiums is a type of life annuity where the payments are made at the beginning of the year. The premiums are obtained by setting the present value of the premiums equal to the present value of the insurance benefits. The annual premium P_x for a whole life insurance is obtained from

$$P_x \ddot{a}_x = A_x$$

where $\ddot{a}_x = a_x + 1$ is the present value of the life annuity with payments made at the beginning of the year. Similarly, the annual premium $P^{1}_{x:\overline{n}|}$ for n-year term insurance is obtained from

$$P^{1}_{x:\overline{n}|}(a_{x:\overline{n-1}|} + 1) = A^{1}_{x:\overline{n}|}.$$

The relationship between whole life insurance and a life annuity can be found in the following way. Since $d_{x+t} = l_{x+t} - l_{x+t+1}$, then

$$\begin{aligned} A_x &= \sum_{t=0}^{\infty} v^{t+1} \frac{l_{x+t} - l_{x+t+1}}{l_x} \\ &= \frac{1}{l_x}(vl_x + v^2 l_{x+1} + v^3 l_{x+2} + \cdots - vl_{x+1} - v^2 l_{x+2} - v^3 l_{x+3} - \cdots) \\ &= v + \frac{1}{l_x}[v(vl_{x+1} + v^2 l_{x+2} + v^3 l_{x+3} + \cdots) - (vl_{x+1} + v^2 l_{x+2} + v^3 l_{x+3} + \cdots)] \\ &= v + (v-1)a_x. \end{aligned}$$

Multiplying both sides of the equation by $1 + i$ and rearranging terms results in

$$(1+i)A_x + ia_x = 1.$$

In Heathcote's and other problems it is of interest to find, for two persons aged x and y, the probability that the person aged y outlives the person aged x, This is given by

$$\sum_{t=0}^{\infty} \frac{d_{x+t}}{l_x} \frac{l_{y+t} + \frac{1}{2} d_{y+t}}{l_y}$$

assuming a uniform distribution of deaths within each year and that a life table is available. The first term in the product under the sum relates to the probability of death of the person aged x. The second term in the product relates to the survival of the person aged y; the addition of the term $d_{y+t}/2$ is to account for both people dying in the same year, assuming equal chances of one predeceasing the other within that year. When $x = y$ the formula simplifies to ½. When a linear survival curve is assumed and $x < y$, then the probability is expressed as

$$\int_y^{\omega} \int_y^{v} \left(\frac{1}{\omega - x}\right) \left(\frac{1}{\omega - y}\right) du dv = \frac{\omega - y}{2(\omega - x)}.$$

In calculating what he thought was the value of a_x, Weyman Lee found the value of m such that $l_{x+m}/l_x = 1/2$ and then set $a_x = a_{\overline{m}|}$. For two lives, one aged x and the other aged y, the probability that they are both dead within m years is

$$\sum_{t=0}^{m} \frac{d_{x+t}}{l_x} \frac{d_{y+t}}{l_y}$$

and the probability that at least one of them is alive within the m years is 1 minus the above probability. Lee argues that a last survivor annuity should be based on the median future lifetime of the two lives. This is calculated by finding the value m such that the above probability is equal to ½ and again setting $a_x = a_{\overline{m}|}$.

Several mathematicians considered a fixed-term annuity with the same value as a_x. They set $a_x = a_{\overline{n}|}$ and solved for n to get the equivalent fixed-term annuity. Others suggested setting the expected future lifetime equal to $a_{\overline{n}|}$ and solving for n. De Moivre argued against this. The expected lifetime of a person aged x is given by

$$e_x = \sum_{t=1}^{\omega - x} \frac{l_{x+t}}{l_x}$$

in standard actuarial notation and the value of a single life annuity is

$$a_x = \sum_{t=1}^{\omega-x} v^t \frac{l_{x+t}}{l_x}.$$

De Moivre argued that if e_x can be set equal to $a_{\overline{n}|}$, then e_x must be considered as an annuity. In that case v_t must be equal to 1 for all t and so the interest rate $i = 0$.

Appendix 2 Life Tables

Halley's life table 1693 completed with reconstructed entries at ages 85 and above

Age x	l_x	Age x	l_x	Age x	l_x	Age x	l_x
1	1 000	26	560	51	335	76	78
2	855	27	553	52	324	77	68
3	798	28	546	53	313	78	58
4	760	29	539	54	302	79	49
5	732	30	531	55	292	80	41
6	710	31	523	56	282	81	34
7	692	32	515	57	272	82	28
8	680	33	507	58	262	83	23
9	670	34	499	59	252	84	20
10	661	35	490	60	242	85	19
11	653	36	481	61	232	86	18
12	646	37	472	62	222	87	17
13	640	38	463	63	212	88	16
14	634	39	454	64	202	89	15
15	628	40	445	65	192	90	13
16	622	41	436	66	182	91	12
17	616	42	427	67	172	92	11
18	610	43	417	68	162	93	10
19	604	44	407	69	152	94	9
20	598	45	397	70	142	95	8
21	592	46	387	71	131	96	6
22	586	47	377	72	120	97	5
23	579	48	367	73	109	98	4
24	573	49	357	74	98	99	3
25	567	50	346	75	88	100	1

Smart's 1738 and Simpson's 1742 life tables

	Simpson	Smart	Simpson and Smart					
Age x	l_x	l_x	Age x	l_x	Age x	l_x	Age x	l_x
0	1 280	1 000	25	426	50	204	75	45
1	870	710	26	418	51	196	76	41
2	700	614	27	410	52	188	77	38
3	635	564	28	402	53	180	78	35
4	600	539	29	394	54	172	79	32
5	580	526	30	385	55	165	80	29
6	564	516	31	376	56	158	81	26
7	551	508	32	367	57	151	82	23
8	541	501	33	358	58	144	83	20
9	532	495	34	349	59	137	84	17
10	524	490	35	340	60	130	85	14
11	517	486	36	331	61	123	86	12
12	510	482	37	322	62	117	87	10
13	504	479	38	313	63	111	88	8
14	498	477	39	304	64	105	89	6
15	492	475	40	294	65	99	90	5
16	486	473	41	284	66	93	91	4
17	480	471	42	274	67	87	92	3
18	474	468	43	264	68	81	93	2
19	468	464	44	255	69	75	94	1
20	462	459	45	246	70	69	95	0
21	455	453	46	237	71	64		
22	448	447	47	228	72	59		
23	441	440	48	220	73	54		
24	434	433	49	212	74	49		

Brakenridge's 1750 life table

Age x	l_x	Age x	l_x	Age x	l_x	Age x	l_x
1	1 000	23	360	45	247	67	108
2	677	24	356	46	241	68	101
3	550	25	352	47	235	69	95
4	505	26	348	48	229	70	89
5	473	27	344	49	222	71	82
6	447	28	340	50	215	72	75
7	434	29	335	51	208	73	68
8	425	30	330	52	201	74	61
9	418	31	325	53	194	75	55
10	412	32	320	54	187	76	49
11	406	33	315	55	181	77	43
12	402	34	310	56	175	78	37
13	398	35	305	57	169	79	31

(*continued*)

Brakenridge's 1750 life table (cont.)

Age x	l_x	Age x	l_x	Age x	l_x	Age x	l_x
14	394	36	299	58	163	80	26
15	390	37	293	59	157	81	22
16	386	38	288	60	151	82	18
17	383	39	282	61	145	83	15
18	379	40	277	62	139	84	13
19	375	41	271	63	132	85	11
20	372	42	265	64	126	86	9
21	368	43	259	65	120	87	7
22	364	44	253	66	114		

Dodson's 1756 life table

Age x	l_x	Age x	l_x	Age x	l_x	Age x	l_x
0	1 400	22	493	44	284	66	98
1	952	23	485	45	273	67	91
2	766	24	477	46	262	68	84
3	695	25	469	47	252	69	77
4	657	26	460	48	242	70	70
5	635	27	451	49	232	71	64
6	618	28	442	50	222	72	58
7	604	29	433	51	213	73	52
8	593	30	424	52	204	74	46
9	583	31	414	53	195	75	40
10	575	32	404	54	186	76	34
11	568	33	394	55	178	77	28
12	561	34	384	56	170	78	22
13	554	35	374	57	162	79	17
14	548	36	364	58	154	80	13
15	542	37	354	59	147	81	9
16	536	38	344	60	140	82	6
17	530	39	334	61	133	83	4
18	523	40	324	62	126	84	3
19	516	41	314	63	119	85	2
20	509	42	304	64	112	86	1
21	501	43	294	65	105	87	0

Price's Northampton life table 1771

Age x	l_x	Age x	l_x	Age x	l_x	Age x	l_x
0	1 149	25	475	50	284	75	83
1	849	26	467	51	275	76	75
2	722	27	459	52	267	77	67
3	672	28	451	53	259	78	60
4	646	29	443	54	251	79	53
5	625	30	435	55	243	80	46
6	609	31	428	56	235	81	39
7	596	32	421	57	227	82	32
8	586	33	414	58	219	83	26
9	577	34	407	59	211	84	21
10	570	35	400	60	203	85	17
11	564	36	393	61	195	86	13
12	558	37	386	62	187	87	10
13	553	38	379	63	179	88	8
14	548	39	372	64	171	89	6
15	543	40	365	65	163	90	4
16	538	41	357	66	155	91	2
17	533	42	349	67	147	92	1
18	528	43	341	68	139		
19	522	44	333	69	131		
20	515	45	325	70	123		
21	507	46	317	71	115		
22	499	47	309	72	107		
23	491	48	301	73	99		
24	483	49	293	74	91		

Price's Northampton life table 1783

Age x	l_x	Age x	l_x	Age x	l_x	Age x	l_x
0	11 650	25	4 760	50	2 857	75	832
1	8 650	26	4 685	51	2 776	76	752
2	7 283	27	4 610	52	2 694	77	675
3	6 781	28	4 535	53	2 612	78	602
4	6 446	29	4 460	54	2 530	79	534
5	6 249	30	4 385	55	2 448	80	469
6	6 065	31	4 310	56	2 366	81	406
7	5 925	32	4 235	57	2 284	82	346
8	5 815	33	4 160	58	2 202	83	289
9	5 735	34	4 085	59	2 120	84	234
10	5 675	35	4 010	60	2 038	85	186
11	5 623	36	3 935	61	1 956	86	145
12	5 573	37	3 860	62	1 874	87	111
13	5 523	38	3 785	63	1 793	88	83

(*continued*)

Price's Northampton life table 1783 (*cont.*)

Age x	l_x	Age x	l_x	Age x	l_x	Age x	l_x
14	5 473	39	3 710	64	1 712	89	62
15	5 423	40	3 635	65	1 632	90	46
16	5 373	41	3 559	66	1 552	91	34
17	5 320	42	3 482	67	1 472	92	24
18	5 262	43	3 404	68	1 392	93	16
19	5 199	44	3 326	69	1 312	94	9
20	5 132	45	3 248	70	1 232	95	4
21	5 060	46	3 170	71	1 152	96	1
22	4 985	47	3 092	72	1 072		
23	4 910	48	3 014	73	992		
24	4 835	49	2 936	74	912		

End Notes

Chapter 1

1. Jordan (1967, pp. 20–21).
2. Hald (1990, p. 509).
3. See, for example, Farren (1844).
4. Daston (1987). Similar ideas are expressed in Daston (1988).
5. Rosenhaft (2010, pp. 17–18).
6. British Library Add. MS 38729.
7. Hayes (1728, pp. 15, 17).
8. Dodson (1752, pp. 333–4).
9. MacKenzie and Phillips (2012, pp. 4–5).
10. For a short description of the various kinds of land tenure in the eighteenth century see Richards (1730); for a modern précis, see Clay (1981).
11. Clay (1981) describes the area as "[w]est of the Pennines ... and of a swathe of country extending south from the Peak District, through the middle Thames valley to the Solent."
12. Evans (1817, pp. 397–8).
13. Lewin and Valois (2003, pp. 83–9) provide a brief description of the development of life tables in the eighteenth century.
14. University College London/Bentham Papers CLXVI/202.
15. The eighteenth-century debate over the size of the population of England and the move to civil registration is described in Glass (1973).

Chapter 2

1. The rise and role of the land surveyor is given in McRae (1996, pp. 169–97).
2. Fitzherbert (1523).
3. See, for example, Kopf (1927) and Poitras (2000).
4. Witt (1613). A biography of Richard Witt is in Lewin (2004).
5. A detailed description of the London book trade from this era is in Bennett (1965) and Bennett (1970).
6. Aldis et al. (1968, pp. 178–9, 225).
7. Stationers' Company (1876, Vol. 3, p. 234).
8. Burke and Burke (1838, p. 161).
9. Blackstone (1794, pp. 318–19).

10. Witt's table (Witt, 1613, p. 95) shows $1.1^{1/4} = 1.0241136$ to seven decimal places. A modern calculation shows that Witt had a small round-off error problem: $1.1^{1/4} = 1.024113689$ to nine decimal places. His calculation of $1.1^{1/2}$ is correct, indicating that his minor problem occurred when finding numerically the square root of a square root.
11. Witt (1613, p. 10).
12. In the title of Clay (1619) there is mention of "certaine briefe and necessarie tables for the valuation of leases, annuities, and purchases, either in present or in reversion." The copy of this book in EEBO and of a later edition in 1621 (Clay, 1621) do not have the tables included. Clay (1622) begins with the title words "Brief, easie, and necessary tables" and does contain the tables within the book, as well as the material in Clay (1619). Some brief information on Clay's work as a land surveyor is in Bendall (1997, p. 100).
13. Aldis et al. (1968, p. 98).
14. Stationers' Company (1876, Vol. 3, p. 296).
15. Pierce and Williams (1990, pp. 147–8).
16. The data for this graph are taken from Clark (2002, p. 297).
17. Ibid. (p. 303). Clark also compares his series to other authors, for example Allen (1992). Clark's estimate of the rise in rent/wage ratio is larger than those of other authors, yet the general pattern is the same. Allen's (1992, p. 286) graph shows an increase between 1550 and 1575 with another in 1600, followed by steady increases thereafter.
18. Hoyle (1992).
19. Overton (1996, pp. 22–36).
20. Ibid. (pp. 147–8).
21. The data on enclosures is taken from Wordie (1983, p. 502).
22. Analyses and discussions of the contents and method of presentation of material in early editions of *Ground of Artes* are in Easton (1967), Wallis (1974), and Fauvel (1989).
23. Record (1582, "third Addition to this Booke," Chapter 11).
24. Ibid. (1623, pp. 604–13).
25. Wingate (1630, pp. 338–87).
26. Bendall (1997, p. 563).
27. Wingate (1650, pp. 273–318).
28. Ibid. (1650, p. 318).
29. Phillippes (1653, pp. 16–17).
30. Ibid. (preface).
31. McKenzie (1960).
32. Mabbut (1686, 1700).

Chapter 3

1. Halley (1693a).
2. Neale was also groom porter. This was a court position whose responsibilities included the settling of disputes at court over card games, dice games, and bowling.

3. Luttrell (1972, pp. 320–23). See also Cruickshanks et al. (2002, Vol. 3, pp. 1057–74, Vol. 4, pp. 1008–14) for entries under Foley and Neale.
4. Great Britain (1963, Vol. 6, pp. 372–8). *Statutes of the Realm 4* William and Mary c. 3.
5. Dickson (1967, pp. 39–46).
6. Great Britain (1963, Vol. 6, pp. 380–7). *Statutes of the Realm 5* William and Mary c. 5.
7. The 1,012 tontine participants are listed in Howard (1694) and the total of £881,493 14s 2d raised by *Statutes of the Realm 4* William and Mary c. 3 is mentioned in *Statutes of the Realm 5* William and Mary c. 5.
8. Graetzer (1883).
9. As defined in the *Oxford English Dictionary.*
10. Person (1635, Lib. 5, p. 17).
11. Strype (1824, p. 331).
12. Dekker (1603).
13. Morgan (1728, p. 293).
14. The route may be pieced together from Harnack (1900, p. 137), Leibniz (1964, p. 605, 1970, pp. 275–9) and Pearson (1978, pp. 75–6).
15. Royal Society Journal Book, Volume 8.
16. Gunther (1935, pp. 207, 212, 220).
17. Ibid. (p. 224).
18. The data are published in Graetzer (1883).
19. In Bellhouse (2011a) there is an example of Halley carrying out an experiment on the evaporation of water from the sea prior to his work on the Breslau mortality data. At a few points in his calculations he rounds his results for ease in future calculations.
20. Graetzer (1883) found the average number of deaths in the first year of life to be 353; the number 348 will be used as it better reproduces Halley's table.
21. Bellhouse (2011a, p. 831).
22. Clark (1999, p. 203).
23. Ibid. (pp. 16–20, 203).
24. Cook (1993, 1998, p. 42).
25. Royal Society Journal Book, Volume 8.
26. Luttrell (1972, p. 389). Notice of the act appeared in *London Gazette*, January 26–30, 1693.
27. The *London Gazette*, May 1–4, 1693, mentions that there were a number of people who had given notice in advance of May 1 that they wished to purchase life annuities.
28. Pearce (1928, p. 125).
29. These widows were referred to as widows of sequestered clergy. The data appear in Stanhope (1698, pp. 28–31).
30. Kennett (1703, p. 17). Kennett also acknowledged that there were several "funds and insurances" where a clergyman could purchase a reversionary annuity for his wife, but dismissed them because they were not charitable organizations.
31. Halley (1693b).
32. De Moivre (1725).

Chapter 4

1. Anonymous (1696).
2. Clark (1999, pp. 203–6).
3. Great Britain (1963, Vol. 6, pp. 483–95). *Statutes of the Realm 5* William and Mary c. 20.
4. Ibid. (Vol. 8, pp. 246–53). *Statutes of the Realm 2* and*3* Anne c. 3.
5. Assheton (1699).
6. Cholmondeley (1713, 1714a, 1714b).
7. The phrase "men with movable property" is attributed to the historian John Brewer by Koehn (1994, p. 18).
8. Assheton (1699). Cholmondeley's benefits are described in Cholmondeley (1714b).
9. Mercers' Company (1708).
10. Cholmondeley (1713, p. 15).
11. See, for example, Dyson (1977, pp. 46–8, 53–4). For contemporary concerns about the British fishery, see Saunders (1708).
12. South Sea Company (1711).
13. In 1719 the South Sea Company competed with the Bank of England to hold the public debt and won the bidding war. The Company convinced many of the government's creditors to trade their assets for shares in the Company on the expectation that the value in the shares would rise. This led to speculation in the shares, which resulted in the share price rising by a factor of seven. When it became apparent that the profitability of the Company could not support the high share price, the value of the stock collapsed. See Hoppit (2002) for an analysis of the South Sea Bubble.
14. Clark (1999, p. 109, fn 53) puts the 12% at the high end of profits earned in trade.
15. Petty (1687, pp. 28–9).
16. Amicable Society (1710).
17. *Post Boy*, March 25, 1714 and *Post Man and the Historical Account*, April 7, 1716.
18. PRO PROB 11/556/318.
19. PRO PROB 18/34/86 and PROB 18/34/108.
20. Clark (1999, p. 140).
21. *London Evening Post*, October 7, 1746; *Whitehall Evening Post or London Intelligencer*, November 25–7, 1746; *St. James's Evening Post*, January 27–9, 1747.
22. The deficit is given in a report to the House of Commons on a petition from the Mercers' Company, March 8, 1747 (old style). See Great Britain, House of Commons (1803, Vol. 25, pp. 539–60). Parliament's monetary support of the failed scheme is documented in City of London Livery Companies Commission (1894, p. 44).
23. The figure is taken from the Mercers' Company records and is quoted in Clark (1999, p. 136).
24. A description and analysis of adverse selection in the government annuities is in Rothschild (2009).
25. Bellhouse (nd).

26. Ward (1707, pp. 245–76).
27. Petty (1674).
28. Ward (1707, p. 274).
29. Ronayne (1717, p. 289).
30. Ibid. (pp. 311–13).
31. Royer (1721, pp. 430–2).
32. Ward (1710, pp. 104–13).
33. Ibid. (1724, pp. 206–13).
34. Ibid. (1710, pp. 106–7).
35. Petty (1674, pp. 82–8).
36. Reference to the first edition is in a newspaper advertisement in *Post Boy*, November 20, 1712. I had access only to the second edition, published in 1714. The material is in Hatton (1714, pp. 113–17).
37. *St. James's Evening Post*, July 3, 1718.
38. His current and previous occupations are on the title page of Ward (1707).
39. What little is known about Edward Hatton's life has been pieced together in Cherry (2001). The reference to Hatton's work as a surveyor for a fire insurance company is in Hawkins (1776, p. 504).
40. Clay (1974).
41. Beckett (1984).
42. Tucker (1960, pp. 6–7).
43. Clay (1980).
44. Laurence (1730).
45. Bendall (2004).
46. Laurence (1727, p. 140).
47. Ibid. (1730, p. 40).
48. Hayes (1727).
49. Hayes's teaching career can be pieced together from various advertisements he placed in London newspapers: *Daily Courant*, October 16, 1717 and May 2, 1718; *Post Boy*, April 19, 1718; *London Gazette*, October 6, 1719; *Daily Post*, July 20, 1727, February 5, 1728, and May 30, 1741; *London Daily Post and General Advertiser*, March 30, 1736.
50. Farren (1844, pp. 54–5).
51. Hayes (1727, p. 5).
52. Ibid. (p. 46).

Chapter 5

1. De Moivre (1725). Biographical information on De Moivre is in Bellhouse and Genest (2007) and Bellhouse (2011b).
2. Ibid. (1711, 1718).
3. Hald (1990, p. 524) has made some similar comparisons, but only to Halley's published values and a 6% rate of interest.
4. Clark (1999, p. 140).
5. Williams (1740, pp. 191–4, 222–33).
6. De Moivre (1743, p. 40).
7. Great Britain, Army (1756, p. 115).

8. Robson (1951, p. 60).
9. Great Britain, Army (1769, p. 27).
10. Vezey (1773, Vol. 2, pp. 422–3).
11. PRO C 12/1820/3.
12. A biography of Morris can be pieced together from the following sources: Bradley (1832), Harris (2004), Hawkins (1776, Vol. 5, p. 411), Martin (1892, p. 144), Watkins (2002), and PRO PROB 11/961/228.
13. A biography of Lee can be pieced together from the following sources: PRO PROB 11/913/443 and *St. James's Chronicle or the British Evening Post* (London, England), November 12–14, 1765.
14. Bendall (1997).
15. Morris (1735, p. 27).
16. Halley (1693a, p. 602).
17. Lee (1737, pp. 165–6).
18. Strange (1755, p. 82).
19. Lee (1737, p. 2).
20. Ibid. (pp. 314–5).
21. Richards (1739, p. 24).
22. De Morgan (1872, pp. 93–4).
23. Canterbury Cathedral Archives CCA-DCc-BB/29/30–36.
24. Bellhouse (2011b, p. 45).

Chapter 6

1. Columbia University Library, David Eugene Smith Collection of Historical Papers, Series I.
2. The frontispiece first appears in De Moivre (1718). Information on De Moivre's scientific connections is in Bellhouse (2011b).
3. *London Daily Post and General Advertiser*, July 11, 1739 and March 13, 1741, and *London Evening Post*, December 10, 1754.
4. *London Evening Post*, September 20, 1755.
5. Columbia University Library, David Eugene Smith Collection of Historical Papers, Series I.
6. Dodson (1752, 1754, 1756).
7. Jones (1706).
8. Cambridge University Library. MS Add. 9597/8/10–12.
9. Bellhouse (nd).
10. Universitätsbibliothek Oldenburg, Cim. 1, 184.
11. *General Evening Post*, December 5–7, 1745.
12. Columbia University Library, David Eugene Smith Collection of Historical Papers, Series I.
13. Staatsbibliothek zu Berlin, Sig. Darmstaedter H 1695.
14. Laurence (1730, p. 19).
15. *London Daily Post and General Advertiser*, March 13, 1741.
16. De Moivre (1738, 1743).
17. Ibid. (1743, pp. 16–18).
18. Ibid. (pp. 86, 91).

19. Ibid. (1744).
20. Dodson (1753, 1755).
21. De Moivre (1744).
22. Columbia University Library, David Eugene Smith Collection of Historical Papers, Series I and Cambridge University Library Add. 9597/8/9. Some of Simpson's letters are transcribed in Clarke (1929).
23. Cambridge University Library Add 9597/8/9.
24. Betham (1803, pp. 2223).
25. I have found a few unverified dates on the Internet for her birth: 1700, ca 1700, and 1702.
26. Cambridge University Library Add 9597/8/9.
27. St. John's College, Cambridge, Library TaylorB/C3.
28. Watkins (1714). Further information on Watkins may be found in Thomas (1718) and Hogg (2011).
29. Brakenridge (1755).
30. Dodson (1756).
31. Simpson (1742).
32. Hatton (1708, p. xxxviii).
33. Smart (1738).
34. Ibid. (1726, p. 113).
35. Pearson (1978, pp. 182–4), Westergaard (1932, p. 67), and Hald (1990, pp. 515–19).
36. Ibid. (p. 183).
37. Simpson (1742, pp. 2–3).
38. *London Evening Post*, October 22–4, 1741.
39. Hald (1990, pp. 525–6).
40. Simpson (1742, p. 62).
41. Ibid. (1752, p. 313).
42. Dodson (1753, p. xix).
43. See, for example, Bellhouse (2011b, pp. 192–4).
44. Lalande (1765).
45. Both definitions of "beggarly" are in *Oxford English Dictionary*, Oxford University Press (2001).
46. Simpson (1752, pp. 323–4).
47. Ibid. (p. 303).
48. Dodson (1753, 1755).
49. *Whitehall Evening Post or London Intelligencer*, February 18–20, 1755.
50. Columbia University Library, David Eugene Smith Collection of Historical Papers, Series I.
51. Dodson (1755, p. 49).

Chapter 7

1. Dodson (1755, pp. 362–6).
2. A list of 60 insurance and annuity societies formed between 1696 and 1721 is found in Clark (1999, pp. 203–6).
3. Carter (ca 1711, p. 3).

4. The construction is in Euclid's *Elements*, Book XIII, Proposition 16.
5. Great Britain (1963, Vol. 6, pp. 447–61). *Statutes of the Realm* 5 William and Mary c. 7. Details of the lottery are also given in Neale (1694).
6. Carter (1695).
7. Details of the schemes are in Bellhouse (2015).
8. Great Britain (1963, Vol. 9, pp. 595–639). *Statutes of the Realm 10* Anne c. 18.
9. Cambridge University Library MS Add.9597/8/4.
10. A detailed analysis of the manuscript is in Bellhouse (2015).
11. Member of the Amicable Society (1706, pp. 2–3).
12. Amicable Society (1721).
13. Whiston (1732).
14. Walford (1871, Vol. 1, p. 82).
15. *Gentleman's Magazine*, 1760, Vol. 30, pp. 9–10, 117–19.
16. Buffon (1749, p. 601).
17. Lee (1754).
18. Anonymous (1949–50).
19. Jordan (1967).
20. Equitable Society (1769a, p. 1).
21. Member of the Amicable Society (1706, pp. 2–3).
22. Brand (1775, p. 45).
23. Gray and McConnell (2004) put his birth year ca 1705.
24. PRO PROB 11/798/37 and PROB 11/834/262.
25. Equitable Society (1762).
26. PRO PROB 11/834/262.
27. Ogborn (1962, p. 83).
28. PRO PROB 11/834/262.
29. London Metropolitan Archives. MS 12806 Vol 11, fol. 321, December 15, 1757 and MS 12819 Vol. 18, fol. 89.
30. Equitable Society (1769b, p. 151).
31. Ogborn (1962, p. 77).
32. British Library Add. MS 38729.
33. London Metropolitan Archives. MS 12806 Vol. 11, fols. 241, 242, 247, 248, 321 and MS 12819 Vol. 18, fol. 89.
34. De Morgan (1882, p. 233).
35. Ogborn (1962, p. 31).
36. Institute and Faculty of Actuaries Archive EL/6/1/2a.
37. Institute and Faculty of Actuaries Archive EL/6/1/3.
38. Asset shares are defined this way by Huffman (1978).
39. Ogborn (1962).
40. Compare Equitable Society (1762, pp. 18–20) and Dodson's *First Lecture on Insurances*, pp. 62–3 in Institute and Faculty of Actuaries Archive EL/6/1/5.
41. Equitable Society (1762).
42. As defined in the *Oxford English Dictionary*, Oxford University Press (2001).
43. The deed of settlement has been reprinted several times. See, for example, Equitable Society (1854). The articles in the deed relating to the position of actuary are in Articles 32–6.

44. Mores (1764).
45. This is argued originally in Ogborn (1962, p. 43) using the same evidence.
46. The list is pieced together from Paterson (1779, pp. 74, 89, 90, 172).

Chapter 8

1. This information can be pieced together from: London Annuity Society (1780, p. ii), Great Britain (1786, p. 83, 1796, p. 84), and PRO PROB 11/1285/184.
2. Macceagh and Sturgess (1949, p. 366).
3. Peach and Thomas state that Rowe was a lawyer (Price, 1983, Vol. 1, p. 293). I can find no evidence to support this statement. Rowe was not a member of any of the four Inns of Court.
4. Bayes (1763) and, for example, Price (1769, 1770, 1775, 1776).
5. Webb (1762).
6. The first edition is Rowe (1751).
7. Royal Society Archives EC/1768/03.
8. Buck (1982).
9. Beyond his work all that is known about Dale is that he lived on Henrietta Street, now Henrietta Place, in the Marylebone area of London. The information is given in his will PRO PROB 11/1285/184, as well as other sources.
10. Laudable Society for the Benefit of Widows (1770).
11. Fisher is listed as secretary in Anonymous (1781, p. 225). His will was granted probate on June 6, 1782. PRO PROB 11/1091/206. The connection of the Fisher who died in 1782 with the Fisher who was secretary can be made through the publication Laudable Society for the Benefit of Widows (ca 1781) and Fisher's will, as Fisher is identified as a lapidary in both places.
12. *Public Advertiser*, June 11, 1760.
13. Price (1771, p. 73).
14. Laudable Society for the Benefit of Widows (1770).
15. In 1810 Francis Baily carried out a similar analysis to mine. It was more limited, in that I have had the benefit of high-speed computing and computer graphics. See Baily (1810, pp. 473–7).
16. London Annuity Society (1765).
17. *Gentleman's Magazine*, 1796, Vol. 66, p. 792.
18. Field appears as the Society's treasurer in London Annuity Society (1765) and as late as 1794 in Anonymous (1794, p. 218).
19. A succinct description of the early design and operation of the fund is given in Lewin (2003, pp. 361–7).
20. Maclaurin (1982, pp. 105–10).
21. Brief reports of meetings leading to the establishment of the fund are in London newspapers: *London Chronicle or Universal Evening Post*, March 7–9, 1765, *Lloyd's Evening Post*, March 27, 1765, *Gazetteer and New Daily Advertiser*, March 29, 1765.

22. A description of how the fund would operate is in Warner (1764). The same fund is suggested more than a decade earlier in Warner (1752). Warner also proposed a scheme based on the Scottish Ministers' Widows Fund; see Fernando Warner (1755).
23. Inner Temple (2016).
24. Cumbria Archive Centre, Carlisle. DHUD 8/68/2.
25. Law Society for the Benefit of Widows (1766).
26. Notice of the Law Society's formation is in *Public Advertiser*, April 24, 1766. A newspaper article referring to the Society's demise is in late 1766 is in *Gazetteer and New Daily Advertiser*, December 31, 1767.
27. Price (1771, p. vii).
28. Morgan (1815, p. 40).
29. Rowe (1776, p. 2).
30. In Rowe (1776, p. 2) the date is given as August 11, 1766; the date of October 11, 1766 appears in the newspaper article in *Gazetteer and New Daily Advertiser*, December 31, 1767.
31. Price (1983, Vol. 1, p. 56).
32. Ibid.
33. Burden (2013, pp. 152–60).
34. Royal Society Journal Book of Scientific Meetings, Vol. 16, and Eames (1739).
35. Royal Society L&P/1/23.
36. Kippis (1784, p. 222).
37. Crane (1966).
38. Rowe (1776). The mention of Simpson as his "late celebrated Friend" is in the preface.
39. Dale (1772, pp. 154–6).
40. Information on the annuities societies can be found as follows: Laudable Society of Annuitants, *Gazetteer and New Daily Advertiser*, August 3, 1767; Amicable Society of Annuitants, *Lloyd's Evening Post*, October 31–November 2, 1770; Provident Society, *Middlesex Journal or Chronicle of Liberty*, July 26–8, 1770; Society of London Annuitants, *Gazetteer and New Daily Advertiser*, May 17, 1770; Equitable Society of Annuitants, *General Evening Post*, September 12–14, 1771; Westminster Union Society, *Gazetteer and New Daily Advertiser*, January 7, 1771; London Union Society, *Gazetteer and New Daily Advertiser*, October 3, 1770; Consolidated Society, *Gazetteer and New Daily Advertiser*, April 22, 1771; Public Annuitant Society, *Middlesex Journal or Chronicle of Liberty*, January 19–22, 1771; Rational Annuity Society, *Public Advertiser*, January 22, 1771; Friendly Society of Annuitants, *London Evening Post*, May 2–4, 1771.
41. Koehn (1994, pp. 3–14, 26–60).
42. Ashton (1955, p. 251).
43. Basic information on Say is in Plomer et al. (1968, p. 222). His appearance before the House of Lords is summarized in Great Britain, House of Lords (1810, p. 373). One account of the Junius affair is in Andrews (1859, pp. 186–90). See also Haig (1960).

44. De Moivre (1731, 1738, 1743, 1750, 1752, 1756).
45. Smollett (1751, pp. 278–9).
46. For example, Hodgson (1747), Stonehouse (1754), and Webb (1762).
47. Hoyle (1754).
48. Fielding (1749, p. 97).
49. The letters are in *Gazetteer and New Daily Advertiser* April 18, 1765, May 17, 1765, May 20, 1765, May 21, 1765, and June 1, 1765.
50. *Gazetteer and New Daily Advertiser*, December 31, 1767. Rowe identifies himself as the writer of this letter in Rowe (1776).
51. These societies do not appear in William Dale's list of societies in 1772 and since the advertisements in London newspaper for these societies ceased in 1767 or 1768, it can be safely assumed that they had ceased their operations by 1770.
52. *Gazetteer and New Daily Advertiser*, November 26, 1766.
53. *Public Advertiser*, June 17, 1767.
54. *Gazetteer and New Daily Advertiser* July 10, 1767.
55. The last advertisement for the Guardian Society appears in *Public Advertiser*, June 29, 1768.
56. Most of the letters, with some minor changes and additional comments, are reprinted in Rowe (1776).
57. Webb initially wrote under the pseudonym "Necrologisticus." The "necro" refers to dead bodies and "logisticus" refers to the ancient mathematician Apollodorus Logisticus, or Apollodorus the calculator.
58. *Gazetteer and New Daily Advertiser*, July 3, 1770.
59. *London Magazine or Gentleman's Monthly Intelligencer*, 1770, Vol. 39, pp. 465–9; *Gentleman's Magazine and Historical Chronicle*, 1770, Vol. 40, pp. 422–5.
60. *Gentleman's Magazine and Historical Chronicle*, 1770, Vol. 40, pp. 524–5.
61. Price (1769).
62. Ibid. (1770). The problems to which Price refers (XVII and XX) are actually from the third edition of the *Doctrine of Chances* (De Moivre, 1756); they appear as Problems XV and XVII in the 2nd through 4th editions of *Annuities upon Lives* (De Moivre, 1743, 1750, 1752).
63. Morgan (1815, p. 39).
64. Price (1771, p. xv).
65. Gloucestershire Archives D2700/RA2/1/13.
66. Dale (1772, pp. 230–47).
67. *Gazetteer and New Daily Advertiser*, September 17, 1771.
68. The job went to John Tipp. See, for example, an advertisement in *Gazetteer and New Daily Advertiser*, January 27, 1772.
69. *Bingley's Journal of Universal Gazette*, June 15–22, 1771.
70. *London Magazine or Gentleman's Monthly Intelligencer*, 1771, Vol. 40, pp. 319–21.
71. *Gazetteer and New Daily Advertiser*, August 27, 1771.
72. *Public Advertiser*, August 17, 1773.
73. Price (1983, p. 102).
74. *Public Advertiser*, November 1, 1771.

Chapter 9

1. The earliest advertisement for its sale that I can find is in *Public Advertiser*, June 6, 1771.
2. The reform is mentioned in a letter to the printer signed "Benevolus" in *Gazetteer and New Daily Advertiser*, February 8, 1772.
3. Price (1773, p. 401).
4. *Morning Chronicle and London Advertiser*, September 8, 1772.
5. *Morning Chronicle and London Advertiser*, September 8, 1772.
6. London Annuity Society (1780).
7. Price (1783).
8. Institute and Faculty of Actuaries Archive EL/6/1/13.
9. Laudable Society for the Benefit of Widows (ca 1781, pp. 32–3).
10. Parts of their report are quoted in a letter to the printer of the *Morning Chronicle and London Advertiser*, October 8, 1772. The highest page number in the report that is referenced is 62.
11. *Morning Chronicle and London Advertiser*, September 22, 1772.
12. *Morning Chronicle and London Advertiser*, October 1, 1772.
13. *Morning Chronicle and London Advertiser*, October 8, 1772.
14. This is attributed to Webb in documents in the Institute and Faculty of Actuaries Archive BV pam 13c1.
15. *Gazetteer and New Daily Advertiser*, October 5, 1772 and October 8, 1772.
16. *Gazetteer and New Daily Advertiser*, October 14, 1772.
17. *Daily Advertiser*, January 15, 1773.
18. This issue of the *Public Ledger* does not seem to be extant. It is quoted in the material from the Institute of Actuaries archive.
19. *Daily Advertiser*, January 20, 1773.
20. Notice of the meeting and reports of it are in *Morning Chronicle and London Advertiser*, January 25, 1773, *Middlesex Journal or Universal Evening Post*, January 26–8, 1773, and *Craftsman or Say's Weekly Journal*, January 30, 1773.
21. *Daily Advertiser*, February 11, 1773.
22. The petitions that were presented to Parliament and the response to them are in Great Britain, House of Commons (1803, Vol. 34, pp. 500, 560, 759–60).
23. Great Britain, House of Commons (1803, Vol. 34, p. 47).
24. Institute and Faculty of Actuaries Archive BV pam 13c1.
25. Price (1773, p. 398).
26. *Gentleman's Magazine*, Vol. 64, 1774, p. 503.
27. *Gentleman's Magazine*, Vol. 65, pp. 79, 124–7.
28. Todhunter (1865, p. 446).
29. *Critical Review or Annals of Literature*, Vol. 44, 1777, p. 367.
30. Dale (1777, p. 8).
31. Ibid. (p. 105–6) and Maitland (1739, p. 537).
32. Ibid. (pp. 70–1).
33. Price (1783, Vol. 1, pp. 145–8).
34. Anonymous (1823, p. 134).
35. Dale (1777, p. 6).

36. His worksheet showing the raw data is inserted between pages 59 and 60 of Dale (1777). The worksheet is reproduced in Haberman and Sibbett (1995, Vol. 4, pp. 26–7) and in Keiding (1987).
37. Biographical information on Maseres can be found in Martin (2004).
38. Price (1983, pp. 99–101). Peach and Thomas dated this letter prior to Eumenes's letter in the *Public Advertiser*. New information puts the letter between July 22, 1771 and October 14, 1771.
39. *Sussex Weekly Advertiser, or Lewes Journal* October 14, 1771 and October 21, 1771. Price's suggestion is also followed in Maseres (1772).
40. *Gazetteer and New Daily Advertiser*, January 8, 1772.
41. Price (1772a, pp. 380–7, 1772b, pp. 38–45).
42. Maseres (1772).
43. American Philosophical Society Library, G: F85 XLIX.36.
44. See, for example, Baxter's writings on "Directions about our Labour and Calling" in Baxter (1773, pp. 447–50).
45. Letter from Franklin to Maseres and Maseres's reply the same day, Packard Humanities Institute (1988).
46. Maseres (1772).
47. Ibid. (1783, p. 34).
48. Cobbett and Hansard (1813, p. 642).
49. Maseres (1773, pp. 13–32).
50. Price (1773, pp. 323, 325) and Simpson (1752, pp. 254, 260). Maseres (1783, p. 629) attributes the tables to Price. The tables attached to the bill, which give no attribution, can be found in Great Britain, House of Commons (1975, pp. 35–148).
51. The bill's journey through Parliament and its ultimate demise can be found in Great Britain, House of Commons (1803, Vol. 34, pp. 47, 62, 120, 136, 152, 166, 171) and Great Britain, House of Lords (1796, pp. 543, 577, 700).
52. Gilbert's efforts at Poor Law reform is described in Tompson (2004).
53. Acland (1786).
54. *Public Advertiser*, December 4, 1786 and December 28, 1786.
55. *World and Fashionable Advertiser*, January 24, 1787.
56. Support for Gilbert's idea appears in letters to newspapers: *Morning Chronicle and London Advertiser*, March 13, 1787, *Whitehall Evening Post*, April 5–7, 1787, and April 14–17, 1787, as well as in Country Gentleman (1787).
57. Considerations of Acland's proposal in parliamentary bills are in Great Britain, House of Commons (1803, Vol. 42, pp. 703–4, 730, 78–787, Vol. 43, pp. 319, 355, and Vol. 44, pp. 212, 370–1, 426, 433, 441 and *Journals of the House of Lords*, Vol. 38, Great Britain, House of Lords (1809, pp. 476, 490).
58. Great Britain, House of Commons (1787, p. 221).
59. Ibid. (1975, Vol. 64).
60. Gosden (1961, p. 100).
61. Price (1792, Vol. 2, pp. 410–11).
62. Ibid. (1771, pp. 317–18).

Chapter 10

1. Price (1771, pp. 121–8).
2. Some modern publications refer to Brand as the Registrar or Register of the Amicable Society. Contemporary sources show he was a clerk who was assistant to the Register. Brown (1819, p. 169), in reporting a 1787 court case, states that Brand was assistant to the Register. An anonymous (1776) London directory lists Brand as the single clerk at the Amicable Society and Joseph Baldwin as the Register.
3. Brand (1775).
4. *The Critical Review: or, Annals of Literature*, Vol. 40, 1775, pp. 111–19.
5. *The Monthly Review; or, Literary Journal*, Vol. 52, 1775, p. 274.
6. *The London Magazine: or, Gentleman's Monthly Intelligencer*, Vol. 44, p. 1775.
7. *The Critical Review: or, Annals of Literature*, Vol. 41, 1776, p. 160.
8. Clark (1999, p. 123).
9. *The Critical Review: or, Annals of Literature*, Vol. 41, 1776, pp. 160–8.
10. Brand (1778).
11. Walford (1871, pp. 81–2).
12. Ibid. (1885).
13. Drew (1928, pp. 60, 84).
14. Bellhouse (2007).
15. London Metropolitan Archives. CLC/192/MS08740/001–006.
16. London Metropolitan Archives. CLC/192/MS08740/006 for 1771–1809.
17. London Assurance (ca 1810).
18. Dale (1777, p. 6).
19. *Gentleman's Magazine, and Historical Chronicle*, Vol. 103, June 133, pp. 569–70, Ogborn (1962, pp. 103–4) and Elderton (1932).
20. Price (1771, p. 255).
21. In a few cases in Tables 10.1 and 10.2 I have rounded a number up rather than rounding it off, so that the totals conform to the total number of deaths or to the radix of the 1771 or 1783 life tables.
22. Price (1783, p. 358).
23. Morgan (1779, pp. xv–xix).
24. Price (1783, Vol. 2, p. 79).
25. Ibid. (p. 358).
26. Ogborn (1962, pp. 110–11).
27. Institute of Actuaries Archives, EL/6/1/7–10.
28. Institute of Actuaries Archives, EL/6/1/10.
29. Royal Society Archives, EC/1790/05.
30. Morgan (1788, 1789, 1791, 1794, 1800).

Chapter 11

1. Exeter Cathedral Archives 7077/104/2.
2. Laurence (1730), p. 7.
3. Hendriks and Rowe (1857).
4. Cornwall Record Office T/1551.

5. Exeter Cathedral Archives 7076/105/155. On the reverse side of a manuscript entitled "Terms of renewing copyhold estates" dated 1812.
6. Exeter Cathedral Archives 7076/105/3. Letter from William Morgan February 22, 1806.
7. Baily (1802).
8. Inwood (1811).
9. Power (1839, p. 155).
10. Hendriks and Rowe (1857, p. 144).
11. Berkshire Record Office D/ESV/M/B11.
12. Hendriks and Rowe (1857, p. 140).
13. Brown (1819, pp. 167–80).
14. Ibid. (p. 175).
15. Kenrick (1788, p. 17).
16. Morgan (1779, p. 269).
17. Great Britain, House of Commons (1777).
18. Institute and Faculty of Actuaries Archive RKN 43915.
19. Clay (1895, p. 632).

Appendix I

1. Kellison (2009).
2. Jordan (1967).

Bibliography

Manuscript Sources

American Philosophical Society Library
G: F85 XLIX.36 Miscellaneous Papers
Berkshire Record Office
D/ESV/M/B11. Letters to Joseph Brooks from Joshua Lucock Wilkinson of Grays Inn, and others, on means of raising money for the Duke of Marlborough apparently for redemption of land tax on his estates
British Library Manuscripts
Add. MS 38729 British Library Add. MS 38729
Cambridge University Library
Macclesfield Collection
MS Add. 9597/8/4. The solution of a question relating to the chances of lives which may serve as a caution to be observed by such as form or are like to be concerned in projects for Insurance of Lives
MS Add. 9597/8/9 (Annuities upon Lives)
MS Add. 9597/8/10 (Simple Interest)
MS Add. 9597/8/11 (Of Annuities in Reversion)
MS Add. 9597/8/12 ("Simple Interest," "Of Purchasing Freehold Estates by the Years Purchase," and "Compound Interest")
Canterbury Cathedral Archives
CCA-DCc-BB/29/30–36 (Notes)
BB/29/33: "On the calculation of fines for the renewal of leases and the valuation of leases for lives"
Centre for Kentish Studies
U1590/C21. Papers by several eminent mathematicians addressed to or collected by Lord Stanhope (contains three letters from De Moivre to Stanhope and several papers by Thomas Bayes)
Columbia University Library
David Eugene Smith Collection of Historical Papers Series I: Catalogued Correspondents Box 21 Thomas Simpson
Cornwall Record Office
T/1551. Case and opinion of William Morgan, actuary to the Equitable Society, concerning leasehold manor, probably Cargoll

Cumbria Archive Centre, Carlisle
DHUD 8/68/2. A Plan of a Society for Granting Annuities to the Widows of Gentlemen of the Law, by Josiah Brown, December 21, 1765
Exeter Cathedral Archives
7076/105/3 and 155. Chapter Clerks Miscellanea
7077/104/2. Terms of renewing Leases adopted by various Cathedrals, 1806
Gloucestershire Archives
D2700/RA2/1/13. Household steward's (William Dale) accounts held at Badminton
Institute and Faculty of Actuaries Archive
BV pam 13c1
EL/6/1/2a. "Tables," by James Dodson Sr
EL/6/1/3. "First Lecture on Insurances," by James Dodson Sr
EL/6/1/5. Book of letters from Richard Price to John Edwards, actuary
EL/6/1/6a. "Observations on the proper method of keeping the accounts, and determining from year to year the state of the Society", by Richard Price
EL/6/1/7. Tables of annual premiums and tables of survivorships, by William Morgan
EL/6/1/8a. "Calculations of premiums" based on the Northampton mortality tables, by William Morgan
EL/6/1/9. Calculations of premiums based on the Northampton mortality tables, by William Morgan
EL/6/1/10. "Table of premiums," by William Morgan
EL/6/1/13. Tables showing the progress of the London Annuity Society in its first 24 years (1765–89)
RKN 43195. Richard Price letter February 28, 1778 accompanies copy of Petition for an Act to enable John Arthur Worsop to settle a Jointure upon any Woman or Women he may hereafter marry on the terms therein mentioned
London Metropolitan Archives
CLC/192/MS08740/001–006 (Assurance Books on Lives. 1733–1809)
MS 12806 Volume 11 (Christ's Hospital Records)
MS 12819 Volume 18 (Christ's Hospital Records)
Public Record Office (PRO)
C 12/1820/3: *Nichols* v. *Gould dep*
PROB 11/556/318: will of Daniel Cholmondeley
PROB 11/811/473: will of Abraham De Moivre
PROB 11/961/228: will of Gael Morris, Broker of London
PROB 11/913/443: will of Weyman Lee of Inner Temple, Middlesex
PROB 11/834/262: will of James Dodson
PROB 11/798/37: will of William Whiston
PROB 11/1285/184: will of William Dale
PROB 11/1091/206: will of Michael Fisher
PROB 18/34/86: *Probate Lawsuit Cholmondeley* v. *Pope* otherwise Cholmondeley and Beachcroft, concerning the deceased Daniel Cholmondeley of St Bride, London. Allegation and interrogatory

PROB 18/34/108: *Probate Lawsuit Cholmondeley* v. *Pope* otherwise Cholmondeley and Beachcroft, concerning the deceased Daniel Cholmondeley of St. Bride, London. Allegation and interrogatory
Royal Society Archives
Election Certificates
EC/1768/03 (James Horsfall)
EC/1790/05 William Morgan
Journal Books of Scientific Meetings: Volumes 8 and 16
L&P/1/23 (undated letter from Willem Kersseboom to John Eames)
Staatsbibliothek zu Berlin – Preußischer Kulturbesitz Handschriftenabteilung
Sig. Darmstaedter H 1695: Moivre, Abraham de
St. John's College Library, Cambridge
TaylorB/C3 (Manuscript notes relating to annuitics)
Universitätsbibliothek Oldenburg
Cim.1, 184 (Leçons sur Algêbre par Mons: Abr: de Moivre à Londres commence le 7me du Mai 1742 fine dans le mois d'Avril 1743)
University College London
Bentham Papers CLXVI/202

Printed Sources

Acland, J. (1786). *A Plan for Rendering the Poor Independent on Public Contribution; Founded on the Basis of the Friendly Societies, Commonly Called Clubs*. Exeter: R. Thorn.

Aldis, H.G., Bowles, R., Dix, E.R.M. et al. (1968). *A Dictionary of Printers and Booksellers in England, Scotland and Ireland, and of Foreign Printers of English Books 1557–1640*. Oxford: The Bibliographical Society.

Allen, R.C. (1992). *Enclosure and the Yeoman*. Oxford: Clarendon Press.

Amicable Society (1710). *The Charter of the Corporation of the Amicable Society for a Perpetual Assurance-Office; Together with the By-Laws Thereunto Belonging*. London: George Sawbridge.

Amicable Society (1721). *A List of the Members of the Corporation of the Amicable Society for a Perpetual Assurance-Office, Who Are Contributors on Their Own Lives, and Have a Right to Vote at the Election of Directors*. London: Mary Matthews.

Andrews, A. (1859). *The History of British Journalism from the Foundation of the Newspaper Press in England, to the Repeal of the Stamp Act in 1855, with Sketches of Press Celebrities*. London: Richard Bentley.

Anonymous (1696). *The Friendly Society for Widows Being a Proposal for Supplying the Defect of Joyntures, and Securing Women from Falling into Poverty and Distress at the Death of Their Husbands*. London: F.C.

Anonymous (1776). *A New Edition (Corrected to 1st of March 1776) of the Court and City Register; or Gentleman's Complete Annual Calendar, for the Year 1776*. London: J. Joliffe.

Anonymous (1781). *A New Edition, Corrected to the 8th of February, of The Royal Kalendar; or Complete and Correct Annual Register for England, Scotland, Ireland, and America for the Year 1781*. London: J. Almon and J. Debrett.

Anonymous (1794). *The Royal Kalendar; or Complete and Correct Annual Register for England, Scotland, Ireland, and America for the Year 1794*. London: J. Debrett.

Anonymous (1823). *The Annual Subscription Charities and Public Societies in London*. London: John Murray.

Anonymous (1949–50). International actuarial notation. *Transactions of the Faculty of Actuaries* 19: 89–99.

Ashton, T.S. (1955). *An Economic History of England: The 18th Century*. London: Methuen.

Assheton, W. (1699). *An Account of Dr Assheton's Proposal (as Improved and Managed by the Worshipful Company of Mercers, London) for the Benefit of Widows of Clergymen and Others; by Settling Joyntures and Annuities at the Rate of Thirty Per cent*. London: B. Aylmer.

Baily, F. (1802). *Tables for the Purchasing and Renewing of Leases for Terms of Years Certain and for Lives*. London: W.J. and J. Richardson.

Baily, F. (1810). *The Doctrine of Life-Annuities and Assurances, Analytically Investigated and Explained*. London: John Richardson.

Baxter, R. (1773), *Christian Directory, or, A Summ of Practical Theologie and Cases of Conscience*. London: Robert White.

Bayes, T. (1763). An essay towards solving a problem in the doctrine of chances. *Philosophical Transactions of the Royal Society* 53: 370–418.

Beckett, J.V. (1984). The pattern of land ownership in England and Wales, 1660–1880. *The Economic History Review* 37: 1–22.

Bellhouse, D.R. (2007). Lord Stanhope's papers on the doctrine of chances. *Historia Mathematica* 34: 173–86.

Bellhouse, D.R. (2011a). A new look at Halley's life table. *Journal of the Royal Statistical Society (A)* 174: 823–32.

Bellhouse, D.R. (2011b). *Abraham De Moivre: Setting the Stage for Classical Probability and Its Applications*. Boca Raton, London: CRC Press.

Bellhouse, D.R. (2015). Mathematicians and the early English life insurance industry. *BSHM Bulletin* 30: 131–42.

Bellhouse, D.R. (n.d.). Mathematics: In *A History of the Dissenting Academies in the British Isles, 1660–1860. Volume 3, The Curricula in the Academies*. I. Rivers and M. Burden (eds.), Cambridge: Cambridge University Press.

Bellhouse, D.R. and Genest, C. (2007). Maty's life of Abraham De Moivre, translated, annotated and augmented. *Statistical Science* 22: 109–36.

Bendall, S. (1997). *Dictionary of Land Surveyors and Local Map-Makers of Great Britain and Ireland 1530–1850*. Vol. 2, 2nd Edition. London: British Library.

Bendall, S. (2004). Laurence, Edward (bap. 1674, d. 1739). *Oxford Dictionary of National Biography*. Oxford: Oxford University Press. Published online at: www.oxforddnb.com/view/article/16125.

Bennett, H.S. (1965). *English Books & Readers 1558 to 1603*. Cambridge: Cambridge University Press.

Bennett, H.S. (1970). *English Books & Readers 1603 to 1640*. Cambridge: Cambridge University Press.

Betham, W. (1803). *The Baronetage of England, or the History of the English Baronets, and Such Baronets of Scotland as Are of English Families*. Vol. 3. London: E. Lloyd.

Blackstone, W. (1794). *Commentaries on the Laws of England. Book II.* 12th Edition. London: A. Strahan and W. Woodfall.
Bradley, J. (1832). *Miscellaneous Works and Correspondence of the Rev. James Bradley, D.D. F.R.S.* S.P. Rigaud (ed.), Oxford: Oxford University Press.
Brakenridge, W. (1755). A letter to the Right Honourable the Earl of Macclesfield, President of the Royal Society, concerning the method of constructing a table for the probabilities of life at London. *Philosophical Transactions* 49: 167–82.
Brand, C. (1775). *A Treatise on Assurances and Annuities on Lives with Several Objections against Dr. Price's Observations on the Amicable Society and Others.* London: Owen.
Brand, C. (1778). *A Table of the Durations of Lives in the Corporation of the Amicable Society for a Perpetual Assurance–Office.* London.
Brown, W. (1819). *Reports of Cases Argued and Determined in the High Court of Chancery during the Time of Lord Chancellor Thurlow, of the Several Lords Commissioner of the Great Seal, and of Lord Chancellor Loughborough, from 1776 to 1794, with an Appendix of Contemporary Cases.* Vol. 2. London: W. Clarke and Sons.
Buck, P. (1982). People who counted: political arithmetic in the eighteenth century. *Isis* 73: 28–45.
Buffon, G.L. Leclerc. (1749). *Histoire naturelle, générale et particulière: avec la description du Cabinet du Roy. Tome Second.* Paris: Imprimerie Royale.
Burden, M. (2013). *A Biographical Dictionary of Tutors at the Dissenters' Private Academies, 1660–1729.* London: Dr Williams's Centre for Dissenting Studies. Published online at: www.qmulreligionandliterature.co.uk/wp-content/uploads/2015/11/bd.pdf.
Burke, J. and Burke, J.B. (1838). *A Genealogical and Heraldic History of the Extinct and Dormant Baronetcies of England.* London: Scott, Webster and Geary.
Carter, R. (1695). *A Beneficial Proposal, Wherein All Adventurers Are Gainers for Exchanging the Blank Tickets, and 10l. Benefit Tickets in the Million-Adventure, by Making Them Much More Valuable Than Now They are, to All Persons that Shall Bring Them into This Proposal, Made by R. Carter, and Others.* London: W. Marshal.
Carter, R. (1711). *A Scheme of a Second State-Lottery.* London.
Cherry, B. (2001). Edward Hatton's new view of London. *Architectural History* 44: 96–105.
Cholmondeley, D. (1713). *A Proposal for Granting Annuities to Raise a Stock for Improving the Fishery of Great-Britain.* London: J. Read.
Cholmondeley, D. (1714a). *The Articles of Settlement of the Benevolent Society for Granting Annuities to Raise a Stock for Improving the Fishery of Great Britain.* London.
Cholmondeley, D. (1714b). *A Sure Way for the Rich to Improve Their Fortunes and to Preserve Others for Wanting Necessaries.* Broadside bound with Cholmondeley (1714a) in the Harry Ransom Center at the University of Texas at Austin.
City of London Livery Companies Commission (1894). *City of London Livery Companies' Commission: Report and Appendix Volume 4.* London: Eyre and Spottiswoode.

Clark, G. (2002). Land rental values and the agrarian economy: England and Wales, 1500–1914. *European Review of Economic History* 6: 281–308.

Clark, G.W. (1999). *Betting on Lives: The Culture of Life insurance in England, 1695–1775*. Manchester: Manchester University Press.

Clarke, F.M. (1929). *Thomas Simpson and His Times*. New York: Waverley Press.

Clay, C. (1974). The price of freehold land in the later seventeenth and eighteenth centuries. *The Economic History Review* 27: 173–89.

Clay, C. (1980). "The greed of Whig bishops"?: church landlords and their lessees 1660–1760. *Past & Present* 87: 128–57.

Clay, C. (1981). Lifeleasehold in the western counties of England 1650–1750. *The Agricultural History Review* 29: 83–96.

Clay, J.W. (1895). *Familiae Minorum Gentium*. Vol. 2. London: Harleian Society.

Clay, T. (1619). *A Chorologicall Discourse of the Well Ordering, Disposing and Gouerning of an Honorable Estate or Reuennue Briefly Describing the Duties of Diuers Officers Therein to Be Imployed*. London: Eld.

Clay, T. (1621). *A Chorologicall Discourse of the Well Ordering, Disposing and Gouerning of an Honorable Estate or Reuennue Briefly Describing the Duties of Diuers Officers Therein to Be Imployed*. London: Eld.

Clay, T. (1622). *Briefe, Easie, and Necessary Tables for the Valuation of Leases, Annuities, and Purchases, Either in Present, or in Reuersion, According to the Rates Now Most in VSE*. London: Eld and Flesher.

Cobbett, W. and Hansard, T.C. (1813). *The Parliamentary History of England, for the Earliest Period to the Year 1803*. Vol. 17. London: Hansard.

Cook, A. (1993). Halley the Londoner: *Notes and Records of the Royal Society of London* 47: 163–77.

Cook, A. (1998). *Edmond Halley: Charting the Heavens and the Seas*. Oxford: Clarendon Press.

Country Gentleman (1787). *A Letter to Thomas Gilbert, Esq; on His Intended Reform of the Poor Laws*. London: Debrett.

Crane, V.W. (1966). The Club of Honest Whigs: friends of science and liberty. *The William and Mary Quarterly* 23: 210–33.

Cruickshanks, E., Handley, S., and Hayton, D.W. (2002). *The History of Parliament: The House of Commons 1690–1715. Volume 3–4*. Cambridge: Cambridge University Press.

Dale, W. (1772). *Calculations Deduced from First Principles in the Most Familiar Manner, by Plain Arithmetic, for the Use of Societies Instituted for the Benefit of Old Age*. London: J. Ridley.

Dale, W. (1777). *A Supplement to Calculations Deduced from First Principles in the Most Familiar Manner, by Plain Arithmetic, for the Use of Societies Instituted for the Benefit of Old Age*. London: J. Ridley.

Daston, L. (1987). The domestication of risk: mathematical probability and insurance 1650–1830. In *The Probabilistic Revolution, Volume 1: Ideas in History*. L. Krüger, L.J. Daston, and M. Heidelberger (eds.), pp. 237–60. Cambridge, MA: MIT Press.

Daston, L. (1988). *Classical Probability in the Enlightenment*. Princeton: Princeton University Press.

De Moivre, A. (1711). De mensura sortis seu; de probabilitate eventum in ludis a casu fortuito pendentibus. *Philosophical Transactions* 27: 213–64.

De Moivre, A. (1718). *The Doctrine of Chances, or, a Method of Calculating the Probability of Events in Play*. London: W. Pearson.

De Moivre, A. (1725). *Annuities upon Lives, or, the Valuation of Annuities upon Any Number of Lives, As Also, of Reversions to Which Is Added, an Appendix Concerning the Expectations of Life, and Probabilities of Survivorship*. London: W.P.

De Moivre, A. (1731). *Annuities upon Lives, or, the Valuation of Annuities upon Any Number of Lives, as also, of Reversions to Which Is Added, an Appendix Concerning the Expectations of Life, and Probabilities of Survivorship*. 2nd Edition. Dublin: Samuel Fuller.

De Moivre, A. (1738). *The Doctrine of Chances: or, a Method of Calculating the Probability of the Events in Play*. 2nd Edition. London: Woodfall.

De Moivre, A. (1743). *Annuities on Lives: Second Edition, Plainer, Fuller, and More Correct than the Former*. London: Woodfall.

De Moivre, A. (1744). A letter from Mr. Abraham De Moivre, F.R.S. to William Jones, Esquire, F.R.S. concerning the easiest method for calculating the value of annuities upon lives, from tables of observations. *Philosophical Transactions* 43: 65–78.

De Moivre, A. (1750). *Annuities on Lives: Third Edition, Plainer, Fuller, and More Correct than the Former*. London: Millar.

De Moivre, A. (1752). *Annuities on Lives: With Several Tables, Exhibiting at One View, the Values of Lives, for Different Rates of Interest*. London: Millar.

De Moivre, A. (1756). *The Doctrine of Chances: Or, a Method of Calculating the Probability of Events in Play*. 3rd Edition. London: Millar.

De Morgan, A. (1872). *A Budget of Paradoxes*. London: Longmans, Green and Co.

De Morgan, S. (1882). *Memoir of Augustus De Morgan*. London: Longman, Green and Co.

Dekker, T. (1603). *The Wonderfull Yeare 1603: Wherein Is Shewed the Picture of London, Lying Sicke of the Plague*. London: Thomas Creede.

Dickson, P.G.M. (1967). *The Financial Revolution in England: A Study in the Development of Public Credit, 1688–1756*. London: Macmillan.

Dodson, J. (1752). A letter from Mr. James Dodson to Mr. John Robertson, F. R. S. concerning an improvement of the bills of mortality. *Philosophical Transactions* 47: 333–40.

Dodson, J. (1753). *The Mathematical Repository. Volume II. Containing Algebraical Solutions of a Great Number of Problems, in Several Branches of the Mathematics*. London: John Nourse.

Dodson, J. (1754). A letter to the Right Honorable George Earl of Macclesfield, P.R.S. concerning the value of an annuity for life, and the probability of survivorship. *Philosophical Transactions* 48: 487–99.

Dodson, J. (1755). *The Mathematical Repository Volume III: Containing Analytical Solutions of a Great Number of the Most Difficult Problems, Relating to Annuities, Reversions, Survivorships, Insurances and Leases Dependent on Lives*. London: John Nourse.

Dodson, J. (1756). A letter to the Reverend William Brakenridge, D. D. Rector of St. Mich. Bassishaw, and F. R. S. with a table of the value of annuities on lives. *Philosophical Transactions* 49: 891–2.

Drew, B. (1928). *The London Assurance: A Chronicle*. Oxford: Kemp Hall Press.

Dyson, J. (1977). *Business in Great Waters: The Story of British Fishermen*. London: Angus and Robertson.

Eames, J. (1739). A short account of Mr. Kersseboom's essay [intituled, Verhandeling tot een Proeve om te weeten de probable Menigte des Volks in de Proventie van Hollandt en Westfrieslandt. Hage 1738. in 4to. door W. Kersseboom] upon the number of people in Holland and West-Friezland, as also in Harlem, Gouda and the Hague; drawn from the Bills of Births, Burials, or Marriages, in those Places. *Philosophical Transactions* 40: 401–6.

Easton, J.B. (1967). The early editions of Robert Recorde's Ground of Artes. *Isis* 58: 515–32.

Elderton, W.P. (1932). William Morgan, F.R.S., 1750–1833. *Transactions of the Faculty of Actuaries* 14: 1–20.

Equitable Society (1762). *A Short Account of the Society for Equitable Assurances on Lives and Survivorships*. London.

Equitable Society (1769a). *The Directors State of the Society for Equitable Assurances on Lives and Survivorships*. London: Kearsley.

Equitable Society (1769b). *Papers relating to the Disputes with the Charter Fund Proprietors in the Equitable Society*. London.

Equitable Society (1854). *The Deed of Settlement of the Society for Equitable Assurances on Lives and Survivorships*. London: Taylor and Francis.

Evans, W.D. (1817). *A Collection of Statutes Connected with the General Administration of the Law*. Vol. I. London: Butterworth.

Farren, E.J. (1844). *Historical Essay on the Rise and Early Progress of the Doctrine of Life-Contingencies in England, Leading to the Establishment of the First Life-Assurance Society in Which Ages Were Distinguished*. London: Smith, Elder & Co.

Fauvel, J. (1989). Platonic rhetoric in distance learning: how Robert Record taught the home learner. *For the Learning of Mathematics* 9: 2–6.

Fielding, H. (1749). *The History of Tom Jones, a Founding*. London: A. Millar.

Fitzherbert, J. (1523). *Here Begynneth a Ryght Frutefull mater: And Hath to Name the Boke of Surveyeng and Improvme[n]tes*. London: Rycharde Pynson.

Glass, D.V. (1973). *Numbering the People: The Eighteenth-Century Population Controversy and the Development of Census and Vital Statistics in Britain*. Farnborough: Saxon House.

Gosden, P.H.J.H. (1961). *The Friendly Societies in England 1815–1875*. Manchester: Manchester University Press.

Graetzer, J. (1883). *Edmund Halley und Caspar Neumann: Ein Beitrag zur Geschichte der Bevölkerungs-statistik*. Breslau: Schottlaender.

Gray, G.J. and McConnell, A. (2004). Dodson, James (c. 1705–57). In *Oxford Dictionary of National Biography*. Oxford: Oxford University Press. Published online at: www.oxforddnb.com/view/article/7756.

Great Britain (1786). *Statutes Relative to the Sewers, within Westminster, and Part of Middlesex*. London.

Great Britain (1796). *Statutes Relative to the Sewers, within Westminster, and Part of Middlesex*. London.

Great Britain (1963). *The Statutes of the Realm. Printed by Command of His Majesty King George the Third*. Vols. 6, 8, and 9. London: Dawsons of Pall Mall.

Great Britain, Army (1756). *A List of the General and Field-Officers as They Rank in the Army*. London: J. Millan.

Great Britain, Army (1769). *The Military Register; or New and Complete Lists of All His Majesty's Land Forces and Marines for the Year 1769*. London: J. Almon.

Great Britain, House of Commons (1777). *An Act to Enable John Arthur Worsop, (Heretofore Called John Arthur) Esquire, to Settle a Jointure upon Any Woman or Women He may Hereafter Marry, on the Terms therein Mentioned. Private Acts 1702–1727 and Private Bills 1727–1814*. In ProQuest. *U.K. Parliamentary Papers*. Published online at: http://parlipapers.proquest.com/parlipapers/search/basic/hcppbasicsearch.

Great Britain, House of Commons (1787). *The Parliamentary Register; or History of the Proceedings and Debates of the House of Commons*, Vol. 22. London: J. Debrett.

Great Britain, House of Commons (1803). *Journals of the House of Commons*. Vols. 25, 34, 42, 43, and 44. London: His Majesty's Stationary Office.

Great Britain, House of Commons (1975). *House of Commons Sessional Papers of the Eighteenth Century*. Vols. 23 and 64. S. Lambert (ed.), Wilmington, Delaware: Scholarly Resources.

Great Britain, House of Lords (1796). *Journals of the House of Lords, Beginning anno undecimo Georgii Tertii, 1770*. Vol. 33. London: His Majesty's Stationery Office.

Great Britain, House of Lords (1809). *Journals of the House of Lords, Beginning anno vicesimo octavo Georgii Tertii, 1783*. Vol. 38. London: His Majesty's Stationery Office.

Great Britain, House of Lords (1810). *Calendar of the Journals of the House of Lords from the Beginning of the Reign of King Henry VIII to 30th August 1642 and from the Restoration in 1660 to 21st January 1808*. London: G. Eyre and A. Strahan.

Gunther, R.T. (1935). *Early Science in Oxford*, Vol. 10. Oxford: University Press.

Haberman, S. and Sibbett, T.A. (1995). *History of Actuarial Science*. Vol. 4. London: W. Pickering & Chatto.

Haig, R.L. (1960). *The Gazetteer, 1735–1797; A Study in the Eighteenth-century English Newspaper*. Carbondale: Southern Illinois University Press.

Hald, A. (1990). *A History of Probability and Statistics and Their Applications before 1750*. New York: John Wiley.

Halley, E. (1693a). An estimate of the degrees of mortality of mankind, drawn from the curious tables of births and funerals in the City of Breslaw; with an attempt to ascertain the price of annuities upon lives. *Philosophical Transactions* 17: 596–610.

Halley, E. (1693b). Some further considerations on the Breslaw bills of mortality. *Philosophical Transactions* 17: 654–56.

Harnack, A. (1900): *Geschichte der Königlich Preussischen Akademie der Wissenschaften zu Berlin*. Vol. 2. Berlin: Reichsdruckerei.

Harris, E.T. (2004). Handel the investor. *Music & Letters* 85: 521–75.

Hatton, E. (1708). *A New View of London, or an Ample Account of that City, in Two Volumes, or Eight Sections*. Vol. 1. London: John Nicholson and Robert Knaplock.

Hatton, E. (1714). *An Index to Interest*. London: Jonas Brown.

Hatton, E. (1721). *An Intire System of Arithmetic*. London: King.

Hawkins, J. (1776). *A General History of the Science and Practice of Music*. Vols. 4 and 5. London: T. Payne and Sons.

Hayes, R. (1727). *A New Method for Valuing of Annuities upon Lives*. London: R. Hayes.

Hayes, R. (1728). *An Estimate of Places for Life: Shewing How Many Years Purchase a Place for Life Is Worth*. London: Meadows.

Hendriks, F. and Rowe, J. (1857). The case book of John Rowe, of London and Exeter, from 1775 to 1790. *The Assurance Magazine, and Journal of the Institute of Actuaries* 7: 136–48.

Hodgson, J. (1747). *The Valuation of Annuities upon Lives; Deduced from the London Bills of Mortality*. London: J. Hinton.

Hogg, B.B. (2011). Freemasons and the Royal Society: Alphabetical List of Fellows of the Royal Society Who Were Freemasons. Published online at: www.freemasonry.london.museum/os/wp-content/resources/frs_freemasons_complete_jan2012.pdf.

Hoppit, J. (2002). The myths of the South Sea Bubble. *Transactions of the Royal Historical Society* 12: 141–65.

Howard, R. (1694). *A Particular Accompt of the Moneys Paid into the Receipt of Exchequer, upon the Late Million Act, for the Benefit of Survivorship*. London: Samuel Heyrick.

Hoyle, E. (1754). *An Essay Towards Making the Doctrine of Chances Easy to Those Who Understand Vulgar Arithmetick Only*. London: J. Jolliff.

Hoyle, R.W. (1992). 'Shearing the hog': the reform of the estates c. 1598–1640. In *The Estates of the English Crown, 1558–1640*. R.W. Hoyle (ed.), pp. 204–62. Cambridge: Cambridge University Press.

Huffman, P.J. (1978). Asset share mathematics. *Transactions of the Society of Actuaries* 30: 277–322.

Inner Temple (2016). *Inner Temple Admissions Database*. Published online at: www.innertemplearchives.org.uk/index.asp.

Inwood, W. (1811). *Tables for the Purchasing of Estates, Freehold, Copyhold or Leasehold, Annuities, &c.* London: J. Taylor.

Jones, W. (1706). *Synopsis Palmariorum Matheseos: or, A New Introduction to the Mathematics: Containing the Principles of Arithmetic & Geometry Demonstrated, in a Short and Easie Method*. London: Matthews.

Jordan, C.W. (1967). *Society of Actuaries Textbook on Life Contingences*. Chicago: Society of Actuaries.

Keiding, N. (1987). The method of expected number of deaths, 1786–1886–1986. *International Statistical Review* 55: 1–20.

Kellison, S.G. (2009), *The Theory of Interest.* 3rd Edition. New York: McGraw-Hill.

Kennett, W. (1703). *A Sermon Preach'd in the Cathedral Church of St. Paul London, before the Sons of the Clergy, December the 3d 1702.* London: Henry Bonwick.

Kenrick, J. (1788). *A State of the Dispute between Sir Robert Clayton, Bart. Sir John Gresham, Bart. Lady Gresham, and Miss Clayton; and John Kenrick, Esq. Relative to the Purchase of the Reversion of the Manor and Borough of Blechingly in the County of Surry, Extracted from the Pleadings in the High Court of Chancery.* London.

Kippis, A. (1784). *Biographia Britannica: or, the Lives of the Most Eminent Persons Who Have Flourished in Great Britain and Ireland, from the Earliest Ages, to the Present Times.* Vol. 3. London: Rivington.

Koehn, N.F. (1994). *The Power of Commerce: Economy and Governance in the First British Empire.* Ithaca and London: Cornell University Press.

Kopf, E.W. (1927). The early history of the annuity. *Proceedings of the Casualty Actuarial Society* 13: 225–66.

Lalande, J.-J. (1765). Remarques sur la vie & les ouvrages de Mrs de la Caille, Bradley, Mayer & Simpson. *Connoissances des mouvemens célestes, pour l'année commune 1767*: 181–204.

Laudable Society for the Benefit of Widows (1770). *An Abstract of the Deed of Settlement of the Laudable-Society for the Benefit of Widows, Which Is Inrolled in the High Court of Chancery, Bearing Date the 18th of March, 1761.* London: Mary Harrison.

Laudable Society for the Benefit of Widows (1781). *Copy of the Deed of Settlement of the Laudable Society for the Benefit of Widows, Inrolled in the High Court of Chancery.* London: Mary Harrison.

Laurence, E. (1727). *The Duty of a Steward to His Lord.* London: John Shuckburgh.

Laurence, E. (1730). *A Dissertation on Estates upon Lives and Years, Whether in Lay or Church-Hands.* London: James and John Knapton.

Law Society for the Benefit of Widows (1766). *The Proposed Deed of Settlement of a Society for Granting Annuities to the Widows of Gentlemen of the Law.* London: William Bunce.

Lee, W. (1737). *An Essay to Ascertain the Value of Leases and Annuities for Years and Lives, and to Estimate the Chances of the Duration of Lives.* London: S. Birt, D. Browne and J. Shuckburgh.

Lee, W. (1754). *A Valuation of Annuities and Leases Certain, for a Single Life.* London: J. Shuckburgh.

Leibniz, G.W. (1964). *Sämtliche Schriften und Briefe. Series 1: Allgemeiner Politischer und Historischer Briefwechsel.* Vol. VII. Berlin: Akademie-Verlag.

Leibniz, G.W. (1970). *Sämtliche Schriften und Briefe. Series 1: Allgemeiner Politischer und Historischer Briefwechsel.* Vol. VIII. Berlin: Akademie-Verlag.

Lewin, C.G. (2003). *Pensions and Insurance before 1800: A Social History.* East Linton, Scotland: Tuckwell Press.

Lewin, C.G. and Valois, M. De (2003). History of actuarial tables. In *The History of Mathematical Tables: From Sumer to Spreadsheets*. M. Campbell-Kelly, M. Croarken, R. Flood, and E. Robson (eds.), pp. 79–103. Oxford: Oxford University Press.

Lewin, C.G. (2004). Witt, Richard (1567/8–1624). In *Oxford Dictionary of National Biography*. Oxford: Oxford University Press. Published online at: www.oxforddnb.com/view/article/38144.

London Annuity Society (1765). *The Plan and Substance of the Deed of Settlement of the London Annuity Society Established to Make Annual Provision for Widows by Deed Inrolled*. London.

London Annuity Society (1780). *The Report of the Committee of the London Annuity Society, Appointed to Examine Their State and Progress and the Ability of Their Fund to Advance the Widow Annuities*. London.

London Assurance (1810). *Proposals of the Corporation of London Assurance of Houses and Goods from Fire, and for Assuring Lives*. London: Henry Teape.

Luttrell, N. (1972). *The Parliamentary Diary of Narcissus Luttrell, 1691–1693*. H. Horwitz (ed.), Oxford: Clarendon Press.

Mabbut, G. (1686). *Tables for Renewing & Purchasing of the Leases of Cathedral-Churches and Colleges According to Several Rates of Interest with Their Construction and Use Explained*. Cambridge: John Hayes.

Mabbut, G. (1700). *Tables for Renewing and Purchasing of the Leases of Cathedral-Churches and Colleges According to Several Rates of Interest with Their Construction and Use Explained*. Cambridge: John Hayes.

Macceagh, H.F. and Sturgess, H.A.C. (1949). *Register of Admissions to the Honourable Society of the Middle Temple*. Vol. 1. London: Butterworth and Co.

MacKenzie, J.-A. and Phillips, M. (2012). *Textbook on Land Law*. Oxford: Oxford University Press.

Maclaurin, C. (1982). *The Collected Letters of Colin MacLaurin*. S. Mills (ed.), Nantwich: Shiva Publishing.

Maitland, W. (1739). *The History of London, from Its Foundation by the Romans, to the Present Time*. London: Samuel Richardson.

Martin, G. (2004). Maseres, Francis (1731–1824). In *Oxford Dictionary of National Biography*. Oxford: Oxford University Press. Published online at: www.oxforddnb.com/view/article/18260.

Martin, J.B. (1892). *'The Grasshopper' in Lombard Street*. London: Leadenhall Press.

Maseres, F. (1772). *A Proposal for Establishing Life-Annuities in Parishes for the Benefit of the Industrious Poor*. London: Benjamin White.

Maseres, F. (1773). *Considerations on the Bill now Depending in the House of Commons, for Enabling Parishes to Grant Life-Annuities to Poor Persons, upon Purchase, in Certain Circumstances and under Certain Restrictions*. London: Benjamin White.

Maseres, F. (1783). *The Principles of the Doctrine of Life-Annuities; Explained in a Familiar Manner, so as to Be Intelligible to Persons not Acquainted with the Doctrine of Chances*. London: White.

McKenzie, D.F. (1960). The author of Tables for Purchasing Leases attributed to Sir Isaac Newton. *Transactions of the Cambridge Bibliographical Society* 3(2): 165–6.

McRae, A. (1996). *God Speed the Plough: The Representation of Agrarian England, 1500–1660.* Cambridge: Cambridge University Press.

Member of the Amicable Society (1706). *A Letter from a Member of the Amicable Society for a Perpetual Assurance; Giving His Friend an Account of that Society, as It Now Stands Incorporated by Her Majesty's Letters Patent.* London.

Mercers' Company (1708). *A Full Account of the Rise, Progress, & Advantages of Dr. Assheton's Proposal (as Now Improved and Managed by the Worshipful Company of Mercers, London) for the Benefit of Widows of Clergy-Men and Others.* London: J.R. Given.

Mores, E.R. (1764). *A List of the Policies and Other Instruments of the Society as Well General as Special.* Oxford: Bodleian Library.

Morgan, J. (1728). *A Complete History of Algiers.* Vol. 1. London: J. Bettenham.

Morgan, W. (1779). *The Doctrine of Annuities and Assurances on Lives and Survivorships, Stated and Explained.* London: T. Cadell.

Morgan, W. (1788). On the probabilities of survivorships between two persons of any given ages, and the method of determining the values of reversions depending on those survivorships. *Philosophical Transactions of the Royal Society of London* 78: 331–49.

Morgan, W. (1789). On the method of determining, from the real probabilities of life, the value of a contingent reversion in which three lives are involved in the survivorship. *Philosophical Transactions of the Royal Society of London* 79: 40–54.

Morgan, W. (1791). On the method of determining, from the real probabilities of life, the value of a contingent reversion in which three lives are involved in the survivorship. *Philosophical Transactions of the Royal Society of London* 81: 246–77.

Morgan, W. (1794). On the method of determining, from the real probabilities of life, the value of a contingent reversion in which three lives are involved in the survivorship. *Philosophical Transactions of the Royal Society of London* 84: 223–61.

Morgan, W. (1800). On the method of determining, from the real probabilities of life, the value of a contingent reversion in which three lives are involved in the survivorship. *Philosophical Transactions of the Royal Society of London* 90: 22–45.

Morgan, W. (1815). *The Life of the Rev. Richard Price, D.D. F.R.S.* London: R. Hunter.

Morris, G. (1735). *Tables for Renewing and Purchasing Leases.* London: J. Brotherton.

Neale, T. (1694). *Anno quinto & sexto Guilielmi & Mariae, by and act pass'd entituled, An act for granting to Their Majesties certain rates and duties upon salt, and upon beer, ale, and other liquors, for securing certain recompentes and advantages in the said Act, mentioned to such persons as shall voluntarily advance the sum of ten hundred thousand pounds, towards carrying on the war against France.* London: Collins.

Ogborn, M.E. (1962). *Equitable Assurances: The Story of Life Assurance in the Experience of the Equitable Life Assurance Society 1762–1962*. London: George Unwin and Allen.

Overton, M. (1996). *Agricultural Revolution in England: The Transformation of the Agrarian Economy 1500–1850*. Cambridge: Cambridge University Press.

Oxford University Press (2001). *Oxford English Dictionary Online*. Oxford: Oxford University Press. Published online at: http://dictionary.oed.com/.

Packard Humanities Institute (1988). *The Papers of Benjamin Franklin*. Published online at: http://franklinpapers.org/franklin/.

Paterson, S. (1779). *Bibliotheca Moresiana: A Catalogue of the Large and Valuable Library of Printed Books, Rare Old Tracts, Manuscripts, Prints and Drawings, Copper Plates, Sundry Antiquities, Philosophical Instruments and Other Curiosities, of that Eminent British Antiquary the Late Rev. and Learned Edward Rowe Mores, Deceased*. London.

Pearce, E.H. (1928). *The Sons of the Clergy: Some Records of Two Hundred and Seventy-Five Years*. London: John Murray.

Pearson, K. (1978). *The History of Statistics in the 17th and 18th Centuries against the Changing Background of Intellectual, Scientific, and Religious Thought: Lectures by Karl Pearson Given at University College, London, during the Academic Sessions, 1921–1933*. E.S. Pearson (ed.), London: Griffin.

Person, D. (1635). *Varieties: Or, A Surveigh of Rare and Excellent Matters Necessary and Delectable for all Sorts of Persons*. London: Richard Badger and Thomas Cotes.

Petty, W. (1674) *The Discourse Made before the Royal Society the 26 of November 1674. Concerning the Use of Duplicate Proportion in Sundry Important Particulars: Together with a New Hypothesis of Springing or Elastique Motions*. London: John Martyn.

Petty, W. (1687). *Five Essays in Political Arithmetick*. London: Henry Mortlock.

Phillippes, H. (1653). *The Purchasers Pattern Shewing the True Value of Any Purchase of Land or Houses, by Lease or Otherwise*. London: R. and W. Leybourn.

Pierce, L.J. and G. Williams (1990). Landlords in Wales, 1500–1640. In *Chapters from the Agrarian History of England and Wales: Volume 2, Rural Society: Landowners, Peasants and Labourers 1500–1750*. C. Clay (ed.), Cambridge: Cambridge University Press.

Plomer, H.R., Bushnell, G.H. and Dix, E.R.M. (1968). *A Dictionary of the Printers and Booksellers Who Were at Work in England, Scotland and Ireland from 1726 to 1775*. Oxford: TRUEXpress.

Poitras, G. (2000). *The Early History of Financial Economics, 1478–1776: From Commercial Arithmetic to Life annuities and Joint Stocks*. Cheltenham: Edward Elgar.

Power, J. (1839). *Church Leases: Report, and Summary of the Evidence and Other Information Appended to the Report, of the Select Committee, Appointed to Enquire into the Management of Ecclesiastical Property in England and Wales*. London: J. Ridgway.

Price, R. (1769). Observations on the expectations of lives, the increase of mankind, the influence of great towns on population, and particularly the state of London with respect to healthfulness and number of inhabitants. *Philosophical Transactions* 59: 89–125.

Price, R. (1770). Observations on the proper method of calculating the values of reversions depending on survivorships. *Philosophical Transactions* 60: 268–76.

Price, R. (1771). *Observations on Reversionary Payments: On Schemes for Providing Annuities for Widows, and for Persons in Old Age; on the Method of Calculating Values of Assurances on Lives; and on the National Debt.* London: T. Cadell.

Price, R. (1772a). *Observations on Reversionary Payments: On Schemes for Providing Annuities for Widows, and for Persons in Old Age; on the Method of Calculating Values of Assurances on Lives; and on the National Debt.* 2nd Edition. London: T. Cadell.

Price, R. (1772b). *A Supplement to the Second Edition of the Treatise on Reversionary Payments &c. Containing Additional Observations and Tables.* London: T. Cadell.

Price, R. (1773). *Observations on Reversionary Payments: On Schemes for Providing Annuities for Widows, and for Persons in Old Age; on the Method of Calculating Values of Assurances on Lives; and on the National Debt.* 3rd Edition. London: T. Cadell.

Price, R. (1775). Observations on the difference between the duration of human life in towns and in country parishes and villages. *Philosophical Transactions* 65: 424–45.

Price, R. (1776). Short and easy theorems for finding, in all cases, the differences between the values of annuities payable yearly, and of the same annuities payable half-yearly, quarterly, or momently. *Philosophical Transactions of the Royal Society of London* 66: 109–28.

Price, R. (1783). *Observations on Reversionary Payments: On Schemes for Providing Annuities for Widows, and for Persons in Old Age; on the Method of Calculating Values of Assurances on Lives; and on the National Debt.* Vols. 1 and 2. 4th Edition. London: T. Cadell.

Price, R. (1792). *Observations on Reversionary Payments: On Schemes for Providing Annuities for Widows, and for Persons in Old Age; on the Method of Calculating Values of Assurances on Lives; and on the National Debt.* Vols. 1 and 2. 5th Edition. London: T. Cadell.

Price, R. (1983–94). *The Correspondence of Richard Price.* Vols. 1–3. W.B. Peach and D.O. Thomas (eds.), Durham, NC: Duke University Press.

Record, R. (1582). *The Ground of Artes Teaching the Perfect Worke and Practise of Arithmeticke.* London: Harrison and Bynneman.

Record, R. (1623). *The Ground of Arts Teaching the Perfect Worke and Practise of Arithmeticke.* London: Beale and Jackson.

Richards, J. (1730). *The Gentleman's Steward and Tenants of Manors Instructed.* London: John Senex.

Richards, J. (1739). *Annuities on Lives, and for Limited Terms of Years, Considered.* London: J. Osborn.

Robson, E. (1951). Purchase and promotion in the British Army in the eighteenth century. *History* 36: 57–72.

Ronayne, P. (1717). *A Treatise of Algebra in Two Books: The First Treating of the Arithmetical, and the Second of the Geometrical Part*. London: W. Innys.

Rosenhaft, E. (2010). How to tame chance: evolving languages of risk, trust, and expertise in eighteenth-century German proto-insurances. In *The Appeal of Insurance*. G. Clark, G. Anderson, C. Thomann, and J.-M. Graf von der Schulenburg (eds.), pp. 16–42. Toronto: University of Toronto Press.

Rothschild, C.G. (2009) Adverse selection in annuity markets: evidence from the British Life Annuity Act of 1808. *Journal of Public Economics* 93: 776–84.

Rowe, J. (1751). *An Introduction to the Doctrine of Fluxions*. London: John Noon.

Rowe, J. (1776). *Letters Relative to Societies for the Benefit of Widows and of Age*. Exeter: Thorn.

Royer, G. (1721). *Arithmetick Compleated in All Its Rules Both Vulgar and Decimal*. London: B. Creake.

Saunders, W. (1708). *An Essay towards the Establishing the Fishery of Great Britain*. London: J. Morphew.

Simpson, T. (1742). *The Doctrine of Annuities and Reversions, Deduced from General and Evident Principles*. London: John Nourse.

Simpson, T. (1752). *Select Exercises for Young Proficients in the Mathematicks*. London: John Nourse.

Smart, J. (1726). *Tables of Interest, Discount, Annuities, &c.* London: J. Darby and T. Browne.

Smart, J. (1738). *An Account of the Number of Persons Dying at the Several Ages Undermentioned for Ten Years Past*. London: Guildhall Library.

Smollett, T. (1751). *The Adventures of Peregrine Pickle*. Vol. 3. London: D. Wilson.

South Sea Company (1711). *Abstract of the Charter of the Governour and Company of Merchants of Great Britain, Trading to the South-Seas, and Other Parts of America, and for Encouraging the Fishery*. London.

Stanhope, G. (1698), *A Sermon Preach'd in St. Paul's Cathedral at the Annual Meeting of the Sons of the Clergy, Tuesday, December vii, 1697*. London: Henry Bonwick.

Stationers' Company (1876). *A Transcript of the Registers of the Company of Stationers of London; 1554–1640 A.D.* Vol. 3. E. Arber (ed.), London: Privately Printed. Reprinted, 1967 by Peter Smith, Gloouceser, MA.

Stonehouse, S. (1754). *The Valuation of Annuities upon Lives, Deduced from the London Bills of Mortality*. London: S. Birt and H. Whitridge.

Strange, J. (1755). *Reports of Adjudged Cases in the Courts of Chancery, King's Bench, Common Pleas and Exchequer, from Trinity Term in the Second Year of King George I to Trinity Term in the Twenty-First Year of King George II*. Vol. 1. London: Henry Lintot.

Strype, J. (1824). *Annals of the Reformation and Establishment of Religion, and Other Various Occurrences in the Church of England, during Queen Elizabeth's Happy Reign*. Vol. 4. Oxford: Clarendon Press.

Thomas, A. (1718). *A List of the Royal Society of London, Instituted by His Majesty King Charles II*. London: J. Morphew.

Timperley, C.H. (1839). *A Dictionary of Printers and Printing with the Progress of Literature, Ancient and Modern*. London: H. Johnson.

Todhunter, I. (1865). *A History of the Mathematical Theory of Probability from the Time of Pascal to that of Laplace*. Cambridge: Cambridge University Press. Reprinted 1965, Chelsea Publishing, New York.

Tompson, R.S. (2004). Gilbert, Thomas (bap. 1720, d. 1798). In *Oxford Dictionary of National Biography*. Oxford: Oxford University Press. Published online at: www.oxforddnb.com/view/article/10703.

Tucker, G.S.L. (1960) *Progress and Profit in British Economic Thought*. Cambridge: Cambridge University Press.

Vezey, F. (1773). *Cases Argued and Determined in the High Court of Chancery, in the Time of Lord Harwicke, from the Year 1746–7, to 1755*. Vol. 2. London: W. Strahan and M. Woodfall.

Walford, C. (1871). History of annuities on lives. In *The Insurance Cyclopædia*. Vol. 1, pp. 98–167. London: Charles and Edwin Layton.

Walford, C. (1885). Chronological table of all the insurance associations. *Post Magazine and Insurance Monitor*, 46: 4–5, 14–15, 26–7, 38–9, 50–1, 62–3, 74.

Wallis, P.J. (1974). Mathematical text books: 1 arithmetical art. *Mathematics in School* 3: 2–4.

Ward, J. (1707). *The Young Mathematician's Guide. Being a Plain and Easie Introduction to the Mathematicks*. London: Edward Midwinter.

Ward, J. (1710). *Clavis Usuræ; or, a Key to Interest, Both Simple and Compound*. London: William Taylor.

Ward, J. (1724). *A Compendium of Algebra: Containing Plain, Easy, and Concise Rules in that Mysterious Science*. London: Daniel Browne.

Warner, F. (1752). *A Scheme of a Fund for the Better Maintenance of the Widows and Children of the Clergy*. London: Whiston and White.

Warner, F. (1755). *An Address to the Clergy; with Some Proposals for Raising and Establishing a Fund, by the Aid of Parliament, to Make Provision for Their Widows and Children*. London: Owen and Payne.

Warner, F. (1764). *A Letter to the Fellows of Sion-College; and to All the Clergy within the Bills of Mortality, and in the County of Middlesex*. London: Charles Say.

Watkins, R. (2002). *Jérôme Lalande, Diary of a Trip to England 1763*. Published online at: www.nawcc-index.net/Articles/Lalande.pdf.

Watkins, T. (1714). Rules for correcting the usual methods of computing amounts and present values, by compound as well as simple interest; and of stating interest accounts. *Philosophical Transactions* 29: 111–27.

Webb, B. (1762). *The Complete Annuitant: Consisting of Tables of Interest, Simple and Compound*. London: J. and W. Oliver.

Westergaard, H. (1932). *Contributions to the History of Statistics*. London: P.S. King and Son.

Whiston, W. (1732). *An Account of the Past and Present State of the Amicable Society for a Perpetual Assurance-Office; With the Occasions of the Low Condition It Is Now in; and Proposals in Order to Recover Its Former Prosperity*. London.

Williams, W.P. (1740). *Reports of Cases Argued and Determined in the High Court of Chancery, and Some Special Cases Adjudged in the Court of King's Bench*. Vol. 2. London: Nutt and Gosling.

Wingate, E. (1630). *Arithmetique Made Easie in Two Books*. London: Flesher, Stephens and Meredith.

Wingate, E. (1650). *Arithmetique Made Easie*. London: Flesher and Stephens.

Witt, R. (1613). *Arithmeticall Questions Touching the Buying or Exchange of Annuities*. Redmer: London.

Wordie, J.R. (1983). The chronology of English enclosure, 1500–1915. *The Economic History Review, New Series* 36: 483–505.

Index